Hybridity, or the Cultural Logic of Globalization

Hybridity,
or the Cultural Logic of Globalization

Marwan M. Kraidy

 Temple University Press
Philadelphia

Marwan M. Kraidy is Assistant Professor of International Communication at the School of International Service, American University. He is co-editor of *Global Media Studies: Ethnographic Perspectives.*

- Dean of Northwestern University in Qatar
- Born June 1972
- leading authority on Arab media

Temple University Press
1601 North Broad Street
Philadelphia PA 19122
www.temple.edu/tempress

Published 2005
Printed in the United States of America

⊗ The paper used in this publication meets the requirements of the American National Standard for Information Sciences—Permanence of Paper for Printed Library Materials, ANSI Z39.48-1992

Library of Congress Cataloging-in-Publication Data

Kraidy, Marwan, 1972–
    Hybridity, or the cultural logic of globalization / Marwan M. Kraidy.
        p.   cm.
    Includes bibliographical references and index.
    ISBN 1-59213-143-3 (cloth : alk. paper) – ISBN 1-59213-144-1 (pbk : alk. paper)
    1. Hybridity (Social sciences).   2. Hybridity (Social sciences)—Case studies.
    I. Title.

    HM1272.K73 2005
    306—dc22

                                                                2004062108

ISBN 978-1-59213-143-3 (cloth : alk. paper)
ISBN 978-1-59213-144-0 (pbk : alk. paper)

032310-P

Contents

Preface

Hybridity is almost a good idea, but not quite.

—Nicholas Thomas

HYBRIDITY IS a risky notion. It comes without guarantees. Rather than a single idea or a unitary concept, hybridity is an association of ideas, concepts, and themes that at once reinforce and contradict each other. The varied and sometimes contradictory nature of its use points to the emptiness of employing hybridity as a universal description of culture. Indeed, we learn very little when we repeat glibly that every culture is hybrid or, as happens too often, when fragments of discourse or data are cobbled together and called hybridity in several registers—historical, rhetorical, existential, economic, and so on. It is therefore imperative to situate every analysis of hybridity in a specific context where the conditions that shape hybridities are addressed.

I hope that this book improves our understanding of the role of communication in the making of hybridities. Communication practices as varied as journalism (Chapter Four), media production (Chapter Five), and media reception (Chapter Six) create hybridity as a notion, an ideology, or an existential experience. Social agents with a variety of motivations and objectives muster communication processes to articulate versions of hybridity that suit their purposes. In colonial Mexico, postcolonial Lebanon, neocolonial Washington, and elsewhere, hybridity comes in different guises and with different effects.

The challenge before us is therefore not to come up with an all-purpose, final definition of hybridity, but to find a way to integrate different types of hybridity in a framework that makes the connections between these types both intelligible and usable. With that goal in mind, I have shaped this book as a reclamation of a critical and historically informed approach to international communication. After dissecting the deficiencies of the cultural imperialism thesis and its would-be substitute "cultural globalization," I propound *critical transculturalism* as a new international communication framework with issues of hybridity at its core. The usage of the word "transculturalism," to be fully explained in the next chapter, conveys a synthetic notion of culture and a dynamic understanding of relations between cultures. As I conceive it, critical transculturalism is at once an engagement with hybridity as a discursive formation, a framework for international communication theory, and an agenda for research.

This book lends support to three general observations that underlie critical transculturalism:

1. Hybridity must be understood historically in a triple context: (a) the development of vocabularies of racial and cultural mixture from the mid–nineteenth century onward; (b) the historical basis of contemporary hybrid identities; and (c) the juncture at which the language of hybridity entered the study of international communication. The first issue is dealt with at length in Chapter Three, and at this point it suffices to remark that discourses of cultural mixture have historically served ideologies of integration and control—not pluralism and empowerment. Chapter Six tackles the second issue, namely, how local history bears upon present-day hybrid identities, which, I contend, should not be viewed as primordial, because ethnic and cultural identities have a strong relational component. The third issue, namely, the timing of the entrance of hybridity into international communication studies and its position vis-à-vis "cultural imperialism" and "cultural globalization," is worth our attention. The discourse of hybridity connects two literatures: anti–"cultural imperialism" and pro–"cultural globalization" writings. Hybridity has emerged as the conceptual linchpin of the latter literature. As this book documents, the thoroughly demonized cultural imperialism thesis is giving way to a benign vision of global cultural diversity, local cultural resistance, and cross-cultural fusion. This cultural pluralism is in my view an inadequate vision for international communication and culture because it ignores power.

2. Hybridity must be understood as a rhetorical notion. This entails comprehension of (a) uses of hybridity in mainstream public discourse, a task that Chapter Four addresses; and (b) the analysis of the advent of hybridity in international communication studies for its rhetorical aspects. If, conceptually, hybridity is invoked in writings unsympathetic to critical approaches to international communication, rhetorically, hybridity facilitates a broader negation

of power in public treatments of intercultural relations. Hybridity, then, may be better understood, following Thomas Nakayama and Robert Krizek's research on whiteness (1995), as a strategic rhetoric. Whiteness, the two U.S.-based rhetorical scholars wrote, "garners its representational power through its ability to be many things at once, to be universal and particular, to be a source of identity and difference" (p. 302). A similar fluidity and polyvalence imbue hybridity with persuasive power. A strategic rhetoric of hybridity frames hybridity as natural, commonplace, and desirable in intercultural relations, and therefore noncontentious. It is one aspect of globalization that represents the whole as egalitarian exchange and positive change. In this respect hybridity is a metonym for globalization.

3. The concept of hybridity must be "operationalized" in case studies. As an emergent phenomenon that eludes easy classification, hybridity poses a challenge to empirical research on media reception and to analyses of media texts. In the first case, there is tension between hybridity's challenge to fixed categories and empirical research's reliance on more-or-less stable classifications. The contrapuntal approach that I posit in Chapter One and execute empirically in Chapter Six is helpful in that regard, but we need to move beyond the merely contrapuntal in order to make hybridity empirically intelligible. As far as textual analysis is concerned, as we see in Chapter Five, intertextual excess and aesthetic eclecticism mark hybrid media texts and introduce an element of arbitrariness to their analysis. Both empirical and textual approaches to hybridity must therefore be situated in a context whose structural elements ought to be explained. The Mexican and Lebanese case studies in Chapters Five and Six substantiate the usefulness of anchoring analyses of cultural hybridity in politico-economic considerations. Nonetheless, there needs to be further methodological experimentation and development in order effectively to integrate hybridity's historical, rhetorical, structural, textual, and empirical dimensions in concrete research studies.

In formulating critical transculturalism, I propose steps toward the full integration of historical, rhetorical, and empirical aspects of hybridity in international communication theory and research. I also explore how analysis of communication processes can improve our understanding of hybridity.

(1) ⸢Chapter One maps the connections that already exist between hybridity and communication, and sets the stage for new links to be established throughout the book.⸥ After describing the rise to prominence of the notion of hybridity in academic and popular discourses, I give a brief etymological exposé of terms used to denote cultural mixture, whose historical development is further discussed in Chapter Three. Then Chapter One turns to a review of approaches to international communication that have mentioned or engaged the notion of hybridity, and to forecast this book's contributions to this debate.

(2) ⸢Chapter Two, "Scenarios of Global Culture," surveys various perspectives on global culture.⸥ After a critique of analytical dichotomies in the study of intercultural relations, it focuses on the connections between, on one hand, "cultural imperialism" and "active audience" theories in media research, and, on the other hand, the debate on global culture. A discussion of the New World Information and Communication Order (NWICO) controversy ensues, in which I highlight the main issues and summarize the historical evolution of this so-called global media debate from its early focus on nation-states to the later shift to transnational corporations and finally the emergence of human rights and public sphere perspectives. I then describe critiques of the cultural imperialism approach and offer my own take on them by way of a comparative analysis of the fields of American studies and international communication, which leads me to revisit some core assumptions of North American mass communication research. ⸢The chapter then turns to an analysis of the shift from "cultural imperialism" to "cultural globalization" and appraises the implications of that change of direction, since this is when media scholars began using the concept of hybridity.⸥

(3) ⸢Chapter Three, "The Trails and Tales of Hybridity," is a multidisciplinary and comparative examination of the applications and critiques of hybridity and equivalent concepts such as syncretism, creolization, *mestizaje, métissage*, transculturation, and others.⸥ The chapter also surveys literary and especially postcolonial theory and its various approaches to hybridity. Beyond Mikhail Bakhtin (1981) and Homi Bhabha (1994), who are credited with taking the concept of hybridity from biology to language and culture, I introduce other writers whose discipline, language, or geographical location may have left them underappreciated in Anglophone studies of hybridity.

Afterward, I explore how hybridity can describe two levels of sociocultural transformation by way of a contrast between the "culture of covering" among radio disc jockeys in post–World War II Italy and the breaking of the Hawaiian taboo system in the wake of Captain Cook's arrival in the Polynesian archipelago. These case studies represent two kinds of hybridity, the former superficial and historically inconsequential, the latter deeply rooted and of epochal significance. They demonstrate that hybridity is of dubious usefulness if employed as a broad conceptual umbrella without concrete historical, geographical, and conceptual grounding.

Indeed, some authors do consider hybridity to be basically useless, and their arguments are given voice in the latter section of Chapter Three. While this "antihybridity backlash" points to some weaknesses in hybridity theory, it largely consists of unconstructive criticism. A more productive corrective to some excesses of hybridity theory can be found in the debate between the African formation of *négritude* and the Caribbean movement of *Créolité*. Both négritude and Créolité are Francophone, interested in Africa and its extensions, and concerned with postcolonial racial and cultural issues. Nonetheless, there are deep differences between the two movements over the ideological implications of hybridity. The significance of the dispute between négritude and Créolité overflows the debate's initial geographical and historical boundaries, because it reflects different interpretations of the connection between hybridity and power.

In search of continuities and discontinuities among mestizaje, métissage, Créolité, creolization, and transculturation, Chapter Four, "Corporate Transculturalism," examines how hybridity is used in contemporary public discourse. Via critical discourse analysis, I examine uses of hybridity in (mostly) U.S. newspapers, magazines, and trade books. These include a series of articles on global popular culture published by the *Washington Post* in 1998; *The Global Me* (Zachary, 2000), a trade book that focuses on hybridity as a commercial asset for multinational corporations; and *Creative Destruction* (Cowen, 2002a), an economic analysis of global culture. The *Washington Post* articles invoke hybridity as a characteristic of intercultural relations and use it to describe how audiences in developing countries interact with American popular culture. Chapter Four grapples with these questions: How does public discourse use hybridity to frame global culture? Does it account for global politico-economic structures? Or does the use of hybridity in public discourse reproduce hegemonic cultural relations, consisting of what Indian-born postcolonial theorist Gayatri Chakravorty Spivak (1999) called "hybridist post-national talk, celebrating globalization as

Americanization" (p. 361)? I find that these publications associate hybridity with assumptions about the benefits of globalization, free trade,
and individual consumer freedom, in effect expressing what I call "corporate transculturalism," hence the title of the chapter.

(5) Chapter Five explores what can be called hybrid media texts that
result from industry practices such as coproduction, format adaptation, and localization. The chapter's title, "The Cultural and Political Economies of Hybrid Media Texts," reflects the importance of the
politico-economic context in which hybrid media programs are created
and consumed. This chapter tackles the following questions: How do
the structural features of the global and national media industries shape
hybrid media texts? What motivates media companies to undertake
what have been called post-Fordist practices such as coproduction and
adaptation? Finally, how can the concept of hybridity be effectively used
to analyze these practices and the media texts they create? After brief
comments on post-Fordism, MTV's localization strategy, and British
television export policies, the bulk of the chapter is devoted to an intriguing case study: the 1999 production and broadcast by Mexican TV
Azteca of *Tele Chobis*, a copycat version of the original British *Teletubbies*.
By way of a textual and semiotic analysis of several episodes of the program, I examine the structural forces—political, economic, regulatory,
and legal—that mold *Tele Chobis*'s hybridity. These include the liberalization of Mexico's economy, the current international copyright regime,
and fierce competition between TV Azteca and Televisa in a changing
media landscape.

(6) Grounded in an ethnographic research project with mostly middle-
class Christian Maronite Lebanese youth that began in 1993, Chapter
Six, "Structure, Reception, and Identity: On Arab-Western Dialogism,"
examines how hybridity is constituted by young Maronites in Lebanon
in relation to Arab and Western worldviews. At the heart of Chapter
Six is an analysis of the links between audience interpretations of media
content and the structures of media policy and ownership. This chapter's
crucial function, therefore, is to examine hybridity at the empirical level.
For young Maronites, identity construction takes place in everyday life
practices of nomadism, mimicry, and consumption. In the process, they
are attracted by hybrid—especially local—cultural texts. To probe the
links between cultural reception and the structure of the Lebanese media, I analyze two "master texts"—a local television series and the lyrics
of a local artist-musician-songwriter—both with dominant hybrid components and both highly popular with my respondents despite their

carrying ideologies that oppose traditional Maronite sensibilities (the two texts were not preselected; I arrived at them by way of interviews and participant observation). This lack of correspondence between audience readings, cultural texts, and media ownership raises provocative questions about theory and policy, which are briefly addressed in Chapter Six and elaborated on in Chapter Seven.

The book's conclusion, Chapter Seven, "Hybridity without Guarantees: Toward Critical Transculturalism," proposes critical transculturalism as a new international communication framework. Because of the openness of discursive formations, hybridity can be appropriated as a strategic rhetoric (Nakayama and Krizek, 1995), aiming in part to become a leading theory not only in international communication but also in the study of the cultural dimensions of globalization. I therefore argue that hybridity is the cultural logic of globalization—hence the title of this book[1]—whose comprehension requires a relational, processual, and contextual approach to hybridity from a critical perspective. This entails that we ought to begin looking at hybridities, each as a particular, localized practice, as opposed to a singular hybridity conceived as an all-inclusive sociocultural order. Hence my call for "Shifting Geertz," in reference to anthropologist Clifford Geertz, by which I mean a renewed emphasis on local knowledge where the notion of the local is reconsidered, followed by reflections on the implications of hybridity for media policy. Contra hybridity as the cultural logic of globalization, this book envisions, by way of critical transculturalism, a hybridity without guarantees.[2]

Acknowledgments

MANY PEOPLE have contributed to this book. Sandra Braman's guidance was instrumental since the book's early stages. John Downing's thorough read of the entire manuscript rescued me from many traps, and Tom Nakayama's encouragement to write a bolder conclusion was critical. Other reviewers for Temple University Press offered a healthy balance of support and skepticism. Patrick Murphy and Raúl Tovares have offered friendship and critical commentary.

For encouragement at crucial stages and for general scholarly counsel, I am grateful to Pat Aufderheide, Michael Beard, Douglas Boyd, Dennis Davis, Larry Grossberg, Drew McDaniel, Toby Miller, Christine Ogan, Lana Rakow, and Josep Rota. I am thankful to Joseph Straubhaar for many edifying chats on cultural hybridity, and to Joe Khalil, Nabil Dajani, and Dima Dabbous-Sensenig for instructive conversations on Arab media and cultures. I am also indebted to all those who generously entrusted me with their feelings and thoughts during my fieldwork in Lebanon.

For inviting me to share portions of the book early on, I thank Radha Hegde at New York University, Hemant Shah at the University of Wisconsin–Madison, Karla Malette at the American University of Beirut, Ramez Maluf at the Lebanese American University, Richard Harvey Brown at the University of Maryland, Henry Jenkins and David Thorburn at the Massachusetts Institute of Technology, and Georgette Wang at Hong Kong Baptist University. I also thank the Senate Scholarly Activities Committee at the University of North Dakota for inviting me to give a Faculty Lecture at the North Dakota Museum of Art, and Jim Mittleman for inviting me to present a summary of the book to the Council for Comparative Studies at American University. Students in my Communication, Culture, and Globalization graduate colloquium at the University of North Dakota and in my Globalization and Culture seminar and Cultural Dimensions of International Politics graduate course at American University have been generous with ideas and comments. Some material in Chapter Four first appeared in "Hybridity in Cultural Globalization" (*Communication Theory* 12[3], pp. 316–339, 2002), and some of the data in Chapter Six were first discussed in "The Global, the Local, and the Hybrid: A Native Ethnography of Glocalization" (*Critical Studies in Mass Communication* 16[4], pp. 458–478, 1999).

I am grateful to Peter Wissoker, my editor and friend, for motivating me to write a stronger and clearer book.

My colleagues at American University provided the intellectual environment and material resources that made completion of this work less arduous. I am indebted to Louis Goodman, Nanette Levinson, Hamid Mowlana, and Shalini Venturelli for their support, to Ivy Broder for awarding me a research leave that accelerated the ultimate revision, and to the colleagues who took over my teaching responsibilities during that time. I am also thankful to a string of diligent research assistants: Tamara Goeddertz, Tim Seidel, Kiran Pervez, Lauhona Ganguly, Dominic De Sapio, and Mike Huston.

Michel, Aida, Ziad, and Ghassan helped in more ways than they can imagine. I am grateful to Ziad and Ghassan for their cheerful hospitality in Paris as I researched French and Francophone writings on hybridity. Aida and Michel warmly opened their home and selflessly provided mental and logistical support during various stays in Lebanon, in addition to numerous television recordings and newspaper clippings. Elke and Walter did the same during various visits to Mexico, offered me Spanish-language books on globalization and culture, and recorded several episodes of *Tele Chobis* for their *nieto*.

Ute, my sharpest and friendliest critic, read successive drafts of the manuscript, discerning the minutest details and prodding me to firm up the overall argument. She put an indelible mark on the book, and for that I am immensely grateful. I completed most of the book between the births of my son, Bruno, and my daughter, Maya, and their early coos and words provided the soundtrack for much of the writing. All three gently put up with my writing-induced mental and physical absences and helped me keep my life in perspective. To them I dedicate this book, with the hope that one day it may help them shorten the distance between our multiple homes.

1 Cultural Hybridity and International Communication

The idea of cultural hybridization is one of those deceptively simple-seeming notions which turns out, on examination, to have lots of tricky connotations and theoretical implications.

—John Tomlinson

HYBRIDITY IS one of the emblematic notions of our era. It captures the spirit of the times with its obligatory celebration of cultural difference and fusion, and it resonates with the globalization mantra of unfettered economic exchanges and the supposedly inevitable transformation of all cultures. At a more prosaic level, since its initial use in Latin to describe the offspring of "a tame sow and a wild boar" (Young, 1995, p. 6),[1] hybridity has proven a useful concept to describe multipurpose electronic gadgets, designer agricultural seeds, environment-friendly cars with dual combustion and electrical engines, companies that blend American and Japanese management practices, multiracial people, dual citizens, and postcolonial cultures. As one journalist put it, the "trend to blend" (Weeks, 2002, p. C2) is upon us.

I favor the term "hybridity" because it has a broader meaning that often encompasses the objects and processes captured by equivalent terms such as "creolization," "mestizaje," and "syncretism." In this preference I am not alone. For example, Argentinian-Mexican cultural critic Néstor García-Canclini (1989/1995) prefers the word "hybridity" because it "includes diverse intercultural mixtures—not only the racial ones to which *mestizaje* tends to be limited—and because it permits the inclusion of the modern forms of hybridization better than does 'syncretism,' a term that almost always refers to religious fusions or traditional symbolic environments" (p. 11). As I use it, "hybridity" refers mostly to culture but retains residual meanings related to the three interconnected realms of race, language, and ethnicity. In this regard, the link between language and race was made explicit in an 1890 entry in the *Oxford English Dictionary*, which read: "The Aryan languages present such indications

1

of hybridity as would correspond with... racial intermixture" (cited in R. Young, 1995, p. 6), thus anticipating the usage of "creolization" in contemporary linguistics. The words "métissage" and "mestizaje," on the other hand, hark back to the Latin *misticum* and *mixticium*, from *miscere*, which means "to mix." The related word *mestif* was used in the regional French language of Old Provençal as early as the mid–twelfth century, while the first confirmed usage of the feminine *métice* can be traced to 1615. The current French usage, Métis, appeared first in 1690, and its pronunciation comes from the thirteenth-century Portuguese *mestiço* or the Spanish *mestizo*, used since 1600 (see Toumson, 1998, pp. 87–95).[2]

This rich vocabulary reflects the historical, geographical, and linguistic diversity of cases of cultural mixture, and mirrors the myriad approaches used to understand it. Indeed, "hybridity" has entered many academic arenas, ranging from traditional disciplines like literature, anthropology, and sociology to interdisciplinary venues such as postcolonial theory and performance studies. "Hybridity" is also employed in less obvious fields such as architecture, tourism, and sports, and in more popular versions in trade books about travel, business, and economics, in addition to mainstream press articles on popular culture.[3] Undoubtedly influenced by this trend, media scholars, as will be elaborated shortly, have begun to use "hybridity."[4] Interest in the topic, as this book will abundantly illustrate, is not restricted to any particular language or location. Indeed, academic journals in Egypt, France, and the United States have devoted special issues to hybridity.[5]

Despite or maybe because of what can be described as an academic stampede, hybridity is controversial. Multiple and often antithetical uses have created a dispute over its meaning, implications, and usefulness. In postcolonial studies, for example, scholars have argued heatedly about the benefits and disadvantages of using "hybridity." As "one of the most widely employed and disputed terms in post-colonial theory" (Ashcroft, Griffiths, and Tiffin, 1998, p. 118), "hybridity" has been characterized as a subversion of political and cultural domination (Bhabha, 1994; Joseph, 1999) or, alternatively, as a retrogressive discourse that celebrates the experience of privileged intellectuals (Friedman, 1997). Other scholars have even accused their colleagues who write positively about cultural hybridity of being complicit with structures of inequality (for example, Ahmad, 1995).[6]

A historical and comparative approach indicates that the present-day controversy over hybridity is a recent manifestation of an old preoccupation with sociocultural change. This concern is shared by scholars whose area of research is not limited to the British colonization of America and India, which have served as the crucible for most Anglophone "postcolonial" scholarship. Indeed, a coterie of thinkers have written about cultural exchange and mixture, including Argentinian-Mexican cultural theorist Néstor García-Canclini (1989), Spanish-Colombian media scholar Jesús Martín-Barbero (1993a), Russian literary theorist Mikhail Bakhtin (1981), French historian Serge Gruzinski (1999) and French philosopher Michel Serres (1969, 1972, 1974, 1977, 1980), French Guyanese literary critic Roger Toumson (1998), Saudi sociologist and novelist Turki al-Hamad (2001), and Iranian intellectual Jalal Al-I Ahmad (1984).

These writers have recognized that cross-cultural encounters are historically pervasive. Encounters between cultures, as U.S. historian Jerry H. Bentley (1993) demonstrates in dozens of richly documented historical case studies, have been so prevalent that the self-enclosed culture is in fact a historical aberration. Hybridizing processes have helped cultural traditions recruit new adherents, but cross-cultural conversion was successful only "when favored by a powerful set of political, social, or economic incentives" (Bentley, 1993, viii). Bentley's focus on premodern times notwithstanding, his work underscores a central nexus of this book: the relationship between hybridity and power.

HYBRIDITY, CULTURE, AND COMMUNICATION IN THE GLOBAL CONTEXT

In the wake of numerous writings on a concept whose definition is maddeningly elastic, whose analytical value is easily questionable, and whose ideological implications are hotly contested, writing yet another book on hybridity is not a self-evident endeavor. This book stems from my belief that the analytical potential of hybridity has not been fully exploited and that international communication analysis can improve our understanding of hybridity. This book is not merely an attempt at mapping the discursive sprawl that is hybridity from the vantage point of communication studies. Rather, the debates that have marked the relatively brief history of the field of international communication—about material and symbolic power, cultural influence and change, social agency, and so on—are serviceable in the interest of a better and more practical understanding of hybridity. Notably, I explore ways in which a communication perspective is particularly helpful in grasping some of the more nebulous aspects of hybridity.

Like the polemic over hybridity in postcolonial studies, a divide exists in international communication research between "dominance" and "pluralism" perspectives. Indeed, theories of cultural domination and resistance have been central to the field of international communication since the 1960s. Though "cultural imperialism" was the reigning thesis during the 1960s and the 1970s, numerous critics have since the 1980s alleged that it no longer reflected the complexity of intercultural relations. The unrelenting announcements that we are now in the "post-imperialist" era have come with a variety of disconnected or antithetical research approaches that have coexisted under a vaguely pluralistic umbrella, bringing back to the fore the congenital instability of international communication theory. British scholar Oliver Boyd-Barrett (1998) captured the situation well:

> [T]here has been a growing consensus in the literature... that previous models of international communication may be abandoned in a process of linear intellectual development that has moved through theories of international communication as propaganda, through to modernization and free flow, to dependency and cultural or media imperialism, supplanted in turn by theories of the 'autonomous reader' and culminating in discourses of globalization that play upon an infinite variety of 'global' and 'local';... intellectual development in the field of international communication appears not to proceed on the basis of exhaustive testing but lurches from one theory, preoccupation, dimension to another with inadequate attention to accumulative construction. (p. 157)

When interdisciplinary cultural theory entered international communication debates in the 1980s, it helped write a pivotal chapter in the eclectic history of international communication. Paradoxically, it was only with the arrival of this so-called cultural turn, which occurred more than a decade after the beginning of cultural imperialism research, that "culture" in contrast to "national development" became a core subject of international communication study. (This paradox is dissected in Chapter Two.) Turning away at once from behaviorist social psychology, positivist political science, and radical political economy, many media scholars borrowed from literary and by extension film theory, in addition to cultural anthropology. This shift, which one scholar labeled "cultural pluralism" (Sreberny-Mohammadi, 1984), signaled a broader engagement with culture than had the structural focus of the cultural imperialism thesis, and ultimately, as I explain in the next chapter, led to the introduction of the notion of hybridity to international communication.

Since hybridity involves the fusion of two hitherto relatively distinct forms, styles, or identities, cross-cultural contact, which often occurs across national borders as well as across cultural boundaries, is a requisite for hybridity. The occurrence of contact typically involves movement of some sort, and in international communication contact entails the movement of cultural commodities such as media programs, or the movement of people through migration. The first is motivated by commerce or geostrategic considerations and occurs primarily through the mass media, but also through exchanges of people, ideas, and practices. The second is motivated by poverty and repression and by the promise of upward mobility and concretely happens through transportation technologies. The former is properly understood as international communication. The latter's relevance to this book is indirect and through one of its consequences, namely the development of migrant or diasporic media.

Though various media researchers have addressed cultural mixture (Boyd-Barrett, 1998; Gillespie, 1995; Kolar-Panov, 1997; P. Lee, 1991; Mattelart, 1994; T. Miller et al., 2001; Morris, 2002; Olson, 1999; Straubhaar, 1991; Tomlinson, 1999), few studies to date have offered a sustained engagement with hybridity or pose it as a central *problématique* (see Kraidy, 1999a, 2002a, 2003a, 2004; Martín-Barbero, 1993a; Naficy, 1993). Media research has to some extent mirrored the debate in postcolonial studies, addressing hybridity alternately as a sign of empowerment or as a symptom of dominance. Most of these researchers have typically analyzed hybridity within a traditional communication framework of production, text/message, and reception. The lion's share of this research has focused on media texts and the dynamics of media reception, and seldom on media production. Rarely have studies analyzed the links between production, message, and reception (Kraidy, 2003a; Martín-Barbero, 1993a; Naficy, 1993), an important endeavor whose scope this book aims to expand.

Most analyses that focus on hybridity in media texts tend to minimize the importance of structural issues. In studies of that type, hybrid texts are often explained as symptoms of cultural pluralism, not indicators of dominance. In this regard, U.S. media researcher Scott Olson (1999) argues that "American media [do] not project American values" (p. 28) and sees hybridity as a hallmark of textual "transparency ... [that] allows [U.S. media narratives] to become stealthy, to be foreign myths that surreptitiously act like indigenous ones" (p. 6). Transparent texts have universal features that in Olson's view give U.S. television and film a "competitive advantage" in the global marketplace, where their popularity creates "polyglot cultures, but not monoculture" (p. 28). The Belgian-born scholar Armand Mattelart agrees with Olson about the popularity of hybrid media texts, casting Brazilian television production as a "remarkable alloying of mass culture and popular cultures" (1994, p. 231) whose vibrancy has made the country's media products globally competitive. In contrast to this optimistic view, Mattelart warns against uncritical interpretations of hybrid cultural productions, because in his view hybridity reflects uneven development within societies like Brazil, where some social groups are caught in relations of "discriminatory 'interdependence'" (p. 232), a process of social segmentation that is recast in terms of market categories by marketing firms that also adapt this strategy internationally. Olson (1999), for his part, dismisses politico-economic approaches to the subject, insisting that "the media texts themselves must provide at least part of the explanation for their global popularity" (p. 11). Olson's overly textualist approach, as T. Miller and colleagues (2001) have correctly argued, underestimates the structural factors which shape global media texts that critical media researchers emphasize.

Hybrid television texts such as the ones that Olson (1999) and Mattelart (1994) (differently) interpret have existed for some time. In fact, the British scholar Jeremy Tunstall (1977) predicted a quarter century ago that regional media centers would produce "hybrid genres" (cited in Sinclair, 1992, p. 106), by which he referred to domesticated versions of successful U.S. and European television formats. Indeed, media-culture industries in regional centers such as Brazil (Oliveira, 1990), Mexico (Sánchez-Ruiz, 2001), and Hong Kong (P. Lee, 1991) have since Tunstall's prognosis increasingly indigenized Western genres. For example, Hong Kong scholar Paul Lee (1991) metaphorizes four patterns of indigenization in Hong Kong; the parrot pattern refers to a wholesale mimicry of foreign culture by local industries—both in form and content; the amoeba pattern describes a modified form but a nonchanging content, such as the adaptation of a foreign movie for local consumption; the coral pattern describes cultural products whose content is changed but whose form is untouched; finally, the butterfly pattern is a radical hybridization that makes the domestic and the foreign indistinguishable.

The boundaries between "domestic" and "foreign" cultural influences are not always clearly demarcated. Hybrid media texts reflect the existence of a variety of historical, economic, and cultural forces whose enmeshments with one another are as manifest at the local, national, and regional levels as they are visible globally. A singular focus on the

mestizaje– interbreeding + cultural intermixing
of spanish + American Indian people. (orig. in mexico)

Cultural Hybridity and Communication   7

media is insufficient to comprehend these complex relations. Rather, we need to situate the media in their societal environment and disentangle various links, processes, and effects between communication practices and social, political, and economic forces. The Spanish-Colombian media scholar Jesús Martín-Barbero (1993a,b; 2000; 2002) has formalized this more productive approach in the core concept of mediations, referring to "the articulations between communication practices and social movements and the articulation of different tempos of development with the plurality of cultural matrices" (1993a, p. 187). At the heart of Martín-Barbero's approach is a critique of dualistic thinking and linear logic in cultural analysis and an emphasis on the numerous forces across time and space that impinge on contemporary cultural identities.

Acknowledging this multiplicity entails abandoning what Martín-Barbero calls "oversimplified Manichaean identifications" (1993a, p. 193) such as popular versus mass culture, cultural versus economic, and foreign versus domestic. The notion of *mestizaje(s)*, whose historical development and current application I discuss in Chapter Three, is Martín-Barbero's second central notion ("mediations" being the first). *Mestizaje* refers to "the sense of continuities in discontinuity and reconciliations between rhythms of life that are mutually exclusive" (p. 188). His use of the concept in the plural, mestizajes, reflects the wide net Martín-Barbero casts to include relations between ethnic groups, cultural beliefs and expressions, social classes, and political constituencies.[7] Despite its broad application, mestizaje for Martín-Barbero is a process and product of mixture whose materialization is best grasped in the analysis of popular culture.

Communication plays a central role in the formation of mestizajes. The significance of communication, in Martín-Barbero's view, lies in its ability to create meanings more than in its capacity to carry information or reinforce an ideology. He therefore repudiates what he describes as "ideologism" or "informationalism" in media theory (Martín-Barbero, 1993a, pp. 204–207). The former's attribution of omnipotence to the media leads to "pure communicationism without any specific communication occurring" (p. 204), and the latter's emphasis on technical efficiency means "the dissolution of political reality" (p. 207). In opposition to the mediacentric premises of these theories—the first reducing culture to its mediated ideologies, and the second reducing society to its information technologies—Martín-Barbero calls for an interdisciplinary approach more attuned to the multiplicity and complexity of contemporary societies, and the removal of the study of communication from a transmission model "into the field of culture: the conflicts which articulate

(margin notes:) major religion, 3rd C, Persian
taught elaborate dualistic cosmology –
good vs evil
light vs dark
spiritual world vs material world

culture, the *mestizajes* which weave it together and the anachronisms which sustain it" (pp. 221–222). Chapter Three includes a historical analysis of the Latin American notion of mestizaje that has led to current-day theories of hybridity (e.g., García-Canclini, 1989/1995).

In Latin America, these manifold aspects of culture and their mutual links can be discerned in the melodrama. The *telenovela*, or Latin American television melodrama, is a hybrid text cast by Martín-Barbero (1993a) as "a new and more Latin American version of magical realism" (p. 227). The telenovela carries residues of older popular genres such as the Mexican *corridos*, the Colombian *vallenatos*, and the Brazilian *cordel*, all of which are characterized as stories that invoke a fantasy past populated by ghosts and lost loved ones. The crucial difference between the telenovela and other Latin American television genres is the telenovela's open time frame and its establishment of basic affective links with its audience that have nothing to do with production values, technical sophistication, or wealth of information. Rather, the telenovela is successful because it activates what Martín-Barbero (1993b) calls "a profound dynamic of memory and imaginaries" (p. 23). The telenovela, then, carries modern stories of upward mobility concurrently with anachronistic narratives of identity. The dynamic links between traditional and modern forms and practices create the peculiar hybrid cultures of Latin America.

While history is replete with media texts such as the telenovela that can be described as hybrid, globalization and the commercial imperative to reach large audiences with minimal investment and risk have made hybrid media forms pervasive. In the case of cultures particularly susceptible to the creation of hybrid forms such as Latin America and Hong Kong, the *longue durée* of history, including colonialism, conquest, and trade, is the scene of a protracted cultural fusion. Clearly, the many Latin American mestizajes and hybridities materialize in societal dynamics shaped by politico-economic forces, and comparable systemic factors mold other communities' hybrid identities, such as the Maronites of Lebanon (explored in Chapter Six). Even in a historically mixed setting like Hong Kong, as Paul Lee (1991) indicates, the factors that shape hybrid media forms are mostly contemporary and economic, including consumer power and the strength of local production, both of which reflect the economic status of a country and its inhabitants. As a small, wealthy, then-British colonial protectorate cum Chinese semi-autonomous region, Hong Kong has the mixture of economic wealth and cultural eclecticism that fosters hybrid media forms.

In contrast, and despite their inclusion of "local" cultural markers, the hybrid texts spawned by today's global media industry are more akin to the technologically sophisticated but historically flat processes of digital superimposition and manipulation that create slick images for international consumption. Politico-economic considerations, then, shape current-day hybrid media, an issue I address at length in Chapter Five.

Free-trade agreements, which seek to integrate markets and industries across large geographical areas, create politico-economic structures that shape media texts, among other cultural commodities. Though official rhetoric tends to focus on the supposed benefits of globalization, namely the growth of exports, and dissident rhetoric emphasizes globalization's dangers, mostly the loss of jobs, the consequences of globalization at the cultural level are not always determined by economics alone. For example, the Canadian political economist Vincent Mosco and his U.S. colleague Dan Schiller have argued that while the North American Free Trade Agreement has economically integrated Canada, Mexico, and the United States, unequal development and cultural differences have persisted. Of immediate relevance to this book is Mosco and Schiller's statement that "cultural practices do not always follow the structure of markets" (2001, p. 29). As a result, the reconstitution of cultural life through continental integration "does not portend a unitary North American monoculture" (p. 4). This recognition notwithstanding, hybrid cultural forms are not anomalies in media globalization. Rather, the pervasiveness of hybridity in some ways reflects the growing synchronization of world markets. This irony is expressed best by Oliver Boyd-Barrett (1998), for whom market forces have contributed to "an increasing hybridity of global culture, ever more complex and more commodified." Nonetheless, this global culture is "everywhere more complex and more commodified in the same sort of way" (p. 174). Indeed, in this book I share the belief that hybridity is fully compatible with globalization. However, whereas, in Boyd-Barrett's view, "media imperialism" can be rehabilitated "by incorporating some of the key concerns of 'globalization' theory, *including hybridity* and the weakening of nation-states (p. 158, emphasis added), I put forth an alternative framework that I call critical transculturalism (elaborated in Chapter Seven). Critical transculturalism shares the broad concerns of "cultural imperialism" about power and cultural change but differs in the way it poses these issues conceptually and tackles them empirically.

Though not traditionally included in international communication research, the movement of people across national and cultural boundaries must be addressed because communication processes spawned by migration are helpful in understanding cultural hybridity. Indeed, the growing trend of migration from the developing world to the West is as much a catalyst of hybrid media forms as are globalization and trade. According to *L'Atlas du monde diplomatique*, the worldwide number of people living outside their native countries has grown from 75 million in 1965 to 120 million in 2000 (Achcar et al., 2003). While there is substantive intraregional migration, North America and western Europe are global immigration magnets: the United States accounts for twenty-five million immigrants, Germany for five, France and the United Kingdom for four each (ibid.). In these countries and elsewhere, two structural aspects make migrant media viable. First, today's migrants are mostly skilled workers (with better socioeconomic conditions than those of yesterday's manual laborers) whose higher incomes make them a target of advertisers. Second, satellite and cable technologies enable audience segmentation so that media operators can target language-specific migrant communities. These mostly commercial media play a crucial role in the formation of migrant identities. As the Indian U.S.-based anthropologist Arjun Appadurai wrote: "media and migration [are] two major, and interconnected diacritics" (1996, p. 3) because they activate the social imagination, which is especially true in the case of migrants whose relationship over distance with the native country has a significant imaginative component.

Hybridity is a central notion in several studies on diasporic media in host countries like the United States (Naficy, 1993), the United Kingdom (Gillespie, 1995), and Australia (Kolar-Panov, 1997). Some have shared media cultural studies' customary focus on reception, such as research on media consumption among Punjabi immigrants who live in Southall, a London neighborhood, that eschews analysis of cultural production and focuses on "the many private lives of Punjabis in Southall—whose trans-cultural experiences . . . constitute the material out of which new pluralist, hybrid cultural forms of expression are being wrought" (Gillespie, 1995, p. 56). This study explores the Indian community's "negotiated" integration into British culture, a process that creates a hybrid identity that draws on countries of both birth and exile. Television consumption is emphasized because viewing rituals are subverted for the benefit of the native culture, as for example when Punjabi families take advantage of British holidays to meet and celebrate the stories, eat the food, and reproduce the narratives of nationhood and identity of the native country (Gillespie, 1995).

These solid insights on migrant media consumption notwithstanding, the main contribution of diasporic media research is in my opinion its focus on production. Key in this regard is the analysis of the practices involved in producing media programs for migrant communities and how these practices lead to hybrid texts that at once appeal to people with hybrid identities and contribute to further cultural hybridization. The Iranian community in Los Angeles, with its elaborate grid of exiles, journalists, political activists, artists, and media entrepreneurs, illustrates the aforementioned processes. To understand the vibrant media scene of what has been dubbed "Tehrangeles," it is necessary to combine research on production and distribution structures with analyses of media texts (Naficy, 1993). The former describes an intricate network of local studios, producers and performers, syndication, and advertising, and the latter examines how hybridity is enacted in processes of mimicry, consisting of pictorial superimposition, ambivalent characters, and incoherent plots and narratives on Iranian television in Los Angeles.

Migrant media practices are not, however, restricted to institutions, commercial or otherwise. With the availability and relative affordability of video cameras, videocassette recorders, and even sound mixers and video-editing consoles, migrants have been known to produce media texts at home. Immigrants to Australia from the former Yugoslavia (Kolar-Panov, 1997) illustrate this phenomenon. Croatian and Macedonian communities in the West Australian city of Perth produce and consume videocassettes—be they family-album tapes of weddings and birthdays or documentary-style tapes about the Yugoslav war—as an active exercise of identity transformation. Migrants use video to create what the author calls "an iconic continuum" (p. 27) between homeland and new country. In doing so they concretize the tensions between the community and the host society that bear upon the creation of a hybrid culture based in the host society but drawing its emotive energy from the native country.

Whereas Gillsepie expands our knowledge of the role of media consumption in the formation of hybrid identities, Naficy (1993) and Kolar-Panov (1997) suggest that analysis of production processes improves our understanding of how broader communication processes shape cultural hybridity. After all, even in its most active and creative moments, media reception for the most part is a reactive process whose parameters are set largely by broader politico-economic and social structures. Though media production is also shaped by structural conditions and could be construed as "reactive" to large-scale forces, it is more proactive in that it involves people who intentionally put their creative energy to work in order to express their existential experience of hybridity. Granted, during reception, viewers can intentionally engage favorite characters or programs and forge strong affective links with media content. However the creation of media texts entails a literally intentional activity that concretely takes shape as production labor, even when the creators are not media professionals. This is more applicable to Croatians in Perth than in the instance of Iranians in Los Angeles, since in the latter case there is a migrant media industry that is to some extent integrated in the commercial system of the host society, while in the former the production of videos is amateurish, home based, personalized, and not integrated in the Australian media sector. Nonetheless, Iranians in Los Angeles, Punjabis in London, and Croatians and Macedonians in Perth actively use media in making sense of the cultural ambivalence of migration.

In general, then, an active role in media production gives the creators of hybrid media more social power than receivers of hybrid media can claim. Chapter Five provides a case study of a hybrid media text, *Tele Chobis,* whose commercial entanglements do not in any way strengthen its viewers' sense of agency beyond addressing them as Mexicans, in contrast to the original *Teletubbies,* whose mode of address, precisely because of the program's commercial objectives, is universal.

Despite their focus on production, studies of diasporic media are of limited applicability because they are concerned with relatively exceptional situations, since migrants constitute only 2 percent of the world's population (Achcar et al., 2003) and therefore make up a small and unrepresentative proportion of media audiences worldwide. Consequently, a more broadly applicable understanding of the local experience of hybridity as a communication issue should be based on audiences that live in their country of origin. Chapter Six, "Structure, Reception, and Identity: On Arab-Western Dialogism," fulfills that objective as it empirically investigates the role of media and communication in the formation of hybridity. A full theoretical dissection of the active links between hybridity, communication, and agency is provided in the formulation in Chapter Seven of critical transculturalism.

CONTRIBUTION AND APPROACH

This book is a reclamation of a critical approach to international communication that is amenable to conceptual nuance and cultural complexity, and therefore capable of explaining the tonalities of hybridity. It assumes that notions of media dominance and audience activity are mutually complementary rather than exclusive because politico-economic structure and sociocultural agency round each other off. Therefore, the framework I envision for hybridity maps out active links between international communication, cultural globalization, international relations, and critical theory, the latter broadly defined to include political economy, media criticism, postcolonial studies, and critical discourse analysis. This approach places the power-hybridity nexus at the core of this book.

My modus operandi is contrapuntal, an approach I adapt from Western classical music by way of Edward Said (1994), who explained that in the counterpoint, "various themes play off one another, with only a provisional privilege being given to any particular one; yet in the resulting polyphony there is concert and order, an organized interplay that derives from the themes, not from rigorous melodic or formal principle outside the work" (p. 51). A contrapuntal approach to hybridity in global media studies has four major advantages.[8] First, contrapuntal methodology helps us focus on a variety of links between institutions, texts, and experiences, at the same time keeping the open trope of hybridity as a unifying element. Second, a contrapuntal approach is well suited for understanding the relational aspects of hybridity because it stresses the formative role of exchanges between participating entities. As will become clear in the case studies in Chapters Four, Five, and Six, this methodology makes possible the integration of material forces and discursive processes. This enables a more complete analysis of global media issues that examines the connections between production, textuality, and reception in the constitution of hybridity. Third, approaching hybridity countrapuntally allows us to eschew the mediacentrism that has bedeviled much media research. Situating media processes in their broader societal context provides a more accurate picture of how a variety of material and symbolic forces shapes communication processes. Finally, a contrapuntal approach helps us move beyond bipolar models of global against local, power versus resistance, imperialism contra hybridity, and focuses instead on complex processes at play.

Approaching hybridity contrapuntally is useful in light of my conception of hybridity as a discursive formation. Foucault (1972) defined a discursive formation as a "system of dispersion" where "one can define a regularity (an order, correlations, positions and functionings, transformations)" between "objects, types of statements, concepts, or thematic choices" (p. 38). "Discursive formation" aptly captures the various types of hybridity analyzed in this book, each type consonant with other types in some aspects and dissonant with other types in other regards, and yet all converging on the central notion of hybridity. According to Foucault, the rules of formation refer to the "conditions to which the ... objects, mode of statement, concept, thematic choices ... are subjected, ... conditions of existence, ... coexistence, maintenance, modification and disappearance" (p. 38). With its focus on relations, processes, and exchanges, a contrapuntal approach is useful for grasping a formation like hybridity because it examines the space in which several objects and ideas related to hybridity emerge, instead of attempting to understand a unique and permanent discourse of hybridity. Throughout the book, my focus on the power-hybridity nexus anchors contrapuntal analysis in the more tangible realm of the material.

The contrapuntal outlook is the reason for my decision to use the term "transculturalism" instead of "internationalism," "transnationalism," or "imperialism." The term "transculturation" is attributed to the Brazilian sociologist Gilberto Freyre (1936/1986) and Cuban legal and social critic Fernando Ortiz (1940/1995), who used it to analyze racial and cultural mixtures in their countries. Its usage became common in the 1990s in interdisciplinary work on culture (Berry and Epstein, 1999; Boggs, 1991; Pratt, 1992; Varan, 1998) and even in mainstream press articles (Terry, 2000) at the same time "transnational" began replacing "international" to reflect, among other things, unofficial relations between nonstate actors (Braman and Sreberny-Mohammadi, 1996; Mattelart, 1983; Miyoshi, 1993; Wilson and Dissanayake, 1996). The prefix "trans-" suggests moving through spaces and across borders, not merely between points. I use "transculturalism" to reflect my vision of culture as a synthetic, not holistic, entity. Unlike cross- or intercultural communication that tends to study contacts between individuals from different cultures that are assumed to be discrete entities, transcultural communication believes all cultures to be inherently mixed. It seeks to understand the depth, scope, and direction of various levels of hybridity at the social—not individual—level. Critical transculturalism integrates both discursive and politico-economic analysis in the study of international communication and culture. For the time being, however, it is useful, indeed necessary, to review various approaches to global culture, a task I turn to in the following chapter.

[handwritten margin note: Discursive analysis may refer to looking at written, visual, or sign language.]

Globalism proponents believe in global citizenship + that humanity's issues could be solved through democratic globalism.

→ All people matter, no matter where they live
→ universal freedom > all mankind.
→ human rights

2   Scenarios of Global Culture

↓
A set of shared experiences, norms, symbols, + ideas that unite people at the global level.

Il faut revendiquer, par rapport à l'idéologie globalitaire, la notion de métissage.... Nous sommes dans des mondes qui ne vont pas vers la globalisation culturelle; il faut être malhonnête intellectuellement pour penser que nous allons vers une culture globale.

(One has to reclaim, in relation to globalist ideology, the notion of hybridity.... We are in worlds that are not heading toward cultural globalization; one has to be intellectually dishonest to think that we are heading toward a global culture.)

—Armand Mattelart

the defining spirit or mood of a particular period of history as shown by the ideas + beliefs of the time.

THE NOTION of global culture is inherent to the contemporary zeitgeist. It conjures up images of a planetary MTV generation listening to Britney Spears on a Sony Walkman in Nike sneakers and Gap sweaters while biting into Big Macs washed down by gulps of Coca-Cola. To some, these snapshots of a global youth consumer culture are unmistakable signs of the fulfillment of McLuhan's global village, where a new generation linked by the language of global popular culture celebrates diversity and thrives in an increasingly interconnected world. To others, these same vignettes are symptoms of a global dystopia where identity, citizenship, and social agency are manipulated by industries of mass persuasion that shape them into niche subcultural markets for a global and soulless capitalism. In spite of their disagreement, both criers of utopia and prophets of dystopia consider transnational media and cultural industries to be major forces in the globalization of culture. Technologies such as satellite television, cellular phones, the Internet, and digital cable have created seamless flows of transnational images, ideas, and ideologies that link scattered locales in what Indian American anthropologist Arjun Appadurai (1996) metaphorized as the "scapes" of globalization. *common to all?*

In the academic world, the idea of global culture—alternatively referred to as "transnational culture," "cultural globalization," or "globalization of culture"—has attracted engagement and speculation

15

complete change of form

across disciplines. Books and conferences in anthropology, comparative literature, cultural studies, communication and media studies, geography, sociology, and other fields have been devoted to understanding the implications of cultural globalization. Deliberations revolve around the global ubiquity of U.S. popular culture and thrash out its consequences for other nations and communities. Opinions have coalesced in two competing scenarios: one views cultural globalization as the transfiguration of worldwide diversity into a pandemic Westernized consumer culture. The other regards cultural globalization as a process of hybridization in which cultural mixture and adaptation continuously transform and renew cultural forms. The first scenario emphasizes the global; the second stresses the local. The former believes that cultural globalization is a process of "saturation"; the latter sees it as a process of "maturation" (Hannerz, 1989). Empirical data are invoked to lend credence to both scenarios, but there is no evidence sufficiently compelling to put the matter to rest. For this reason, I prefer to use "scenarios" in reference to conceptions of global culture. A scenario is, according to the 1984 edition of *Webster's II*, "an outline of a hypothesized or projected chain of events." More modest than "paradigm," less academic than "thesis," and less banal than "perspective," "scenario" captures the speculative nature and tentative ontology of theories of global culture.

Being everywhere or very common

Cultural Dichotomies in International Relations

Scenarios of global culture are intrinsically political. They echo rival visions of the world and the power practices deployed to create and sustain those schemes while at the same time they attempt to discredit and dismiss alternative views. Thus in the "international information flows" debate of the 1970s and 1980s, the United States advocated a "free flow" of information in tandem with its demands to liberalize media and information worldwide. The "free flow" ideology clashed with the "fair and balanced flow" doctrine advocated by many other states, both Western liberal democracies and developing countries. Cold War superpower rivalry was a powerful undertow in this quarrel, with U.S. business interests and concerns over Soviet manipulation clashing with the rest of the world's resistance to unbridled media capitalism. Scenarios of global culture are also political in a more elementary sense, in that political leaders invoke these scenarios to justify state policies. They believe that global culture is relevant to issues of governance, since it is alternatively perceived to be a threat to national identity or to provide an opportunity to expand a nation's sphere of influence. Thus, while in the past the French polity used Gallic culture as a tool for spreading a humanist message it believed to be universal, contemporary France sees the Americanization of global media culture as a dual threat to French cultural identity within France and to the *rayonnement* of French culture abroad. This explains why, in the wake of the global information "war" that followed the destruction of Taliban rule in Afghanistan in 2002 and Saddam Hussein's regime in Iraq in 2003, French officials have called for bids by the private sector to create a "French CNN," a twenty-four-hour Francophone news network that would give France leverage in international "public diplomacy." Scenarios of global culture are political in a third way, relating to academic politics, where intellectual discourses are never insulated from the national and global environment in which they develop. The rejection of the "cultural imperialism thesis" in U.S. mass communication research, for instance, reflects the national political climate and ideological reluctance to admit to the existence of global American power projection, as much as it is a product of empirical research and theoretical development. Similarly, some formulations of postmodernism in the 1980s exhibited an uncanny compatibility with neoliberal tenets: cultural fragmentation fit neatly with niche marketing, reader agency related to individual consumer autonomy, and "decentering" and "deterritorialization" tied in with post-Fordist business practices (the last to be explained in Chapter Five). Whether the topic is global culture or global warming, ideological riptides often dispose intellectual formations, and the ensuing politicization turns discussions into polemical arguments that undermine substantive deliberation.

The notion of culture has enjoyed sustained interest over the past decade, and this attention has drawn it from its academic quarters into public discourse. In the last decade, a few widely circulated publications, such as Benjamin Barber's *Jihad vs. McWorld* (1996) and Samuel Huntington's *The Clash of Civilizations and the Remaking of World Order* (1996), have treated culture as a key explanatory variable in world affairs. Because of their commercial success and influential ideas, these books help us understand some of the prevailing ideas associated with cultural globalization. Both volumes have regained importance—and been reissued—in a wounded post–September 11 United States attempting to make sense of its newly felt vulnerability, seeking solace in "cultural" explanations of the behavior of nation-states and nonstate actors.

In *Jihad vs. McWorld*, political scientist Benjamin Barber conceives of global culture in bipolar terms. The book's subtitle, *How Globalism and Tribalism Are Reshaping the World*, bespeaks its vision of a struggle over world culture between the consumerist utopia of "McWorld" and the fundamentalist dystopia of "Jihad." Admittedly, Barber is right when he points to transnational capitalism as the driving engine that brings what he calls "Jihad" and "McWorld" in contact and shapes their interaction. Nonetheless, two facets of his model are unhelpful. The first is its positing of "Jihad," defined as ethnic and religious tribalism, against "McWorld," a transnational capitalism driven by consumerism, with no space for any alternative. Writes Barber: "[O]ur *only choices* are the secular universalism of the cosmopolitan market and the everyday particularism of the fractious tribe" (1996, p. 7, emphasis added). Barber attempts to exit this diametrical opposition, in a chapter titled "Jihad via McWorld," when he postulates that Jihad stands in "less of a stark opposition than a subtle counterpoint" (p. 157) to McWorld. Nevertheless, Barber unwittingly contradicts that claim by offering plethoric evidence in support of a bipolar, rather than a multipolar and contrapuntal, understanding of cultural globalization.

This scenario emphasizes the global at the expense of the local, since it believes that globalization rules via transnational capitalism. The local impulses of Jihad, in Barber's view, are no match for McWorld's powerful global market forces. Clearly, it would be naïve to invest excessive credence in local abilities to "resist" the global. But Barber merely brushes off a vast multidisciplinary corpus on the dynamism of cultures and their ability to negotiate foreign influence. His assumptions about audiences' reactions to "the seductive lifestyle trinity of sex, violence and money" (p. 90) offered by an "information telesector" with an American face are redolent of the mass society paradigm whose proponents believe people to be passive and vulnerable. Thus he writes: "Infantilism is a state of mind dear to McWorld, for it is defined by 'I want, I want, I want'" (p. 93), reducing audiences to infantile cultural dupes, defenseless against the pernicious ideology of consumption. Barber recognizes that consumerism and fundamentalism feed off each other's energies, writing that "Jihad not only revolts against but abets McWorld, while McWorld not only imperils but re-creates and reinforces Jihad" (p. 5). However, his conclusion veers toward immoderate formulae in which the interaction of Jihad with McWorld creates "startling forms of inadvertent tyranny" that range from "an invisibly constraining consumerism to an all too palpable barbarism" (p. 220). These issues notwithstanding,

Jihad vs. McWorld's provocative thesis, broad sweep, accessible style, and wealth of information have made it a classic work.

The "clash of civilizations" thesis propounded by political scientist Samuel Huntington has come to the fore as both retroactive premonition and rationale for the September 11, 2001, attacks and their aftermath. As Dutch sociologist Jan Nederveen Pieterse (1996) reminds us, there is a long tradition among historians of dividing the world into neatly defined civilizational spheres (the phrase "clash of civilizations" itself was coined by Middle East historian Bernard Lewis). After his initial article in *Foreign Affairs* (Huntington, 1993), that bastion of the U.S. foreign policy establishment, Huntington expanded his thesis into a book published in 1996. In the article, "The Clash of Civilizations?" Huntington (1993) had written that a clash of civilizations was to occupy the center of world politics. He had explained that "with the end of the cold war, international politics moves out of its Western phase, and its centre piece becomes the interaction between the West and non-Western civilizations and among non-Western civilizations." In the subsequent book, where the question mark after "The Clash of Civilizations" revealingly disappeared from the title, Huntington broadened his argument to a sweeping culturalist thesis, in which all differences among nations are determined by "culture."

The self-evident premise of the book that the non-Western world has only "entered" international relations after the Cold War notwithstanding, Huntington (1996) writes that "the central theme of the book is that culture and cultural identities, which at the broadest level are civilization identities, are shaping the patterns of cohesion, disintegration, and conflict in the post-Cold War era" (p. 20). The building blocks of Huntington's thesis can be summarized as follows. First, in coming conflicts, civilizational culture—however nebulously defined—will shape alliances between states, but these states will remain the leading political agents operating from and within civilizational spheres. Second, although six or seven civilizations will compete for power, the main fault line will be between the West and the Rest, especially between the Western and Islamic civilizations. Third, the West, and especially the United States, should reject multiculturalism and universalism and instead should focus on strengthening putative core Western values such as liberty, capitalism, the rule of law, and human rights.

Huntington's thesis stirred controversy for several reasons. Intellectually, his division of the world into neatly separated civilizational blocks is not representative of global cultural complexity. Huntington uses "civilization" and "culture" in a manner that suits the examples he offers to support his thesis. While his use of "civilization" is hazy, his use of "culture" is wanting in its assumption of cultural homogeneity. As an example, communities and nations as fundamentally diverse as the Shiites of Lebanon and Iran, the Malays in Malaysia, and the Wahhabi Sunnis in Saudi Arabia are lumped under the monolith of Islamic civilization. In addition, the intercivilizational borders that form the foundations of Huntington's edifice are arbitrary. If Western civilization's core identifier is Christianity, as Huntington assumes, why is Latin America, with its hundreds of millions of Catholics, excluded from Western civilization? Skidmore traced Huntington's cosmetic attempts to remedy these unfortunate contradictions between the article, where China and its sphere of influence were referred to as Confucianist civilization, and the book, where Huntington replaced "Confucianist" with the even vaguer characterization "Sinic" (Skidmore, 1998, p. 182).

The notion of "clash of civilizations" advances a political agenda with domestic and foreign policy components. Notably, Huntington's simultaneous dismissal of multiculturalism and internationalism stands out in its oscillation between isolationism and triumphalism:

> Some Americans have promoted multiculturalism at home; some have promoted universalism abroad; and some have done both. Multiculturalism at home threatens the United States and the West; universalism abroad threatens the West and the world. Both deny the uniqueness of Western culture. The global monoculturalists want to make the world like America. The domestic multiculturalists want to make America like the world. A multicultural America is impossible because a non-Western America is not American. A multicultural world is unavoidable because global empire is impossible. The preservation of the United States and the West requires the renewal of Western identity. The security of the world requires acceptance of global multiculturality. (1996, p. 318)

Huntington accomplishes the feat of dismissing notions of both homogenization and hybridization in favor of a model of civilizational conflict that is intellectually parochial, empirically untenable, and politically dogmatic. Both universalism and relativism are therefore repudiated, lest they interfere with the hermetic categorization that lies at the heart of the book. Writes Nederveen Pieterse (1996): "[I]t is the blatant admixture of security interests with a crude rendition of civilizational difference that makes Huntington's position stand out for its demagogic character" (p. 1389).[1]

Huntington's thesis is the least helpful of these perspectives for un-derstanding intercultural relations. While competing forces do shape cultural globalization, they come as multifaceted and internally diverse constellations of various forces that work on numerous registers with different intensities, and rarely if ever do they come as neatly prepack-aged and unitary categories. These include the constellations of local, national, regional, and global; economy, politics, society, culture; and power, accommodation, appropriation, resistance. The civilizational clash thesis fails to account for the mediations between the dual forces of universalism and particularism, homogenization and hybridization, that weave the fabric of global culture.[2]

In contrast to the bipolarity embodied in *The Clash of Civilizations*, my objective is to understand the complexity and polyvalence of intercul-tural relations. An exploration of the homogenization and hybridization scenarios is thus necessary but not sufficient, since my main interest lies in the role the mass media play in these scenarios. To this end, after exploring scenarios of global culture I revisit two schools of thought in media and communication research that are broadly associated with homogenization and hybridization: (1) the cultural imperialism the-sis, rooted in the critical political economy of international communi-cation; and (2) the active audience school, grounded in reception the-ory and cultural studies. I address questions such as: How do these two "paradigms" relate to the homogenization and hybridization scenarios? How have "cultural imperialism" and "active audience" formulated cross-cultural media influence? Finally, how do these two approaches inform an analysis of hybridity as a communicative phenomenon?

Both homogenization and hybridization acknowledge that global culture has been in the making for centuries; they both also regard transnational media, especially audiovisual media like television and film, as active shapers of contemporary culture. The importance of elec-tronic media stems from their ability to connect hitherto relatively iso-lated spheres of life with relatively continuous streams of sounds, im-ages, ideas, and information. This heightened "complex connectivity" (Tomlinson, 1999) links a multitude of "local" communities, thus form-ing the communicative space of global culture. Because of the ability of contemporary technologies to transcend time and space, they have accelerated the process of cultural globalization and at the same time expanded its range.

Agreement on the general premise that electronic media perform an active role in the globalization of culture does not preclude divergences on the intensity, scope, and desirability of the media's impact, issues grounded in larger geopolitical considerations and revolving around power and identity. These questions remain controversial: Is there an emerging global culture? What does the globalization of culture entail for local diversities? Does cultural globalization extend the political, economic, and technological power of dominant countries to the cultural domain, or, to the contrary, does it stimulate local renewal? Does this process lead to homogenization, or is it spawning a multitude of hybrid cultures?

THE GLOBAL MEDIA DEBATE AND THE RISE OF "CULTURAL IMPERIALISM"

The cultural imperialism position emerged in the early 1970s as a radical critique of functionalist international communication research (see Tomlinson, 1991, for a comprehensive treatment of cultural imperialism). Grounded in an understanding of media as cultural industries that harks back to the Frankfurt School, cultural imperialism is firmly rooted in the critical political economy tradition. Researchers working within this scenario have focused on systemic issues such as capital, infrastructure, and politico-economic concentration of power as determinants of international communication processes. Their basic assumption is that economic and political relations of dependency between first and third world create vast inequities—cultural among others—between nations. The founding texts of the cultural imperialism thesis were published in the 1970s and included Herbert Schiller's *Mass Communication and American Empire* (1971/1992) and *Communication and Cultural Domination* (1976), Jeremy Tunstall's *The Media Are American* (1977), and Armand Mattelart's *Multinational Corporations and the Control of Culture* (1979). Also influential in establishing this research tradition were Ariel Dorfman's and Armand Mattelart's *Para Leer al Pato Donald* (1971), Oliver Boyd-Barrett's chapter "Media Imperialism" (1977), and Johann Galtung's *Journal of Peace Research* article "A Structural Theory of Imperialism" (1971).

The first wave of research focused on nation-states as primary actors in international relations, alleging that rich Western nation-states exported their cultural products and imposed their sociocultural values on poorer nations in the developing world (Schiller, 1971/1992). This group produced a number of studies that demonstrated that the flow of broadcast news and entertainment was biased in favor of industrialized countries, both quantitatively, since most media flows were exported by the Western countries and imported by developing nations, and qualitatively, since developing nations received scant and prejudicial news coverage in Western media (Charles, Shore, and Todd, 1979; Larson, 1979; Varis, 1974, 1984).

Concerns about unequal international media flows ushered in the New World Information Order debate, or NWIO, later known as the New World Information and Communication Order, or NWICO. The 1976 Nairobi, Kenya, Nineteenth General Conference of the United Nations Educational, Scientific, and Cultural Organization (UNESCO), whose mission as a specialized agency of the United Nations encompasses issues of communication and culture, passed a resolution adopting NWICO by consensus, and the thirty-first UN General Assembly shortly followed suit. In 1977, UNESCO appointed Irish statesman Sean McBride chair of a newly created International Commission for the Study of Communication Problems, known as the McBride Commission, to follow up on the resolutions. At first focused on news flows between the North and the South, the NWICO debate evolved to include all international media flows. This change occurred because news and entertainment flows were both unequal, and also because (then) new media technologies such as communication satellites and videocassette players and recorders made the international media landscape more complex. Strong differences polarized conference attendees in two groups. Comprising the United States and the United Kingdom, the first group insisted on the "free flow of information" doctrine that advocates unfettered market processes in information and media programs. The second group, a coalition of Western, Communist, and developing countries, perceived the "free flow of information" ideology as a justification for continued Anglo-American economic and cultural domination, what Mattelart (1994) retrospectively derided as "the free fox in the free chicken house" (p. 236). The latter group argued instead for a "free and balanced flow" of information (Masmoudi, 1979; Schiller, 1974; Zassoursky and Losev, 1981). It is important to emphasize that this was not a West-versus-Rest debate, since Canada and France, for example, often opposed the United States and the United Kingdom. It is equally crucial not to underestimate the influence of cold-war rivalry between the United States and the Soviet Union, and the legitimate American concerns about authoritarian control of information.

In addition to geopolitical competition, the chasm between the two sides was anchored in two different conceptions of culture. According to the United States and Great Britain, cultural products were private commodities to be sold and bought according to market mechanisms. The other camp argued that culture was a public resource to be protected by the state from market forces because cultural products concretize a country's national identity and cultural distinctiveness. One of the first UNESCO reports, the result of a conference on culture and identity, reflected those concerns:

> Culture belongs to man, to all men. The conference was unanimous in recognizing and reaffirming with conviction and force the equal dignity of all cultures, rejecting any hierarchy in that area . . . . It therefore reaffirmed the duty of each to respect all cultures. It could be clearly seen that the affirmation of cultural identity had become a permanent requirement, both for individuals and for groups and nations . . . . Cultural identity [is] the defence of traditions, of history and of the moral, spiritual and ethical values handed down by past generations. (UNESCO, 1982, p. 8)

Besides the report's asserting that culture was a public resource, the strong feelings suggested by its language are grounded in an unstated definition of culture as national culture. This view is also based on the assumption that national culture is a unitary entity that carries a repertoire of beliefs and traditions that require an active role by the state to protect the authenticity of national culture from endogenous corruption, a holistic conception of culture that, I argue in Chapter Seven, offers little help in understanding contemporary intercultural relations. Within this approach, when external influence or foreign influence was mentioned, it customarily referred to the United States, whose commercial popular culture has been the bête noire of governments and scholars alike. Information was subjected to a similar controversy between those who advocated a public service and educational role, and those who argued for the commercial exploitation of information resources. The passage in 1977 of a UN resolution that supported NWICO reflected widespread international (1) acceptance of the holistic conception of culture and (2) opposition to the free flow principle advocated by the United States.

Despite the fact that UNESCO and UN resolutions on the subject were neither legally binding nor practically feasible, both the U.S. government and nonstate actors in the United States fought the New World Information and Communication Order. The Reagan administration called on UNESCO to stop its efforts to "control press freedom," and then assistant secretary of state Elliot Abrams counseled UNESCO to look for a solution to world communication problems in the First Amendment of the Constitution of the United States (Kleinwachter, 1994). U.S.

press coverage was in line with U.S. government policy, epitomized in a *New York Times* editorial that some considered the first public call for withdrawal from UNESCO. "If it turns out to be impossible to reject this attempt to tamper with our basic principles," the *New York Times* wrote, "there is always the alternative of rejecting UNESCO itself" (quoted in Gerbner, 1994, p. 114). Indeed, the controversy eventually led to the withdrawal from UNESCO of the United States and the United Kingdom, and to the de facto decline of the global media debate.[3]

In the aftermath of the NWICO debate, the notion of cultural imperialism became a rallying cry for developing countries in their attempt to formulate an alternative to the globally pervasive Anglo-American media. The enduring resonance of imperialism rhetoric and its effectiveness at mobilizing disparate interests of relatively weak developing nations remains evident, although this discourse no longer prevails in international organizations. For example, UNESCO publications nowadays speak of hybridity instead of dominance (see Brunel and Lefort, 2000; Portella, 2000), which may explain why the United States rejoined UNESCO in 2002—in the famous "Axis of Evil" speech by U.S. president George W. Bush. This, however, is a moot point, since international media and cultural flows are no longer regulated by states but are now deregulated under the sway of the World Trade Organization and the International Monetary Fund. Clearly, the idea of cultural imperialism has been losing its political luster.

"CULTURAL IMPERIALISM" IN QUESTION

The intellectual cachet of "cultural imperialism" did not stem from rigorous theoretical definition, because as a notion the term suffered from a polysemic ambiguity that wrapped the thesis itself in controversy. The thesis's founding narratives (Boyd-Barrett, 1977; Galtung, 1971; Mattelart, 1979; Schiller, 1971/1992, 1976; Tunstall, 1977) contained a variety of definitions whose differences ranged from subtle nuances to more substantial divergences. In one of the first published and most frequently cited definitions, U.S. media critic Herbert Schiller wrote in his seminal *Communication and Cultural Domination* (1976): "The concept of cultural imperialism . . . best describes the sum of the processes by which a society is brought into the modern world system and how its dominating stratum is attracted, pressured, forced and sometimes bribed into shaping social institutions to correspond to, or even promote, the value and structures of the dominating center of the system" (p. 9). While ushering in an era of radical critique of global power structures, Schiller's definition revealed some of the contradictions that were to bedevil the cultural imperialism thesis. He essentially described a structural socioeconomic process while referring to it as *cultural* imperialism. The language he used—"world system," "social institutions," "structures," and "center"—does not directly address the notion of "culture" in cultural imperialism, with the exception of a mention of the "values" of the center. British researcher Jeremy Tunstall (1977) included culture more explicitly in his definition of cultural imperialism, which stated that "authentic, traditional and local culture . . . is being battered out of existence by the indiscriminate dumping of large quantities of slick commercial and media products, mainly from the United States" (p. 57). One year later, Bolivian writer Luis Ramiro Beltrán (1978b) defined cultural imperialism as "a verifiable process of social influence by which a nation imposes on other countries its set of beliefs, values, knowledge, and behavioral norms as well as its overall style of life" (p. 184).

These definitions set the tone for the emerging thesis and simultaneously showed the first cracks in its edifice. First, there is the unarticulated conception of culture as a holistic, organic entity that is closely associated with the nation-state. Emerging in tandem with the NWICO debate, this view is problematical because it glosses over the cultural diversity and fusion that exist within most nation-states, and for other reasons elaborated on in Chapter Seven. Besides, critics were quick to accuse proponents of the cultural imperialism thesis of ideological rigidity and bipolar thinking. The cultural imperialism approach's claims of cultural authenticity were synchronic, while assertions of cultural imposition and erasure were allegedly reminiscent of early theorizing in mass communication, such as the "magic bullet" and "hypodermic needle" models that treated audiences as passive cultural dupes. Early warning signals about the ambiguity of the concept came from its own advocates. The Belgian-born critic Armand Mattelart (1979), co-author with the Chilean-born Ariel Dorfman of *Para Leer al Pato Donald* (1971), raised concerns about cultural imperialism's ambiguity, and wrote that the concept has "too often been used with ill-defined meaning" (p. 57). In a sweeping assessment, U.S.-based media scholar Fred Fejes (1981) warned of the absence of rigorous conceptual work and called for innovative theory construction. Fejes advocated research on the national aspects of domination, and a historical perspective on the "extremely complex interrelationships" (p. 286) between mass media and dominance. He also called for expanding cultural imperialism research from the mass media to other areas, such as professional training and information data transfers. Most relevant to this book, Fejes argued for the necessity of a sophisticated understanding of the concept of culture. He thus encapsulated a major weakness of the thesis under critique:

> [A] great deal of the concern over media imperialism is motivated by a fear ... of the threat that such media poses to the integrity and the development of viable national cultures in Third World societies. All too often the institutional aspects of transnational media receive the major attention while the cultural impact, which one assumes to occur, goes unaddressed in any detailed manner. Generally a perception of the cultural consequences of the contents of various media products is based on a view of the mass media as primarily manipulative agents capable of having direct, unmediated effects on the audience's behavior and world view. (p. 287)

Fejes concluded his statement by pointing to what he saw to be promising developments in literary scholarship on culture, a nod that in retrospect was prescient to the extent that it came on the heels of nascent theoretical (Hall, 1980/1997) and empirical (D. Morley, 1980) developments that would turn out to be influential in media studies.

By the 1990s, critics of the cultural imperialism perspective—both in media and interdisciplinary venues—were legion. The thesis of Herbert Schiller and his colleagues was dismissed as a monolithic theory that lacked subtlety, and it was increasingly questioned by empirical research. Titles such as *Media Imperialism Reconsidered* (C. Lee, 1980), *The Decentering of Cultural Imperialism* (Sinclair, 1992), "Beyond Cultural Imperialism" (Golding and Harris, 1997; Straubhaar, 1991), "Media Imperialism Reformulated" (Boyd-Barrett, 1998), and "Media Imperialism Revisited" (Chadha and Kavoori, 2000) have appeared with increasing regularity, underscoring an unequivocally revisionist trend. Some scholars (C. Lee, 1980; Salwen, 1991; Sreberny-Mohammadi, 1997; Straubhaar, 1991) criticized the cultural imperialism approach for failing to adapt to changes in international media flows, while others (Elasmar and Hunter, 1997; Willnat, He, and Xiaoming, 1998) argued that the cultural imperialism scenario was unsubstantiated by empirical data. Sreberny-Mohammadi concluded that cultural imperialism has "lost much of its critical bite and historic validity" (1997, p. 47). While there is some truth in most of these writings, the fact that many critics still spend substantial print space outlining the deficiencies of cultural imperialism has imbued the thesis with a residual life-after-death attraction and continues to expose the lack of a solid alternative.

Because of their size and resources, countries like Brazil (Straubhaar, 1984, 1991) and China (C. Lee, 1980) raise questions about the cultural imperialism thesis. Both China and Brazil have substantial domestic audiences, strong cultural traditions, and resources relatively proportional to their size. With the world's largest population, a strong economic growth rate, a nuclear arsenal, and a permanent seat on the UN Security Council, China is a great power en route to superpower status. With Latin America's largest economy and dominant military forces, a population close to 175 million, and a thriving creative tradition of television drama, Brazil is an emerging giant.

The cases of China and Brazil offer a corrective to the broad brush of the cultural imperialism thesis, but their main contribution is to stimulate new theoretical debates. For example, in his examination of Brazil, U.S. scholar Joseph Straubhaar (1991) introduced new theoretical material by reinterpreting the Norwegian scholar Johann Galtung's (1971) concept of "asymmetrical interdependence" as a characteristic of international media relations whereby countries have multiple relationships and differential degrees of cultural, economic, and cultural power.[4] Some scholars met the notion of interdependence with skepticism, with Mattelart, for example, arguing that it is a "leitmotif at the heart of the doctrine of soft power" (2002, p. 600), which in Mattelart's view serves to deny the existence of a hierarchy of nation-states and to absolve dominant countries from responsibility and accountability. Nonetheless, whether one focuses on the power imbalances that "asymmetrical" suggests or the two-way interactions that "interdependence" connotes, the debate on intercultural media relations has moved into more nuanced terrain.

Salwen (1991) for instance, argued that exposure to foreign media is only one of several factors that may weaken cultural identities and transform social values. However, Salwen cites cases (Granzberg, 1982; Kang and Morgan, 1988; Tan, Tan, and Tan, 1987) where Western cultural influence did create "personal conflicts and social disruptions" (p. 39). For further research into this phenomenon, Salwen advocated widening the scope of methods and approaches involved in the study of cultural imperialism beyond critical political economy because "the phenomenon of cultural imperialism is far too important and far-reaching for its analysis to be limited to any single . . . subdiscipline" (p. 36). This statement is at once an acknowledgment of inequality in intercultural relations and an invitation for further interdisciplinary research.

What transpires from these analyses is that the shortcomings of "cultural imperialism" do not warrant a sweeping dismissal. As explained in Chapter One, several leading figures in the cultural imperialism scenario since the 1970s (Boyd-Barrett, 1998; Mattelart, 1994, 1998) have acknowledged the need to revise the dominance perspective and recognize the notion of hybridity, with the caveat that cultural imperialism as a general framework should not be dismissed. This shift reflects a more nuanced understanding of culture within the political economy tradition (Mosco and Schiller, 2001) and a blending of political economy and cultural studies approaches (Miller et al., 2001), concretizing an evolution (in the critical political economy tradition) that considers, in Edward Comor's words, "the multiple and integrated levels of both structure and agency" (2002, p. 320).[5]

Reconsidering the cultural imperialism thesis and elucidating some of its blind spots are therefore more useful than rejecting it wholesale. Notably, that thesis's most important contribution transcends criticism: the argument that power pervades international communication processes. For instance, writers in that tradition have analyzed Western government intervention on behalf of cultural industries (Comor, 1997; Fehrenbach and Poiger, 2000a; Herman and McChesney, 1997; Mattelart, 1994; Schiller, 1991), some contending that the free flow doctrine is partly a rhetorical strategy that serves corporate media interests at the expense of nation-states and citizens. Finally, these researchers have paved the way for the argument that the right to communicate is as important as the right to freedom from oppression and the right to a clean environment, that the right to communicate is a civil right that ought not be subordinated to commercial interests.

The evolution of the debate is therefore a redirection of emphasis rather than a paradigm shift. There is growing interest in communicational dimensions of social justice, human rights, global civil society, and the transnational public sphere (Braman and Sreberny-Mohammadi, 1996; Thussu, 1998). This new direction has benefited from the theoretical and empirical contributions of feminism, postcolonial thought, cultural studies, and critical perspectives on development. The journal *Public Culture*, published by Duke University Press for the Society of Transnational Cultural Studies, focuses on issues of civil society and the public sphere from a variety of interdisciplinary perspectives located at the intersection of the critical social sciences and interpretive humanities. *Public Culture* has institutionalized, perhaps more than any other forum, the language of transnationalism (Chuh, 1996; Rouse, 1995) and a new "critical" perspective on internationalism (B. Lee, 1994). Other arenas where global issues of power and culture can be addressed critically from standpoints outside the cultural imperialism thesis *strictu sensu* include the special issue of *Communication Theory* on postcolonialism and the *Journal of International Communication*.[6]

Questioning the Postimperialist Blues

Retrospectives on the cultural imperialism school have summarized and synthesized critiques directed against it (Roach, 1997; Tomlinson, 1991), but few have explored the institutional and disciplinary bases of the anti–cultural imperialism discourse. As mentioned earlier, theoretical perspectives are influenced by the environment in which they develop, in that the institutional space where a discourse arises exerts a formative influence on the tenor of that discourse. In that regard, what is the significance of the fact that many critics of the cultural imperialism thesis's hailing from North American mainstream mass communication research (with some notable exceptions: C. Lee, 1980; Salwen, 1991; Straubhaar, 1991) have not fully engaged the tenets of cultural imperialism research? Indeed, most critics have claimed that the cultural imperialism thesis is rhetorical rather than scientific, ideological rather than empirical. For example, in their introduction to the special issue "Media Flows of Latin America" of the journal *Communication Research*, U.S.-based scholars Everett Rogers and Jorge Schement (1984) write that "[m]any publications are of a polemic nature, selecting facts mainly to support one position or another, and aiming at political persuasion rather than at the scientific testing of hypotheses. When a theoretical viewpoint has been utilized, such as dependency theory, empirical data have not always been brought to bear on theoretical hypotheses" (p. 161). Subsequent critiques of the cultural imperialism thesis echo this perspective by pointing to scarce empirical support or by asserting the weakness of foreign television influence (Elasmar and Hunter, 1997; Willnat, He, and Xiaoming, 1998).

Repeated criticism compelled exponents of cultural imperialism to defend (Schiller, 1991) or reformulate (Boyd-Barrett, 1998; Mattelart, 1994) their claims. However, the critics' preoccupation with empirical—in other words, statistical—validation or invalidation of the tenets of cultural imperialism, while on the surface illustrating methodological differences, exposes deeper epistemological and ontological divergences, which then U.S.-based German scholar Hanno Hardt (1988) fleshes out in his critical review of comparative mainstream mass communication research in the United States: "This tradition fails to consider historical growth as an indissoluble process that cannot be dissected into empirical parts or facts and prefers to treat communication and media studies in terms of a series of specific, isolated social phenomena. In this context, it seems that the field suffers not only from a cultural bias but also from a social scientific bias toward searching for laws governing the relationship of media and society. As a result, empirical research techniques obscure cultural differences" (p. 138). The rejection of the radical agenda of the cultural imperialism thesis was also grounded in the political context of post–World War II social science research in the United States. According to Hardt (1988), U.S. international communication research has developed in response to the needs of the U.S. government and not as an autonomous area of knowledge. It is true that U.S. policy makers viewed the global spread of American television as both a commercial opportunity and a strategic advantage. U.S. media scholar Michael Curtin (1993) argued that Federal Communication Commission officials were keenly aware of these advantages and ensured that the international regulatory environment was suitable to U.S. governments and corporations. The American policy discourse that emerged in the 1950s is best described, according to Curtin, as "official internationalism," a doctrine dedicated to enhancing U.S. leadership and later serving as the framework for the notion of free flow of information.

This policy discourse on global television can be understood within a broad historical pattern that some critics have identified in public discourse in the United States as the denial of empire. Literary scholars Amy Kaplan and Donald Pease argue that the absence of empire is an enduring characteristic of the study of U.S. culture. In their view, American studies and diplomatic history "mirror one another in their respective blind spots to the cultures of US imperialism" (1993, p. 11), because the resilience of the idea of U.S. exceptionalism articulates imperial practice with academic discourse. Kaplan (1993) claims that this discourse is grounded in two historical eras: the struggle for independence from the British, and the Cold War against the Soviets, when the United States saw itself as resisting imperial domination. The passing of these two eras did not entail the waning of empire denial. Kaplan cites a *New York Times* opinion piece whose author refutes the claim that the 1991 Gulf War was imperialistic and argues for a distinction between unipolarity and U.S. dominance, explaining that "a unipolar world is not the same as a hierarchical system dominated by a single power that creates the rules as well as enforces them" (quoted in Kaplan, 1993, p. 13). Kaplan reads this explanation as a double dynamic of displacement and denial that replaces notions of imperialism and empire with euphemisms such as "unipolarity" and "world power."

This analysis of imperial practices within a body of knowledge that, according to Kaplan (1993), has systematically refused to acknowledge the presence of these practices is emblematic of a critical and interpretive turn in the human and social sciences. It is remarkable that mainstream international communication research has entered its putative postim-perialist era at precisely the point in time when other disciplines have come to terms with power relations in their fields. The field of American studies is an interesting exemplar of this trend, because arguably no other area in the social sciences and humanities is as inextricably bound to the history and national identity of the United States. In a landmark article in *American Quarterly*, American studies scholars Jane Desmond and Virginia Domínguez (1996) called for relocating American studies in a "critical internationalism" (p. 475), a notion borrowed from cultural critic Benjamin Lee (1995). From the onset, the authors draw a clear distinction between critical internationalism and a superficial internationalization that merely adds a few international courses to the curriculum and a few non-American scholars to the faculty. According to Desmond and Domínguez (1996), this internationalization movement remains U.S.-centric and immune to analyses of the United States from other countries and intellectual traditions.

They call for a dynamic interface between U.S. and non-U.S. scholars that would establish new sites for the production of knowledge, and for a clear engagement with issues that may not be of immediate concern and interest to the domestic U.S. sphere. This globalist outlook, according to these American studies scholars, is best achieved by the adoption of a comparative epistemology, which to succeed must engage and respect scholarship about the United States produced by non-U.S. scholars, and not ghettoize these scholars and their intellectual traditions according to geographical or political criteria. It is significant that American studies—a field whose focus is by definition the national sphere of the United States—would enter such a critical moment of increased self-reflexivity and international engagement, when international communication—a field that by name is indubitably cosmopolitan and whose scope is nominally the world—would retreat from a critical and globally engaged agenda.

Developments in American studies can serve as a departure point from which to reform the cultural imperialism thesis and revisit some of its core beliefs in the wake of the current interest in "cultural globalization." Before examining the assumptions of the cultural globalization literature vis-à-vis cultural imperialism and its critics, it is important to understand the contributions of the active audience group to the study of transnational communication and culture. Just as the critical movement in American studies helped restore the agency of the Other in U.S. history and foreign policy, active audience research, as we will shortly see, restored a sense of social agency to audiences that cultural imperialism scholarship had—paradoxically, in light of its progressive agenda—denied them.

THE ACTIVE AUDIENCE AND GLOBAL MEDIA STUDIES

The history of audience research has oscillated between approaches that emphasized the media's persuasive power and perspectives that stressed audience activity. While a teleological origin is impossible to pinpoint, the Frankfurt School in Germany played a pioneering role in focusing on the media audience, since the school's critical perspective associated instrumental uses of communication with the rise of fascist exploitation of the masses and the concomitant loss of individual agency. In an environment of modernization and urbanization, traditional social mediators between leaders and the people crumbled, and as a result alienated individuals succumbed to targeted persuasion campaigns. The Frankfurt School approach's deep gloominess stems from its grounding in the totalitarian experience of Nazism. When its leading figures Theodor Adorno, Max Horkheimer, and Herbert Marcuse escaped from Nazi persecution to New York in the late 1930s, they stirred a debate about the role of the mass media in society.

North American–based researchers such as Elihu Katz, Paul Lazarsfeld, and Robert Merton refuted the Frankfurt School's attribution of powerful effects to the mass media and disagreed with their German colleagues' assessment of social mediators between politicians and the people. These two lines of thought can be found in Lazarsfeld and colleagues' *The People's Choice* (1944) and Katz and Lazarsfeld's *Personal Influence* (1955), which developed the "two-step" flow idea of mediated influence to counter the Frankfurt School's belief in unmediated communication between leaders and their constituencies. Contra the philosophically grounded and theoretically informed critical methods of Frankfurt School scholars, U.S. researchers advocated functionalist approaches to mass media effects. In 1946, Merton published *Mass Persuasion*, a study of the Kate Smith war-bond broadcasts in the United States. Reviewing these developments, British media cultural studies scholar David Morley (1994) pointed out that Merton (1946) presciently called for an emphasis on the actual process of communication, at a time when most researchers focused on the content (Berelson, 1952) of the mass media, but that Merton's call for a new direction led to an unintended switch from content to effects, often studied from a behaviorist perspective (for example, see Bandura, 1961). By emphasizing limited media effects, these studies prepared the ground for notions of audience activity.

The "uses and gratifications" tradition developed in the environment hostile to Frankfurt School–inspired models of powerful media effects and passive audiences. Dennis McQuail (1984) traced the beginnings of "uses and gratifications" to the 1940s, when early studies of radio looked into the social environment of listeners. A broad and eclectic literature concerned with the motivations of media users (see Klapper, 1960) ensued, whose central concern was the "functions" of the media, expressed by Katz when he made his famous pronouncement that "less attention [should be paid] to what media do to people and more to what people do with the media" (1959, p. 2). Katz was in fact arguing that media-effects research should presume that audience behavior is selective, launching "uses and gratifications."

There are several strands of uses-and-gratifications research (McQuail, 1984; McQuail and Gurevitch, 1974), whose core assumptions are that individuals in the audience (1) are motivated to make conscious choices about which media to use, and (2) know how to use them in order to obtain gratification. Early formulations emphasized a psychological approach (Katz, Blumler, and Gurevitch, 1974) that focused on needs and the expectations they create, within a functionalist framework that influenced later research (Liebes and Katz, 1990; Rosengren, Wenner, and Palmgreen, 1985). No longer as prevalent as it once was, "uses and gratifications" still occasionally frames research on "new" technologies such as the cellular phone (Leung and Wei, 2000) and the Internet (Papacharisi and Rubin, 2000).

Since the 1970s, postfunctionalist developments within mass communication research have challenged the uses-and-gratifications perspective. These approaches include cultural studies, semiotics, symbolic interactionism, and even mainstream mass communication and political communication research (Ang, 1991, 1996; Carey and Kreiling, 1974; Chaney, 1972; Downing, 1996; Elliott, 1974; Hall, 1980/1997; Morley, 1980, 1992; Nightingale, 1996; Swanson, 1977). Uses-and-gratifications scholars were themselves dissatisfied with aspects of the theory (see McQuail, 1984 and Rosengren et al., 1985). Critics focused on the theoretical thinness of the uses-and-gratifications approach, its methodological flaws, its individualistic psychological focus associated with a lack of attention to power and structural issues, its assumption of a stable, conflict-free social environment, and the consumerist connotations of its language. Criticism of the uses-and-gratifications perspective was somewhat concurrent with the development of the active audience formation in cultural studies, which shares uses-and-gratifications' basic assumption of audience activity, but has substantially different theoretical positions, methodological tools, and political sensibilities.

To understand audience studies in their historical context, it may be useful to go back to mid-twentieth-century Europe. Concerns with "Americanization" can be traced back to interwar Europe, when fascist governments adapted U.S. media-production strategies for propaganda purposes (Fehrenbach and Poigier, 2000b). These concerns turned into a widespread preoccupation in post–World War II Europe when U.S. soldiers introduced American consumer icons—most famously Coca-Cola. At that time, American popular culture was perceived to be "here, there, and everywhere" (Wagnleitner and May, 2000), and as a result was met with hostility in European countries struggling to rebuild their states and societies (Fehrenbach and Poiger, 2000b), leading to a variety of anti-American discourses (Ellwood, 2000). However, post–World War II European reactions to U.S. culture were ambiguous, at once rejection and acceptance, and may be better understood if we situate them in the internal dynamics of some European countries. For example, while the reconstruction of German cinema was shrouded in fears of Americanization, Fehrenbach (2000) has argued that the real cause of these concerns was anxiety about post-Nazi German identity. Similarly, debates about limiting U.S. popular music on French radios conveniently deflected attention from internal French struggles (Petterson, 2000), while disputes over U.S. popular music in 1940s Britain highlighted class differences in British society (Hebdige, 1988). Nonetheless, perception of U.S. cultural influence was a unifying theme in Europe in the 1940s and 1950s, and to some extent is still a factor in present-day Europe.

More importantly, U.S. social science provided a counter-template for European audience research. Theoretically, the cybernetic communication model (Shannon and Weaver, 1949) subsumed the audience under the individualistic term "receiver," while mass media organizations were described as "senders." Communication was a process of transmission that took place through "message" and "feedback" in a "channel" where the process could be challenged by "noise." This mechanistic model thus reduced audience activity to "feedback," presumably to be provided by audience surveys. Though this model dominated North American media research, it was less influential in Europe, where it nonetheless was engaged by scholars like the British Richard Hoggart and the Italian Umberto Eco (see Nightingale, 1996, for a more elaborate discussion of this issue). Nonetheless, Shannon and Weaver (1949) was explicitly taken as a counter-model in cultural studies approaches to audience activity.[7]

British cultural studies scholar Stuart Hall counterposed his encoding-decoding approach (1980/1997) to the cybernetic model. Hall conceived of the process of communication as a "complex structure in dominance" (p. 91) that consists of four distinct but connected "moments"—production, circulation, distribution/consumption, and reproduction. Each of these stages, in Hall's view, is necessary "to the circuit as a whole," but none of the stages predetermines the next, even if the moments of encoding and decoding are "determinate" (p. 91). Hall proposed three hypothetical decoding positions: a "dominant-hegemonic" code, a negotiated code, and an oppositional code. Dominant meanings are those that "win plausibility for and command as legitimate a *decoding* of the event within the limits of dominant definitions" (p. 99). This formulation can be seen as the beginning of the notion of "no necessary correspondence," through which Hall (1985, 1986) expressed his theory of articulation based on notions of Gramscian hegemony as opposed to the more necessary correspondence between institutional practices and social effects seen in the Althusserian notion of interpellation.

The encoding/decoding proposal had a significant influence on the then nascent audience-research tradition in cultural studies. In the 1980s, half a dozen empirical studies crystallized the empirical implications of Hall's theory. The founding cohort included David Morley and Charlotte Brunsdon's *Everyday Television "Nationwide"* (1978), Morley's *The "Nationwide" Audience* (1980), Dorothy Hobson's *Crossroads: The Drama of a Soap Opera* (1982), Ien Ang's *Watching Dallas: Soap Opera and the Melodramatic Imagination* (1985), and David Buckingham's *Public Secrets: EastEnders and Its Audience* (1987). This first wave was mostly British and focused on single television programs. Contrary to conventional wisdom, however, not all these studies were concerned with reception. In fact, as Australian scholar Virginia Nightingale (1996) reminds us, some of these studies focused substantively on media production.

The central theoretical and epistemological questions of the active audience design were taken up in North America in a special issue of the *Journal of Communication Inquiry*, "Cultural Studies and Ethnography" (1989), and a symposium organized around a provocative piece by Canada-based Martin Allor (1988) in *Critical Studies in Mass Communication*. These two scholarly events, among other publications and conferences, signaled a transatlantic migration and a subsequent institutional recognition of audience ethnography in North America. This recognition was foretold by literary scholar Janice Radway's *Reading the Romance* (1984), although in that book Radway focused on romance novels and not on television. There was also James Lull's *World Families Watch Television* (1988), with a symbolic interactionist bent, and Liebes and Katz's *The Export of Meaning* (1990), grounded in a modified uses-and-gratifications perspective. These developments were anticipated by earlier studies on media reception that were often unacknowledged (see Curran, 1990).

Though American versions shared the British school's focus on audience activity, they did not place equal weight on exploring how media reception reproduces ideological structures. Neither did most U.S. active audience studies account for the material realities that frame media consumption. Rather, this research focused on what it saw as the empowering attributes of subversive interpretations of media texts, which led some critics to bemoan what they saw as a "cultural populism" (McGuigan, 1992) that was "pointless" (Seamann, 1992). In fact, both U.K. and U.S. variants of active audience research suffered from the critiques leveled at cultural studies in general, namely, according exaggerated importance to discursive processes at the expense of structural forces (see the various contributions to Ferguson and Golding, 1997). Morley, an audience-research pioneer who nonetheless warned elsewhere of the "pitfalls" of audience activity (Morley, 1995), encapsulated the core argument against (most) North American audience research as follows: "One of the crucial features of the American (and predominantly literary) appropriation of British cultural studies has been the loss of any sense of culture and communications as having material roots, in broader social and political processes and structures, so that the discursive process of the constitution of meanings often becomes the exclusive focus on analysis, without any reference to its institutional or economic setting" (Morley, 1997, p. 123). However, though Morley acknowledged the "unhelpful romanticization of consumer freedoms" (p. 137) in some active audience studies, he nonetheless warned of an artificial separation between what he considered to be complementary micro- and macroprocesses.

This "debate" between—and also within—North American and British approaches to the audience, joined by scholars from India, Latin America, and Scandinavia (see Murphy and Kraidy, 2003b), underscores that the audience is, explicitly or latently, the linchpin of research on media influence. Indeed, the cultural imperialism perspective was predicated on an unstated audience, which was putatively assumed to be dependent, passive, and vulnerable. But does recognition of audience activity, which opens the possibility of some kind of social agency, fatally undermine the cultural imperialism thesis? Or does such recognition usher in a more urbane methodology to tackle cultural dominance? In fact, the radical critique of transnational cultural power initiated by cultural imperialism scholars may be more crucial at a time when "globalization," with its ideological baggage and economic bases, is promoted as an alternative framework for international communication studies.

FROM "CULTURAL IMPERIALISM" TO "CULTURAL GLOBALIZATION"?

Globalization has become, in the terms of world-system theorist Immanuel Wallerstein (2000), an "enormous recent furor" (p. xix) in the human and social sciences. The word "global" is more than four centuries old, but its derivatives "globalize" and "globalization" appeared only in the late 1950s, and in 1961 *Webster's* was the first major dictionary to define "globalization" (Waters, 1995). Two decades later the word had already entered academic parlance, but it is the 1990s that witnessed the rise to prominence of the notions "global culture" and "cultural globalization." As an innately interdisciplinary constellation of concepts and perspectives, "cultural globalization" differs from both the cultural imperialism thesis and the active audience group. That dissimilarity, however, should not distract from the intellectual debt that cultural globalization owes to both aforementioned media-research traditions, as global culture scholars have implicitly borrowed and adapted ideas from writings on both cultural imperialism and audience activity.

Like "imperialism" in the 1970s and "postmodernism" in the 1980s, "globalization" is an infamously ambiguous word, "a maddeningly euphemistic term laden with desire, fantasy, fear, attraction—and intellectual imprecision about what it is supposed to describe" (Miller et al., 2001, p. 18). Its founding sociological narratives culminated in the early 1990s, when British sociologist Anthony Giddens (1990) described globalization as the "intensification of world-wide social relations which link distant localities in such a way that local happenings are shaped by events occurring many miles away and vice versa" (p. 64), and U.S. sociologist Roland Robertson (1992) defined it as "the compression of the world and the intensification of consciousness of the world as a whole" (p. 8). Swedish anthropologist Ulf Hannerz's definition of a global "ecumene" as a "region of persistent culture interaction and exchange" (Hannerz, 1994, p. 137) reflects its anthropological underpinnings, conceived of by Arjun Appadurai (1994) in terms of disjunctive flows of people, capital, technology, images, and ideologies.

Global culture gained recognition as a salient social science research issue in a 1990 double issue of the journal *Theory, Culture, and Society*, subsequently reissued as a book (Featherstone, 1994). In that volume, British sociologist Anthony Smith (1994) expressed some trepidation toward the concept of "global culture." If culture meant a collectivity's way of life, Smith argued, then it is impossible to speak of a global culture, because there are many different ways of life and therefore *many* cultures. Nonetheless, Smith acknowledged a developing global culture that "is tied to *no place or period. It is context-less*, a true melange of disparate components drawn from everywhere and nowhere, borne upon the modern chariots of global telecommunication systems" (p. 177, my emphasis), effectively introducing, without naming it, the idea of deterritorialization and its more controversial cousin, hybridity.

The volume *Global Culture: Nationalism, Globalization, and Modernity* (Featherstone, 1994) instituted the vocabulary of the Anglophone debate on the tension in global culture between cohesion and dispersal, homogenization and heterogenization. In addition to Anthony Smith's contribution (1994), Arjun Appadurai expounded his now famous notion of "disjuncture," Zygmunt Bauman (1994) underscored the "ambivalence" of modernity, and Immanuel Wallerstein (1994) famously cast culture as "the ideological battleground of the modern world-system" (p. 31). Besides setting the parameters of the debate, the volume (Featherstone, 1994) questioned the idea of global cultural uniformity, paving the way for the hybridity discourse. In his extensively cited and anthologized

article "Disjuncture and Difference in the Global Cultural Economy"—
reprinted in his *Modernity at Large* (1996)—Appadurai proffered his
landscape metaphors (ethnoscapes, mediascapes, financescapes, etc.)
to illustrate deterritorialization, and held that cross-cultural exchanges
"play havoc with the hegemony of Eurochronology" (Appadurai, 1996,
p. 30).

Another seminal volume on global culture carried the proceedings
of an international symposium held in Binghamton, New York, in 1989.
Culture, Globalization, and the World-System (King, 1990/1997) regroups
some of the contributors to the global culture issue of *Theory, Culture,
and Society* with other scholars. While it shares the Featherstone (1994)
collection's concern with the relationship of the global and the local,
King's volume is more inclusive in that contributors hail from both the
humanities and social sciences. In contrast to the former's inclusion of
mostly sociologists and anthropologists, the latter gathered art historians (Barbara Abou-El-Haj and John Tagg) and visual media scholars
(Janet Wolff and Maureen Turin) in addition to sociologists (Roland
Robertson and Immanuel Wallerstein) and anthropologist Ulf Hannerz.
Many of the authors have interdisciplinary affiliations: Robertson is also
a professor of religious studies, King holds a joint appointment in sociology and in art history, Wallerstein is a political economist, and Hall is
probably the world's preeminent cultural studies scholar.

The two books (Featherstone, 1994; King, 1990/1997) shaped the cultural globalization debate into the mid- to late 1990s, when the publication of Rob Wilson and Wimal Dissanayake's *Global/Local: Cultural
Production and the Transnational Imaginary* (1996) and Fredric Jameson
and Masao Miyoshi's *The Cultures of Globalization* (1998) instituted the
study of globalization and culture in the humanities. *Public Culture*, the
journal of the Society for Transnational Cultural Studies, also engaged
the debate. The *Publication of the Modern Language Association* (*PMLA*)
published a special issue, "Globalizing Literary Studies" (2001), that
featured an essay by Edward Said, "Globalizing Literary Study," and
both the journals *International Sociology* (2000) and *Third World Quarterly*
(2000) published special issues on globalization. Within the span of a
decade, globalization had become a pandisciplinary preoccupation.

A similar debate arose in international communication scholarship,
where several factors explain the advocacy of "cultural globalization" as
an alternative to "cultural imperialism." First, the end of the Cold War
as a global framework for ideological, geopolitical, and economic competition catalyzed a rethinking of conceptual approaches and analytical

categories. By giving rise to the United States as the lone superpower and at the same time leaving the world politically fragmented, the complexity of the post–Cold War era presents tension between global forces of cohesion and local reactions of dispersal. In this intricate arrangement of interlocking subnational, national, and supranational forces, the nation-state no longer monopolizes political agency. Globalization thus allegedly replaced cultural imperialism because it conveys a process (or more accurately, many interlocking processes) with less coherence and direction (Tomlinson, 1991), weakening the cultural unity of all nation-states, not only those in the developing world. Whereas the term "imperialism" reflects an intentional and systematic endeavor, "globalization" refers to a more complex phenomenon, "a dialectical process because . . . local happenings may move in an obverse direction" (Giddens, 1990, p. 64).

The opening of the field of international communication to approaches beyond social psychology and political economy is the second factor behind the switch from imperialism to globalization. Notably, the irruption of cultural sociology and anthropology, in addition to cultural studies and its combination of literary criticism, semiotics, and Marxist cultural interpretation, contributed to moving the relatively contained field of international communication into a more explicitly interdisciplinary configuration of approaches that, as mentioned earlier, I have referred to as global media studies (see Kraidy, 2002c). The recognition by theorists of global culture—hailing from anthropology (Appadurai, 1996), sociology (Bamyeh, 2000) or literary studies (Jameson, 1998)—of the importance of the communicative dimensions of globalization is the third factor contributing to the shift from imperialism to globalization. This recognition reflects a growing awareness that many of the economic, political, and ideological aspects of globalization are predicated on gathering, encoding, manipulating, disseminating, decoding, restricting, resisting, countering, marketing, selling, and buying information.[8]

In his exploration of the connections between globalization and culture, British media scholar John Tomlinson (1999) argued that an understanding of the "complex connectivity" (p. 2) of globalization is impossible to achieve outside "the conceptual vocabularies of culture" (p. 1). Tentacular networks that carry information, ideas, images, commodities, and people across national borders create an intricate level of connectivity that forms the backbone of globalization. By increasing the interconnections between various localities and by intensifying the quality of these contacts, globalization connotes closeness, or "global spatial-proximity" (p. 3). Tomlinson views proximity as a primarily phenomenological issue that arises in people's lived experience of globalization as inherently local and embodied.

If globalization is experienced locally, then each place encounters globalization differently. While nodes on the network of global connectivity—such as large cosmopolitan airports—are relatively standardized, local communities, according to Tomlinson (1999), retain their diversity, because of the continuing centrality of local life. While Tomlinson, following Robertson (1992), acknowledges that globalization has an inherent drive toward "global unicity" (1999, p. 10), he is nonetheless critical of the cultural imperialism thesis because in his view it implies an unjustified logical chain that links connectivity, proximity, and uniformity. Tomlinson laudably emphasizes the need to "unravel from the complexly intertwined practices of the cultural, the economic and the political, a sense of *purpose* of the cultural—that of making life meaningful" (p. 18, emphasis in original), an unpacking that requires the explicit recognition of the diversity of local engagements with the multiple dimensions of globalization.

Tomlinson spells out a medial position when it comes to the importance of culture in globalization. On one hand, he criticizes Giddens (1990) for subsuming culture to technology in his treatment of globalization. Indeed, Giddens's *The Consequences of Modernity* (1990) contains a sole mention of the cultural realm; the prominent sociologist, as if in an afterthought, recognizes culture as "a fundamental aspect of globalization" (p. 77). On the other hand, Tomlinson is equally critical of those who privilege culture over other dimensions of globalization, as illustrated in the statement that "[w]e can expect the economy and the polity to be globalized to the extent that they are culturalized, that is to the extent that the exchanges that take place within them are accomplished symbolically" (Waters, 1995, pp. 9–10, quoted in Tomlinson, 1999, p. 22). Waters's claim, as Tomlinson himself points out, is strongly idealist and neglects the political economy of globalization; it also espouses the old distinction between the cultural, political, and economic spheres, a separation that is arguably no longer tenable because of the complex links between these spheres of human life (see Jameson, 1998). Shunning both cultural fetishism and material determinism, Tomlinson draws a distinction between culture as "instrumental symbolization," which he attributes to Waters, and his own understanding of culture as "existentially significant meaning-construction" (1999, p. 23). "Instrumental symbolization" refers to the ways in which communication and cultural codes are used to facilitate political and economic processes of globalization. In contrast, a view of culture as an existentially significant process of meaning construction typifies a phenomenological approach committed to understanding locality. Meaning construction should not be misconstrued as mere symbolic play subjected to the determining forces of globalization. Rather, culture is *"consequential"* (Tomlinson, 1999, p. 24, emphasis in original) because it affects weighty individual and social actions. Though culture does not determine other aspects of globalization, it is indispensable for understanding them.

Moving from imperialism to globalization as a framework for international communication research is, however, problematical, because the two schemes occupy conflicting positions on the ideological spectrum. Thus the teleological argument that international communication has evolved from a paradigm of imperialism to one of globalization is not a natural development, but a substantively, though not exclusively, ideological shift. To that effect Curran and Park (2000) decry narratives of "linear development in which those mired in the error of media imperialism theory have been corrected by the sages of cultural globalization" (p. 8) and conclude that the cultural globalization approach neglects history and power.

In this regard the role of the state, an issue growing in salience in international communication research (Braman, 2002; Curran and Park, 2000; Morris and Waisbord, 2001; Nordenstreng, 2001), is an important point of friction between the cultural imperialism and cultural globalization approaches. The former regards powerful Western states as complicitous with transnational corporations in exploiting weaker states in developing nations with the help of accommodating elites, while in the latter the state is increasingly invisible or, when present, plays an allegedly protectionist or authoritarian role. Again, Curran and Park (2000) are instructive in this regard: "In the cultural globalization literature, the state and nation tend to be associated with hierarchy, monolithic structures, historically contingent identities, repressive cultures, spatial competition, and war. Indeed, cultural globalization is viewed as positive precisely because it is thought to weaken the nation" (p. 11). It is true that the analysis of contemporary cultural flow and hybrid forms requires a more polished framework than the cultural imperialism thesis. However, because it tends to celebrate the weak state, cultural globalization theory may be justly regarded as a discourse whose bases are more ideological than empirical. In effect, "cultural globalization" elicits the same sort of criticism that has riddled "cultural imperialism" since the 1980s: in addition to being ideologically motivated, it tends to be conceptually ill defined because its arguments tend to be general and ungrounded in concrete settings. Because of this baggage, the cultural globalization approach is less than ideal for a *critical* understanding of contemporary hybrid cultures.

Is there an alternative to the cultural globalization perspective, one that would give adequate attention to cultural hybridity and at the same time address political and economic power and recognize an important, albeit changed, role for the state? The 1970s were the decade of "cultural imperialism," the 1980s of the "active audience," the 1990s of "cultural globalization." The verdict is still out on which discourse of global culture will capture the first decade of the twenty-first century. Without succumbing to the temptation of an illusory teleological ordering of scenarios of global culture, presently available options are not satisfactory. The remaining chapters of this book explore the imbrication of hybridity and power in communicative and cultural processes, leading to the formulation in the ultimate chapter of *critical transculturalism* as a framework for the study of global communication and culture. Before reaching that point, however, it is essential to trace the genealogy of the idea of cultural mixture in intellectual and public discourse. The next chapter explores the historical development, applications, and critiques of the notions of hybridity, miscegenation, syncretism, mestizaje, transculturation, creolization, métissage, Créolité, and négritude.

3   The Trails and Tales of Hybridity

I consider the social science study of syncretism to be crucially about the various discourses that seek to control the definition of syncretism.
—Charles Stewart

[C]reolisation, métissage, mestizaje, and hybridity . . . are . . . rather unsatisfactory ways of naming the processes of cultural mutation and restless (dis)continuity that exceed racial discourse and avoid capture by its agents.
—Paul Gilroy

Speaking with virtually mindless pleasure of transnational cultural hybridity, and of politics of contingency, amounts, in effect, to endorsing the cultural claims of transnational capital itself.
—Aijaz Ahmad

CONTEMPORARY WRITING on globalization and culture suggests the demise of the modern notion of a universal culture, in both its utopian and dystopian varieties. Both the French Enlightenment vision of a universal civilization predicated on human rights, scientific rationalism, and material progress (the utopian version) and the Romantic German notion of an authentic national culture threatened by the spread of soulless global forms (the dystopian variant) are outdated. Taking their place is a growing consensus in the social and human sciences that global culture is hybrid, mixing heterogeneous elements into recombinant forms. This position is more akin to the metaphor of polyglot ancient Babel than to the *civilisation* of French rationalism or the *Kultur* of German romanticism. It is skeptical of claims that foreign influence eradicates local traditions, and at the same time it is ambivalent toward the notion of local resilience. Its call for "openness" opposes notions of "delinking" originated by Egyptian political economist Samir Amin and taken up by Dutch international communication scholar Cees Hamelink (1983), who sees delinking as the only way for nations to avoid "cultural synchronization" (p. 22). In contrast, anthropologists have argued, at least since U.S. anthropologists Marshall Sahlins and Clifford Geertz, against a direct correspondence between economics and culture.[1]

There is growing recognition that hybridity is a prima facie global condition caused by voluntary and forced migration, wars, invasions, slavery, intermarriages, and trade. Mexican American performance artist Guillermo Gómez-Peña (1996) opposes the idea of the New World Order with the notion of the New World *Border*.[2] Instead of a monocentric homogenization, Gómez-Peña sees a hybrid transnational culture where "Spanglish, Franglé, and Gringoñol are *linguas francas*" (p. 7) are the norm, and where the only resistance comes from a reactionary minority of purity advocates. Even materialist anticolonial critic Aijaz Ahmad, who is no fan of hybridity talk, echoes Gómez-Peña when he writes that the "cross-fertilization of cultures has been endemic to all movements of people" (1995, p. 18). Chicano critical anthropologist Renato Rosaldo (1995) reflects the widespread recognition that hybridity is a master trope in cultural formations when he writes that "instead of hybridity versus plurality, . . . it is hybridity all the way down" (p. xv). While recognition of the hybrid fabric of global culture is inevitable, it should not harden the variegated elements of hybridity into a definite and therefore fossilized discourse, but should serve as a point of departure for renewed scrutiny of the conditions and bases of hybridity.

The contemporaneous salience of hybridity should not obscure the long history of intercultural borrowing and fusion. In English-speaking theory circles, Russian literary theorist Mikhail Bakhtin (1981) and Indian American postcolonial critic Homi Bhabha (1994) are often credited with dislocating the concept of hybridity from the biological domain of miscegenation to the cultural field of power. In the interdisciplinary social sciences, Argentinian-Mexican cultural critic Néstor García-Canclini (1989) articulated the most systematic treatment of cultural hybridity, grounded in Latin American politics and culture. For decades, however, writers, scientists, and ideologues across the world have developed concepts such as syncretism, *mestizaje*, and creolization to capture cultural mixture. Bhabha's conception of hybridity in cultural politics and García-Canclini's articulation of cultural hybridity with political culture actually stand on the shoulders of various European, Latin American, and other thinkers, going as far back as the eighteenth-century French mathematician, naturalist, and racialist theorist George Buffon and the late nineteenth-century liberal Berlin School of Ethnology directed by Rudolf Virchow and Adolf Bastian. My approach to hybridity will therefore be both historicist, grounding theories in their sociohistorical circumstances, and comparative, drawing on a global and multidisciplinary literature.

In *Old World Encounters: Cross-cultural Contacts and Exchanges in Premodern Times*, U.S.-based historian Jerry Bentley (1993) asserts that "cross-cultural encounters have been a regular feature of world history since the earliest days of the human species' existence" (p. vii). Beyond the de facto recognition by theorists of contemporary culture that cultural hybridity is a historical reality, Bentley demonstrates it in an encyclopedic array of historical case studies of cultural hybridity that range from South America to China. For instance, Bentley explains that Islam spread rapidly in sub-Saharan Africa because local elites converted voluntarily to enhance trade with Muslim merchants and because Islam was the dominant mode of sociopolitical organization of the world that surrounded sub-Saharan Africa. Also, rulers and the elite were motivated to convert to Islam because the recognition by powerful Islamic states to the north and east strengthened their local power and prestige. Hence Islam's successful expansion out of its original territory of Arabia and its dominant commingling with local traditions in Africa. Bentley also relates the syncretic practices of the Manicheans who migrated from Central Asia to China and integrated Daoist and Buddhist communities in the seventh century. These were a few among many historical episodes of mutual cultural appropriation of vocabularies and symbols. Indeed, Bentley's entire book is an exploration of hybridity in the *longue durée*, charting the trajectory of cultural mixture in world history.

Historicizing the terms used to represent cultural mixture is an essential prerequisite for engaging the politically charged and conceptually unstable trope of hybridity. Knowledge of how the notion of hybridity and its antecedents emerged, developed, and mutated is crucial for a diachronic comprehension of cross-cultural encounters. Most importantly for a critical theory of hybridity, a foregrounding of the historical trajectory of terms of cultural mixture can help illuminate the role of power in the transcultural processes that weave the hybrid fabric of transnational culture. This entails the following questions: What is the historical trajectory of the vocabulary of cultural mixture? What are the conceptual and terminological antecedents of hybridity? What are the historical factors at play in the adoption and contestation of this controversial concept? More importantly, how have terms of cultural mixture defined the world in which they were deployed? Addressing these questions paves the way for the elaboration in the final chapter of the notion of critical transculturalism, based on a communication-driven process of hybridization.

MISCEGENATION: HYBRIDITY AND BIOLOGY

The modern debate on hybridity emerged in the eighteenth century in the context of interracial contact that resulted from overseas conquest and population displacement in Britain, France, and the United States. For example, French racialist theory developed during the Siècle des Lumières, the eighteenth-century Enlightenment and its progressive principles that catalyzed the French Revolution. Puzzlement is a natural first reaction when one considers that emancipatory discourses of rationalism, human rights, and political equality went in tandem with racialist theories of European superiority. One of the least known of these theorists is Georges-Louis Leclerc, Comte de Buffon, known as Buffon, a friend of Denis Diderot, the French Enlightenment author who supervised the writing of the *Encyclopédie*. At the heart of Buffon's theory of race, developed during the 1740s at the conclusion of several works on natural history and the animal world, is the premise that all humans are part of one species, and that different races are individuated subgroups of that common species. Individuation occurs as an evolutionary reaction to environmental constraints. Hence Buffon's infamous theory that Africans' black skin is a protective measure against extreme heat. Processes of individuation, however, correspond to a hierarchy among the races, whose top and bottom are occupied by white Europeans and the indigenous peoples of America and Australia respectively, while the middle positions are filled by Africans and Asians (Toumson, 1998).

One derivative of Buffon's theory, unimportant at the time but decisive in the development of subsequent racialist theory, is that since all races are part of the same species, sexual unions between individuals from different races lead to procreation. Unlike Buffon, Joseph Ernest Renan, French historian and theorist of nationalism and collective identities *avant la lettre*, believed that human races were actually different species. However, both French racial theorists elevated white Europeans to the top of the hierarchy, but Renan demoted black Africans to the bottom of the hierarchy, which they shared with Native Americans and Australians. It logically followed that the mixing of races would lead to the degeneration of superior races.[3]

Grounded in pseudo-scientific concepts of anatomy and craniometry, these early speculations on the hybrid were chiefly concerned with the contamination of white Europeans by the races they colonized. Differences of opinion on the vitality of hybrids, oscillating between "hybrid sterility," which was the initial consensus perspective, and "hybrid vigor," were overshadowed by ideologies of racial superiority that warned of the danger of "miscegenation." A typical argument in that debate can be found in the writing of the Edinburgh racial theorist Robert Knox (1850) who argued that hybridity was "a degradation of humanity and . . . was rejected by nature" (p. 497, quoted in Young, 1995, p. 15) and found its literary counterpart in what Kipling described as the "monstrous hybridism of East and West" (1901, p. 341, quoted in Young, 1995, p. 3). This early hybridity discourse was symptomatic of the Enlightenment's failure, despite its otherwise progressive agenda, to come to terms with its racist underside, a dereliction manifest most clearly in the refusal of most Enlightenment thinkers to condemn slavery.

SYNCRETISM: HYBRIDITY AND RELIGION

In the first century AD, the Greek philosopher Plutarch coined the word "syncretism" to describe the union of hitherto separated peoples of Crete to confront external enemies (*sunkrtismos* means "union") (Moreau, 2000; Stewart, 1999), and the Renaissance humanist Erasmus (1466–1536) later used "syncretism" to refer to the fusion of divergent ideas. Since the seventeenth century, syncretism has served as a framework for the study of interreligious borrowing and intrareligious fusion (Moreau, 2000). In a seminal article titled "Zum Verständnis des Synkretismus" (translated as "On Understanding Syncretism" [Baines, 1999a]), German Egyptologist Hans Bonnet (Baines, 1999a) laid the foundations for the modern study of syncretism. Bonnet believed that the tendency toward syncretism was a fundamental dimension of polytheistic Egyptian religion, characterized by "the fusion of names of Egyptian deities" (Baines, 1999b, p. 204). Ancient Egyptians, according to Bonnet, resorted to syncretism in order to manage polytheism, using syncretism as a framework for theological unity. Though central to Egyptian religion, syncretism was "double-sided" not only in its "nature" but also in its "effects" (p. 198), since syncretism advanced Egyptian religion to its peak through the integration of various deities and ideas, but also precipitated its decline by causing fatal fragmentation. Bonnet's insights have historical value, but their applicability is limited because of his focus on religious syncretism within one sociocultural system, and also due to his ideational focus on religious thought more than on syncretism's social and political bearings (see Baines, 1999b, for more on this issue). It is in Christianity, especially Catholicism, that the concept of syncretism began to carry negative connotations, because it generally referred to the degree to which church doctrine was contaminated by nonchurch beliefs as Christianity entered new territories opened up by colonialism. Anthropologist Charles Stewart (1999) writes that "[s]*yncretism* became a term of abuse often applied to castigate colonial local churches that had burst out of the sphere of mission control and begun to 'illegitimately' indigenize Christianity instead of properly reproducing the European form of Christianity they had originally been offered" (p. 46). This issue remains a source of contention between the Vatican and Catholic churches in rural and predominantly indigenous southern Mexico, where local deacons tend to deviate from standard Catholic doctrine (Thompson, 2002). The deacons' "special brand of evangelism, infused with the tenets of liberation theology as well as pre-Columbian symbols and songs," has provoked the Vatican into ordering the Diocese of San Cristóbal in the state of Chiapas—where poverty among the rural and mostly indigenous population and its neglect by federal Mexican authorities led to the well-known Zapatista movement—not to ordain any deacons for at least five years. The letter issuing the order states that "the perceived danger is . . . sending an implicit message from the Holy See to other ecclesiastical groups for an 'alternative' church model that could seem convenient for '*cultural situations and particular ethnic groups*'" (Thompson, 2002, emphasis mine). Paradoxically, the letter's content was widely circulated in Chiapas within the same week as the pope's announcement of his plan to canonize the first Native Mexican (Indian) saint, Juan Diego, during a summer 2002 visit to Mexico. "Syncretism" thus refers to a border zone of tension between religious universalism and particularism.

At the beginning of the twenty-first century, syncretism is still a salient concern of Christian churches and missionaries and a subject of debate in Christian publications such as the *International Bulletin of Missionary Research*. While some recent discussions have advocated abandoning the concept of syncretism because of its charged history and pejorative connotation (Schineller, 1992), others have relocated syncretism from its strictly theological dimension to the notion of inculturation—not to be confused with enculturation—defined as "the development of a response to the Gospel that is rooted in a specific time and place" (Schreiter, 1993, p. 50). This application of syncretism has expanded its scope from a strictly religious concern to include broader cultural processes of interest to anthropologists (Stewart, 1999), linguists (Blevins, 1995), and historians (Drell, 1999).[4] The ensuing multiplicity of meanings and uses heightens the importance of contextualizing the use of "syncretism," as suggested by the Latin American experience with "mestizaje."

HYBRIDITY AND THE NATION: MESTIZAJE AND TRANSCULTURATION

In the wake of postimperial decolonization movements in the Americas, racial and cultural mixture emerged to the forefront of national policy. In the United States, the ideology of the melting pot was adopted as a nation-building strategy used to integrate ethnic difference. Across Latin America, states adopted mestizaje as the official ideology of nation building in their bids to forge national identities distinct from mere provincial status in the Spanish empire. As a Latin American "foundational theme" (Martínez-Echazábal, 1998), mestizaje was an attempt to mitigate tensions between the indigenous populations and the descendants of Spanish colonists by positing the new nations as hybrids of both worlds (see, for instance, Anderson, 1993; Archetti, 1999; Doremus, 2001; Hale, 1999; Mignolo, 2000). While the concept of mestizaje contains residual imperial relations, it has nonetheless helped scholars like Martín-Barbero (1993a, b), as explicated in Chapter One, to make sense of Latin American historical and sociocultural fusions. Nonetheless, some Afrocentric critics have attacked the concept of mestizaje, which they believe represents the erasure of the African black heritage in Latin America (Rosa, 1996).

Most historians of race and ethnicity in Latin America subscribe to a more complex understanding of constructions of racial mixture, one where race enters a volatile mix with gender, class, and nationalism (Bolke Turner and Turner, 1994; Doremus, 2001; Gruzinski, 1999; Hale, 1999; Kellogg, 2000; Martínez-Echazábal, 1998). This complexity has endowed "mestizaje" with different connotations compatible with various Latin American national experiences. Mexican history provides a genealogy of mestizaje as official state ideology. According to French historian Serge Gruzinski (1995), rulers in colonial Mexico deployed images to carry out "a policy of cultural mestizaje" (p. 53) that amounted to the Westernization and Christianization of Mexico's indigenous population. In Gruzinski's view, this was nothing short of a visual invasion of Mexico by a "Western imaginaire" that entailed a fundamental albeit subtle reorganization of the "humanist relationship to the real" (p. 56). On the ground, this was accomplished by enlisting artists whose work created a baroque image that blended Catholic religious themes with native iconography, leading to the development of a "hybrid imagery" (p. 70) in the seventeenth century. The dark-skinned, barefooted Virgen de Guadalupe, now the patron saint of Mexico, was the ultimate syncretic icon, which, according to Gruzinski, connected native America to Christian Europe. The objective of this strategy was the creation of a stable Mexican identity that incorporated heterogenous elements. In Gruzinski's opinion: "the miraculous image played a great role in unifying and homogenizing colonial society and its commingled cultures, mixing processions and official ceremonies with an inexhaustible series of popular entertainments and Indian dances" (p. 65).

In the early decades of the twentieth century, Mexican intellectuals revived the mestizaje ideology at a crucial time, when Mexico was redefining itself as a new nation, mainly through the 1910–1921 Revolución. Book titles such as *Los grandes problemas nacionales* (Molina-Enríquez, 1909/1978) and *Forjando patria* (Gamio, 1916/1992) played up mestizaje as a central characteristic of Mexican identity. Most widely known was *La raza cósmica* (Vasconcelos, 1925/1997), whose author posits Mexico as a pioneering example of a hybrid cosmic race. Mostly concerned with the management of racial and ethnic difference for the purpose of national integration, this discourse had three interlocked implications. First, it switched the focus of mestizaje from biology to ethnicity culture. The second implication derives from the first: mestizaje is made easier to achieve since, relocating it to the less politicized realm of culture, it was no longer exclusively based in racial mixing. Third, it reclassified many indigenous people as mestizos, thus officially shrinking the size of the native community while swelling the number of mestizos (Doremus, 2001). The integrative dimension of mestizaje is enshrined in the Plaza de las Tres Culturas in Mexico City, where a precolonial pyramid, a colonial church, and a modern building stand contiguously, a record of the historical trajectory of Mexico as a hybrid nation, a mixture of its three cultures. This monument is in effect an outdoor museum in a metropolis whose museums García-Canclini (1989) analyzes as central to the creation of the Mexican nation through an exhibitive dialectic that arranges elements from the miniature (in museums) to the monumental in a cultural narrative of a mestizo nation. Elsewhere in Latin America, mestizaje takes on several connotations and various levels of complexity as it is situated within the historical peculiarities of nations like Cuba (Martínez-Echazábal, 1998), Guatemala (Hale, 1999), Paraguay (Bolke Turner and Turner, 1994). In most of these nations, mestizaje is a deeply racialized discourse whose progressive surface has a reactionary undertow.

The notion of transculturation came forth in Cuba and Brazil in the mid-1930s and early 1940s as a variant of mestizage. Cuban legal scholar and cultural critic Fernando Ortiz (1940/1995)—not to be confused with the Brazilian scholar Renato Ortiz, who still writes today on national identity and culture—developed the notion of transculturation to understand Cuba's experience with racial and cultural encounters, while Brazilian sociologist Gilberto Freyre (1936/1986) used it to explain racial and class dynamics in his country. Transculturation entails "a kind of brokerage, an exchange, a give-and-take, a process whereby both parts of the cultural equation are modified and give way to a new sociocultural conglomerate" (Martínez-Echazábal, 1998) and is thus different from both acculturation and assimilation. Contra prevailing ideologies of cultural purity represented by conservative Cuban critic Sánchez de Fuente, Fernando Ortiz posited the African element at the heart of scholarly inquiry and public debate on Cuban national identity. He asserted that it was inevitable that Cuban culture would be mixed, an argument he fleshed out in his analysis of mixed Cuban musical forms (Boggs, 1991; Ortiz, 1952).

More recently, "transculturation" was appropriated to denote cultural mixture in literature and music. In conjunction with the Russian culturalist school, a circle of humanities scholars dedicated to the study of cultural interactions following Mikhail Bakhtin, transculture is used to understand "the Western postmodern condition" (Berry and Epstein, 1999, p. 79) by resolving the contradiction between multiculturalism's push for communal identities and deconstruction's imperative to excavate internal differences in identity. In other contexts transculturation describes emerging forms of "world music" (Wallis and Malm, 1990) and literary renditions of colonial encounters (Pratt, 1992). Clearly, transculturation has not escaped the multiplicity of meanings and applications that riddled its predecessors.

Like mestizaje, however, transculturation was an integrative discourse in sync with the interests of dominant strata of Latin American societies. By displacing mixture from race to culture, and by selectively welcoming and rejecting native traditions, Latin American ideologists of mestizaje (and transculturation) saw institutionalized cultural mixture as a sure way to effect the slow decay of precolonial cultures and integrate them in the dominant society, which welcomed their non-threatening arts, crafts, and selected rituals, while imposing on them the

Spanish or Portuguese language, the Catholic faith, and colonial political and social organization. As a discourse that recognizes, even celebrates, cultural difference, mestizaje in effect is a tool for "bleaching" all but the most benign practices that gave precolonial natives their identities. Cultural mixture within the emerging nation-states thus obeyed a residual colonial logic.

In contrast to mestizaje's ostensible recognition of diversity in the context of ideologies of integration in the emerging Latin American nation-states, current conceptions view hybridity as a progressive citizenly discourse (Gómez-Peña, 1996; Joseph and Fink, 1999; Werbner and Modood, 1997). According to performance studies scholar May Joseph (1999), hybridity can be an anti-imperialist, participatory discourse of cultural citizenship. As a "democratic expression of multiple affiliations" (Joseph, 1999, p. 2), hybrid identity can be asserted for political—used here in its strict meaning of institutions and practices of governance—advantage. This multiplicity of links between citizens and cultural identities can, in the view of British-based social anthropologist Pnina Werbner, be an effective counterweight to xenophobic forces. If hybridity is understood as a "theoretical metaconstruction of social order" (Werbner, 1997, p. 1), its political potential lies in its ability to subvert binary categories.

In distinction from the interpretive approach of performance studies scholars and sociologists, some political theorists have applied a normative framework to intercultural relations within the nation-state. Though in general these writers have not focused on cultural mixture, Turkish American scholar Seyla Benhabib (2002) explicitly discusses the notion of hybridity as she teases out aspects of a citizenly discourse premised on fluid cultural identities. Indeed, in *The Claims of Culture* (2002) Benhabib argues against the "faulty epistemic premises" of the holistic conception of cultures and advocates instead "recognition of the radical hybridity and polyvocality of all cultures" (p. 4). Cultures, she argues "are not holistic but ... multilayered, decentered and fractured systems of action and signification" (p. 25). In contradistinction to scholars who have used hybridity as a metadescriptive device and in contrast to those for whom hybridity is an assertion of resilient localism, Benhabib seeks to reconcile universalist ideals of equality with relativist manifestations of identity. To come to terms with this global-local tension, Benhabib puts forth normative rules that in her opinion enable us to use cultural hybridity as a practicable aspect of citizenship.

Three normative requisites, in Benhabib's view (2002), enable societies at once to recognize hybrid identities and to be compatible with universally acknowledged human rights and democratic standards. These conditions are (1) egalitarian reciprocity, (2) voluntary self-ascription, and (3) freedom of exit or association. The first normative condition calls for equal rights for all communities, including minorities. Voluntary self-ascription entails that membership in a group must be through self-identification, not through an inflexible system that traps individuals in irreversible birth identities, hence the third rule, which guarantees the ability of individuals to affiliate with groups they were not born in. When these conditions are secured, pluralistic societies can engage in what Benhabib calls "complex cultural dialogues" (p. 22), an egalitarian process of exchange that leads to mutual transformation of its participants. This idea lies at the heart of Benhabib's invitation to political theorists to consider identity groups as complex and dynamic movements whose political outlook is not predetermined by their ethnicity, religion, or race.

For complex cultural dialogues to have concrete effects, Benhabib (2002) advocates "a legal pluralism that would countenance a coexistence of jurisdictional systems for different cultural and religious traditions and accept varieties of institutional design for societies with strong ethnic, cultural, and linguistic cleavages" (p. 19). For hybridity to be a bona fide progressive citizenly discourse, then, the state has to play an active role in its legislative, regulatory, and juridical institutions. Even though recognition of fluid identities by the state remains controversial, as the wrangling surrounding the "multiracial" categories in the 2000 U.S. Census demonstrates, I believe that Benhabib proposes a valid and usable scheme for the actual usefulness of hybridity in politics.[5] Therefore, in Chapter Seven, I draw on Benhabib's framework in my discussion of how media policy can integrate, at the normative level, a positive notion of hybridity in communication processes.

HYBRIDITY, LANGUAGE, AND CULTURE: CREOLIZATION

The concept of creolization (Chaudenson, 1992; Jourdan, 1991; Valdman, 1978) shares the historical trajectory of mestizaje and transculturation. Like them, it came to life in the wake of European colonialism in the New World and has now diffused into a few distinct usages linked by a shared history of political and cultural struggles with Europe's empires.

The term "creole" stems from the Portuguese *crioulo* or the Spanish *criollo*. *Criar* is the Spanish verb "to raise" or "to breed," deriving from the Latin *creare*, "to create." Initially describing African slaves relocated on the American continent (Stewart, 1999), "Creole" came to connote someone "born in the country" (Toumson, 1998, p. 120), in reference to those people born in Europe's colonial possessions. In anthropologist Charles Stewart's words, "creolization" reflected "a connection between New World birth and deculturation" (1999, p. 44). As we will briefly see, the term has carried a variety of meanings linked to geography, race, culture, and language.

In his now famous treatise on nationalism, Benedict Anderson (1993) devotes a chapter to what he calls the "Creole pioneers" who led the establishment of nationalism on the American continent and the states it created. In Anderson's view, they were all Creole states, because they were "formed and led by people who shared a common language and a common descent with those against whom they fought" (p. 47). One of the most interesting dimensions of Latin American creolism as explicated by Anderson is that it was in fact the source of a movement of national coalescence and unity, a centripetal force of homogenization whose project was the establishment of independent nation-states. Remarkably, according to Anderson, Creole communities developed a national awareness *"well before most of Europe"* (p. 50, emphasis in original). They gravitated toward republicanism and, with the temporary exception of Brazil, did not replicate the royal dynastic systems of the Old Continent. Anderson's definition of "Creole" is based on birthplace, where a common identity derives from "the shared fatality of extra-Spanish birth" (p. 63).

Whereas in Anderson's usage, creolism is the social equivalent of mestizaje, in the United States creolism is associated with the state of Louisiana, a place whose confluence of British, French, and African elements has received significant scholarly attention (Domínguez, 1986; Chaudenson, 1992; Henry and Bankston, 1998). Advocates of a structural approach to the phenomenon propose four dimensions of creole identity: "birthplace, ancestry and race and culture" (Henry and Bankston, 1998, p. 560). In this analysis, a Creole was historically born in colonial territories from parents born away. Race and culture, which are collapsed as one dimension, was a less straightforward issue because it had diametrically opposed meanings for whites and blacks. For the former, Creole meant white purity and elite political and socioeconomic status, while for the latter it denoted racial mixture and a subordinate social position. A more revealing difference is that whites understood creolism to be indicative of purity, while for blacks it was "a matter of continuum" (Henry and Bankston, 1998, p. 563).

The multiple usages of "creolization," like those of other terms of cultural mixture like "syncretism," "mestizaje," and "hybridity," has led to a confusing situation where the expanding scope of the concept dilutes its meaning. The term's numerous meanings hark back to the middle of the twentieth century (see Arron, 1951), and more than five decades later it is a source of confusion. In present-day Louisiana, the label "Creole" has been appropriated by the touristic and culinary sectors. In academic parlance, "creolization" oftentimes refers to cultural mixture at large, a usage mostly visible in Ulf Hannerz's (1987) advocacy of creolization as "our most promising root metaphor" (p. 551). The term has been also used to refer to mixed musical styles and genres (Salamone, 1998) and retains an association with linguistics. However, creolization is a contested notion. Stewart (1999) criticizes Hannerz's choice of creolization (1987) as reflecting a "general state of confusion in social science terminology" (p. 45). Stewart argues that the word "creolization," like "hybridization" and "mongrelization," is burdened with a colonial and biologistic weight, and is not therefore the salutary metaphor that Hannerz claims it to be. Similarly, Henry and Bankston (1998) recognize that "the accumulation of referents and shifts in meanings have made *creole* a multilayered term and dulled its effectiveness as an identifier" (p. 563). Seemingly oblivious to the semantic and conceptual slippage in the vocabulary of cultural mixture, the original term of mixture—"hybridity"—has enjoyed a vigorous renascence in postcolonial theory.

HYBRIDITY AND POSTCOLONIAL THEORY

The postcolonial turn took up hybridity as a central dimension of the literary and cultural productions of Africa, Latin America, Asia, and diasporas in the West. Standing on the shoulders of the disciplines that debated syncretism, mestizaje, and creolization, postcolonial theory re-popularized the term "hybridity" to explicate cultural fusion. British sociologist Paul Gilroy cast *The Black Atlantic*, his book about the history of demographic and ideological movements between Europe, Africa, and the Americas (1993), as "an essay about the inescapable hybridity and intermixture of ideas" (p. xi). Conceptualizing the "Black Atlantic" as a "counterculture of modernity," Gilroy examines the transatlantic flows of people, ideas, and culture that began with the slave trade, arguing that it has been significant for cultural renewal in Europe, Africa, the Caribbean, and America. Gilroy argues against what—after Sollors (1986)— he calls "cultural insiderism" (p. 3), or the various forms of ethnic essentialism and nationalism that expound ethnicity and identity as immutable categories set against markers of Otherness in binary oppositions such as black versus white. Recognizing "the tragic popularity" (p. 7) of notions of cultural purity, which usually couple an emphatic assertion of identity with an equally strong rejection of difference, Gilroy argues for an alternative and more challenging understanding of intercultural contact, "the theorization of creolisation, métissage, mestizaje, and hybridity" (p. 2), which he initiates with the image of the ship. As a moving object, the ship symbolizes the trajectory between point of departure and destination, a liminal in-between that captures the spirit of the "Black Atlantic." As a carrier of people, a ship also represents the idea that entire life worlds can be in motion, such as is the case for the myriad experience of forced, semi-forced, and voluntary migrations that are a hallmark of the modern, hybrid world.[6]

While Gilroy focuses on narratives of the historical entanglement of Europe, Africa, and America, Bhabha (1994) explores hybridity in the context of the postcolonial novel and celebrates it as a symptom of resistance by the colonized, as the contamination of imperial ideology, aesthetics, and identity by natives striking back at colonial domination. He emphasizes hybridity's ability to subvert dominant discourses and reappropriate them to create what he calls "cultures of postcolonial *contra-modernity*" (p. 6, emphasis in original). This reinscription is found in Bhabha's analysis of mimicry as a hybridizing process. "Mimicry," Bhabha argues, "emerges as the representation of a difference that is itself a process of disavowal." As a result, mimicry "'appropriates' the other as it visualizes power" (p. 86). As a process of cultural repetition rather than representation, mimicry undermines the authority of colonial representation because it brings to light the ambivalence of colonial discourse. As such, according to Bhabha, it opens up a space for alternative forms of agency by highlighting colonial culture's "insurgent counter-appeal" (p. 91). The cultural hybridity enacted in mimicry, best captured by Bhabha's notion of "third space," is thus understood as a subversive practice of resistance. It is this highly textualist formulation of hybridity as resistance that has subjected Bhabha to critiques of poststructuralist license and a lack of sensitivity to the material inequalities that riddle the previously colonized world.

Homi Bhabha's fervent embrace differs sharply from Edward Said's decreasingly ambivalent engagement with hybridity. Between the

Palestinian American scholar's magnum opus, *Orientalism* (1978), and his other major work, *Culture and Imperialism* (1994), unfolds an increasingly explicit recognition of hybridity as a fundamental dimension of intercultural relations, albeit a hybridity that is firmly grounded in imperial dynamics. This is a major shift between the two books, one of many changes that, according to Tanzanian-British scholar Bart Moore-Gilbert (1997), warrant a distinction between an early and a late Said. The early Said (1978) draws on Michel Foucault's conception of discourse and Antonio Gramsci's view of hegemony to argue that the political, military, and economic drives of empire go in tandem with a discursive regime that compels, supports, justifies, even ennobles—and ultimately underscores the inevitability of—colonialism and imperialism. This discourse, which he calls Orientalism, can be encountered not only in the West's relations with the Arab and Muslim worlds, Said's initial locus of analysis, but in any locale touched by Western conquest.

Drawing on a vast cornucopia of fiction, scholarship, and public discourse, Said (1978) paints a veritable discursive machine dedicated to making the non-West a subordinate Other. In the early Said's view, the will to dominate that animates much of Western narrative production about the non-West is concretized in the dichotomy the West establishes between itself and the rest of the world. It is a binary opposition in which the former is granted the upper hand in nearly all realms of life: morality, religion, justice, science, customs, and traditions. The imperial West, which in *Orientalism* concretely means Britain, France, and the United States, is largely oblivious to attempts to resist its discursive grip. It is this last aspect of Said's argument that made him a target of detractors who pointed out that he was articulating a totalistic logic, representing the West exactly as he claims it has represented the East. In *Orientalism*, the West and the Rest are separated by a wall of prejudice and suspicion, largely of the West's making. Herein resides the significance of Said's shift between *Orientalism* (1978) and *Culture and Imperialism* (1994). Unlike the former's portrayal of an unbridgeable gap between West and East, the latter is replete with endorsements of interaction and exchange. On this register, the late Said is unequivocal and persistent. Early in *Culture and Imperialism* the author credited with starting postcolonialism writes that "all cultures are involved in one another, none is single and pure, all are hybrid, heterogenous, extraordinarily differentiated, and unmonolithic" (1994, p. xxv). Some pages later, Said reiterates that "we have never before been as aware as we now are of how oddly hybrid historical and cultural experiences are, of how they partake of many often contradictory experiences and domains, cross national boundaries, defy the *police* action of simple dogma and loud patriotism. Far from being unitary or monolithic or autonomous things, cultures actually assume more foreign elements, alterities, differences, than they consciously exclude" (p. 15, emphasis in original).

Said understands that this entanglement is the result of imperial conquest and the various processes of accommodation, appropriation, and resistance triggered by colonialism and imperialism. However, unlike *Orientalism, Culture and Imperialism* accounts for indigenous, non-Western literary and cultural creativity. The late Said (1994) also exhibits a stronger appreciation for resistance to domination, even arguing that, in the long run, colonialism and imperialism can be defeated by those who suffer under them. In doing that Said moves further from Foucault's conception of dominance in history—from whom he had already distanced himself in *The World, the Text, and the Critic* (1984)—and moves closer to Gramsci's more optimistic outlook as to the potential of resistance. Said's often stated commitment to a universal humanism leads him in his later work to a more hopeful outlook manifest in his recognition of hybridity and mutual reliance, nonetheless without abandoning his focus on power and domination.

Hybridity and Sociocultural Transformation

The hybridizing processes that pervade human history have created uneven cultural mixtures, some superficial and others significant enough to shake a society's cultural foundations. The reception of U.S. music in post–World War II Italy is an example of the former. After American soldiers brought their music with them to Europe in the 1940s, disc jockeys changed the names of U.S. singers to mitigate the sense of otherness many Italians felt toward American popular culture. To make them more Italian sounding, "Louis Armstrong became Luigi Braccioforte, Benny Goodman was Beniamino Buonomo, Hoagy Carmichael turned into Carmelito, Duke Ellington became Del Duca, Coleman Hawkins was Coléma" (Minganti, 2000, p. 151). Historians call this phenomenon "covering," which evolved in more than mere name changing. Covering combined imitation and mitigation, admiration and derision, and was mocked by some Italians as a pathetic imitation of all things American, as illustrated in the famous 1957 Renato Carosone song "Tu vuo' fa l'americano" (You Pretend to Be an American). While making fun of the Americanness that many Italians aspired to in the fifties and sixties, the song was clearly influenced more by rock 'n' roll than by traditional Italian music. As a hybrid text that mixes American music with Italian lyrics, it pays tribute to U.S. popular culture and simultaneously derides it, also expressing ambivalence toward Italians seduced by American culture.

Other examples of hybridity reflect deep social change, such as U.S. anthropologist Marshall Sahlins's study of the Hawaiian encounter with Europeans (1981, 1985). Central to Sahlins's study of the cultural impact of Captain Cook's visits to the Hawaiian Islands in 1778–1779 is the concept of mythopraxis, which refers to the ways in which ancient myths are reenacted in the present. Among the insights of Sahlins's historical anthropology, of particular interest to this book is the explanation he offers for the perplexing tendency of the Hawaiian aristocracy to mimic English royalty's sartorial style and even to adopt the names of English kings. According to Sahlins, these hybridizing practices— he did not call them that—reflect a fundamental sociocultural change caused by the encounter. True to his culturalist principles, Sahlins attributes this change not to any immediate material factors but to the breaking of the Hawaiian taboo system, which prohibited men and women from eating together. When Cook's sailors disembarked, they feasted with Hawaiian women, who did not repel the Englishmen because Hawaiians supposedly believed Cook to be the god Lono. Sahlins argues that the relationships between Hawaiian women and Hawaiian men, Hawaiian commoners and Hawaiian royalty, and Hawaiian royalty and English royalty, are structurally parallel and interlinked. When Hawaiian women shared meals with English sailors, they broke the traditional rules of gender relations, which in turn changed how Hawaiian commoners related to their kings. In order to maintain their superior status among commoners, Hawaiian kings in turn broke the cultural distance between themselves and English royalty by imitating their clothing style and adopting their names.

In Sahlins's analysis (1981, 1985), alteration in one relationship in the Hawaiian sociocultural structure led to sweeping systemic change. Unlike the culture of covering in post–World War 2 Italy, the hybridity inherent in the practices of the Hawaiian ruling class is symptomatic of deeply rooted cultural changes. Formally acknowledging the impact of their encounters with the English, Hawaiian kings abolished the entire taboo system in 1819 (Kuper, 2000). If we bracket for a moment the political implications of Sahlins's analysis—made public in the heated controversy which opposed him to the Princeton-based Sri Lankan anthropologist Gananath Obeyesekere, who argued that Sahlins's analysis was rooted more in a white man's colonial fantasy than in empirical evidence (1992)—we are faced with a historical case study where symbolic factors played an important role in social change, albeit triggered by the all-too-material arrival of well-armed English sailors hungry for food, sex, and conquest.

For reasons of the scope, diversity, and complexity of the factors involved, Latin America rather than Hawaii has been a cardinal site for the study of cultural hybridity. The historical development of the discourse of mestizaje, discussed earlier in this chapter, has culminated in contemporary writings on hybridity, conceived in broader terms than mestizaje's mostly racial and ethnic connotations to include the fine arts, comics, graffiti, museums, and cultural consumption writ large (notably, García-Canclini, 1989/1995, and Martín-Barbero, 1993a, the latter discussed in Chapter One). In the influential *Culturas Híbridas* (García-Canclini, 1989; English translation, García-Canclini, 1995); Néstor García-Canclini offers one of the most systematic treatments of hybridity, grounded in Latin American arts, cultures, and politics. In García-Canclini's view, theories of dependency and magical realism fail to understand the complex Latin American reality, where authoritarianism mixes with liberalism and democracy with paternalism. The central inadequacy of these theories is their conception of the relation between culture and socioeconomic development,

> the thesis that the disagreements between cultural modernism and social modernization make a defective version of the modernity canonized by the metropolis. Or the inverse: that for being the land of pastiche and bricolage, where many periods and aesthetics are cited, we have had the pride of being postmodern for centuries, and in a unique way. Neither the "paradigm" of imitation, nor that of originality, nor the "theory" that attributes everything to dependency, nor the one that lazily wants to explain us by the "marvelously real" or a Latin American surrealism, are able to account for our hybrid cultures. (p. 6)[7]

For García-Canclini, then, the notion of hybridity is helpful precisely because it is an analytical tool for understanding a mixed reality created by dynamic links, on the one hand, between different historical periods and, on the other hand, between present-day politics, culture, and economics. The former produce "multitemporal heterogeneity" (see pp. 9, 47), caused by the fact that in Latin America only rarely has modernization replaced tradition, and the latter creates what the author calls "impure genres" (p. 249).

The idea of multitemporal heterogeneity, or *tiempos mixtos*, reflects at once the continuing relevance of the indigenous, colonial, and post-colonial cultural sediments in Latin American societies, and the fact that

"Latin America [is] a ... complex articulation of traditions and modernities (diverse and unequal), a heterogenous continent consisting of countries in each of which coexist multiple logics of development" (García-
Canclini, (1989/1995, p. 9). In the author's view, the aforementioned
contradictions between modernism and modernization explain why, for
example, the Brazilian Constitution of 1824 integrated the Declaration
of the Rights of Man while slavery was still a reality in Brazilian society,
or, more recently, why middle-class households in cities from Santiago
to Mexico City contain books in several languages, colonial furniture,
indigenous crafts, personal finance magazines, and satellite television.
This makes the middle classes feel that they are cultured, since "[b]eing
cultured—including being cultured in the modern era—implies not so
much associating oneself with a repertory of exclusively modern objects
and messages, but rather knowing how to incorporate the art and literature of the vanguard, as well as technological advances, into traditional
matrices of social privilege and symbolic distinction (pp. 46–47).

This mixed reality that in the bourgeoisie finds its expression in a
mundane, everyday life eclecticism shows how little, García-Canclini
points out, the binary opposition between "tradition" and "modernity"
contributes to our understanding of social dynamics.

Graffiti and comics are examples of cultural impurity. These "con-
stitutionally hybrid genres" (García-Canclini, 1989/1995, p. 249) result
from contradictions within and between the economic, political, and
cultural realms. As a mode of expression of those who do not have access to public means of communication, such as youth, the urban poor,
or political dissidents, graffiti is a hybrid in both style and intent (readers
interested in comics may look at pp. 254–257). Graffiti "affirms territory
but destructures the collections of material and symbolic goods" (p. 249)
by claiming a public wall as property but imbuing it with content that
escapes and in some cases even counters prevalent meanings and ideologies. For example, during a 1986 papal visit to Colombia, the walls of
Bogotá intoned, "God does not do his job. Not even on Sunday," and
"Don't believe anymore: Go for a walk," clear expressions of disillu-
sionment with the country's intractable problems. Three years later in
hyperinflation-wracked Argentina, graffiti alternately expressed indig-
nation: "Put your representative to work: don't reelect him"; or hope-
lessness: "Yankees go home, and take us with you" (p. 251), the latter
example illustrating an ironic twist on dependency theory. Stylistically,
graffiti fuse typography, color, and words in fragmented messages, and
when several graffiti artists use the same space, the superimposition

of several styles is compared by García-Canclini to the "incongruent rhythm of the video" (p. 249). Hence the author's characterization of graffiti as "a syncretic and transcultural medium" (p. 251). (In Chapter Five, stylistic fusions and discontinuities form a major component of my analysis of *Tele Chobis*, the Mexican copycat version of *Teletubbies*.)

In Latin America, then, hybridity is shaped at once by ancient intercultural encounters and contemporary social dynamics. In García-Canclini's view (1989/1995), hybridity helps us understand the uncertainty that surrounds modernity in Latin America, since hybridity highlights the mixtures and discontinuities that have characterized at once the encounter between the modern and the traditional in history, and the interactions between the global, regional, national, and local that continue to this day. Hence García-Canclini's guarded engagement with postmodernism, which he conceives as a lens through which to revisit the exclusionary and reappropriative ways in which modernity has related to traditions. Whether in the form of state institutions and official discourse, or since the 1980s in the form of corporate practices and media-propagated consumerist ideology, Latin American modernity and modernism have integrated traditions rather than caused their demise.

The discontinuous, selective, and unequal processes through which this integration has been accomplished, and its outcome, can be grasped only through a "transdisciplinary" approach, which García-Canclini (1989/1995) expresses first in a transportation and communication metaphor: "The anthropologist arrives in the city by foot, the sociologist by car and via the main highway, the communications specialist by plane" (p. 4). His second metaphor is architectural, since understanding processes of hybridization requires mixed methodologies that hitherto have addressed separate realms of knowledge, which he compares with a building's floors. In contrast, today we need "nomad sciences capable of circulating through the staircases that connect these floors" (p. 2). An interdisciplinary approach with an empirical and not merely textual focus, the author concludes, establishes crucial connections between the cultural and political realms.

A notion of hybridity grounded in a concrete socio-politico-economic context is central to the interdisciplinary approach García-Canclini (1989/1995) advocates. Compared to the more celebratory conceptions of hybridity discussed earlier, García-Canclini warns against uncritical celebrations of cultural pluralism and mixture, and he is circumspect about cultural hybridity's potential in terms of political empowerment.

His conception of hybridity is political, in the sense that he fully accounts for the fact that hybridity's constitutive processes entail both inclusion and exclusion of traditional forms into modern practices, and reflect both hybridization and separation between various social strata and their cultural expressions. The hybrid is also political, because it helps elite groups integrate memory and the cultural artifacts reminiscent of the past into a hegemonic national framework, an issue discussed at length in my earlier analysis of the discourse of mestizaje. It is to underscore this point that García-Canclini writes of "the *cultural* need to confer a denser meaning on the present and the *political* need to legitimize the current hegemony by means of the prestige of the historical patrimony" (p. 28, emphasis in original).

The notion of hybridity as used by García-Canclini (1989/1995) captures what he calls oblique power (p. 258), by which he means the subtle and refracted ways in which power operates in historically mixed, culturally hybrid, and politically transitioning societies like Latin America's. We cannot understand power in terms of "confrontations and vertical actions" (p. 259), because power's effectiveness stems from the interweaving of relations of power between one social class and another, one ethnic group and another, one generation and another, and the interactions among these pairs. In this view it is important to fully account for the structures through which the convoluted power vectors mentioned earlier operate. In other words, he calls for a critical, and not merely interpretive, exploration of hybridity as a social condition: "One may forget about totality when one is interested only in the differences among people, not when one is also concerned with inequality" (p. 11). García-Canclini's vision of hybridity is more difficult to criticize as textualist or populist, because it integrates the political-economic context of hybridity. Nonetheless, as we shall see in the following section, opponents of hybridity do not have the patience for such intricate differences and have usually attacked the idea of hybridity at large.

THE "ANTIHYBRIDITY BACKLASH"

The widespread use of the concept of hybridity has attracted critiques whose tones have ranged from cautionary to scathing. Strong divergences on its meaning and implications mire hybridity in two paradoxes. First, hybridity is believed to be both subversive and pervasive, exceptional and ordinary, marginal yet mainstream. Second, foggy conceptual boundaries and extreme semantic openness invite arbitrary and at times exclusionary usage. "Hybridity," as Mexican American performance artist Guillermo Gómez-Peña (1996) put it, "can be appropriated by anyone to mean practically anything" (pp. 12–13). These contradictions have enabled critics to depict hybridity theory as poststructuralist license, and to impute to its proponents reactionary politics wrapped in trendy jargon. This hostility against hybridity is founded on (1) allegations of theoretical uselessness; (2) suspicion toward the high priests of hybridity—expatriate, Western-based intellectuals; and (3) perhaps most importantly, the charge that hybridity rhetoric embraces the logic of transnational capitalism and is therefore "neocolonial." As the next pages show, the "anti-hybridity backlash" (Nederveen-Pieterse, 2001, p. 221) sees hybridity at best as academic nonsense, at worst as a pernicious affirmation of hegemonic power.

Since all cultures are always hybrid, the assumption of erstwhile purity is untenable, and as a result hybridity is conceptually dispensable (Nederveen-Pieterse, 2001). This point's apparent simplicity underscores a deeper problem. The notion of hybridity invokes the fusion of two (or more) components into a third term irreducible to the sum of its parts. By unhinging the identities of its ingredients without congealing into a stable third term, hybridity enters a vicious circle where its condition of existence is at the same time its kiss of death. Another cause of alleged theoretical futility is hybridity's appropriation in areas that range from theology to biology. When a concept means so many different things to so many different people in so many different fields and so many different contexts, it ceases to have any meaning whatsoever. Hybridity's extreme polysemy has in effect morphed it into a floating signifier, a situation that undermines the explanatory power and parsimony that concepts usually have. And yet, in spite of this seemingly intractable paradox, hybridity remains an appealing concept, as the burgeoning written record unmistakably demonstrates.

Hybridity is also decried as a self-gratifying discourse by emigré intellectuals who indulge in fancy theorizing, seen as a form of "moral self-congratulation" (Werbner, 1997, p. 22) that is politically vacuous (Friedman, 1997; Hutnyk, 1997). In a hard-hitting essay in *Race and Class*, Aijaz Ahmad (1995) writes that "between postcoloniality as it exists in a former colony like India, and postcoloniality as the condition of discourse practiced by such critics as Homi Bhabha, there would appear to be a considerable gap" (p. 10). This is Ahmad at his most euphemistic toward Bhabha, who embodies what Ahmad derogatorily calls "the migrant intellectual" (p. 13) who (falsely) enunciates hybridity as a universal experience. From their privileged Western location, intellectuals like Bhabha, Ahmad intones, have abdicated their critical role and been co-opted by their success in Western academe. In Bhabha's work, this positionality manifests itself in his associating hybridity with contingency, contingency with agency, and in turn agency with counterhegemonic resistance. Ahmad is right to point out that postcolonial intellectual discourses of hybridity and mimicry sharply contrast with the living conditions of millions of people whose energies are devoted to securing the barest conditions of survival, but his charge of reactionary intellectual politics stops short of engaging the complexity of the issue, an intricacy which is explored in the Francophone argument between Créolité and négritude. The next section uses this dispute to explore the links between hybridity and hegemony and to conclude this chapter.

HYBRIDITY AND HEGEMONY: MÉTISSAGE, CRÉOLITÉ, AND NÉGRITUDE

In *Writing Diaspora* (1993), Hong Kong–born cultural critic Rey Chow contends that "[w]hat Bhabha's word 'hybridity' [revives], in the masquerade of deconstructing anti-imperialism, and 'difficult' theory, is an old functionalist notion of what a dominant culture permits in the interest of maintaining its own equilibrium" (p. 35). The claim that hybridity is hegemonically constructed in the interest of dominant societal sectors resonates with my ulterior analysis of the Latin American ideology of mestizaje. By displacing mixture from race to culture and selectively appropriating native traditions, Latin American ideologists of mestizaje integrated precolonial cultures in the dominant society. This process allowed nonthreatening arts, crafts, and rituals, but imposed the Spanish language, the Catholic faith, and colonial political and social organization. As a discourse that recognizes, even celebrates, cultural difference, mestizaje in effect is a tool for "bleaching" all but the most benign practices that gave pre-Hispanic natives their identities. In the name of cultural mixture within the emerging nation-states, the pre-Hispanic life world was reordered by the descendants of the Conquistadores according to a residual colonial logic.

The dispute between proponents of Créolité and négritude illustrates the tension between hybridity's progressive and hegemonic aspects. In *Mythologie du métissage* [Mythology of Hybridity] (1998)—whose title reveals a skeptical outlook—Roger Toumson, a professor of comparative French and Francophone literatures at the University of the Antilles, describes hybridity as a "lyrical illusion" (p. 11).[8] Contending that hybridity is a discourse of power, Toumson sets out to understand how and why hybridity emerged as a discourse that is well adapted to the complexities of the contemporary world. While Toumson agrees with the premise that all cultures are hybrid, he sees the deployment of such a rhetoric as a cosmopolitanism that is at best apolitical, at worst hypocritical. He therefore dismisses the premise expressed in the title of René Duboux's book, *Métissage ou barbarie* (1994), that the two alternatives for the world are hybridity or barbarism—a premise Toumson dismisses as "an antiphilosophy of identity" (p. 64). In Toumson's view, asserting that "we are all hybrids" is at the heart of a new planetary ideology whose basic aim is to avoid addressing highly political issues such as racial and colonial oppression. What if, asks Toumson, we would insist that, for instance, Italian culture and language are hybrid? This would reverse the hybridity discourse in the sense that while denotatively we can repeat that all cultures are hybrid, we have in fact used hybridity as a framework for studying and defining postcolonial nations and cultures. In other words, hybridity is a discourse with a particular geopolitical directionality, and as a result should be treated with suspicion.

In pursuing his argument, Toumson contrasts two discourses of cultural identity born in what was the French colonial empire: Créolité and négritude. Against Créolité's celebrations of hybridity as the distinguishing feature of international relations, a perspective embodied in Édouard Glissant's *Le discours Antillais* (1981) and his later work (Glissant, 1993), and more recently in the volume *Éloge de la créolité* (In Praise of Créolité) (Bernabé, Chamoiseau, and Confiant, 1989), Toumson (1998) argues that hybridity is a discourse of "voluntary amnesia" (p. 28) that covers past and lingering racial inequities. Glissant (1993), the Martinique-born high priest of the Créolité movement in Caribbean French postcolonies, sees the mutual interpenetration of cultures as the engine of history, and the discourse of hybridity as a guarantee against intolerance. Toumson faults Glissant for glossing over the inequality that characterizes intercultural dynamics in a world defined by a hierarchical system of international relations. More important, Toumson argues that Glissant's view of history ignores the heterogenous and antagonist forces unleashed by the "homogenizing and dissolving power of the monocentric technoculture" (p. 58).

Born in Africa in the 1950s, the négritude movement is grounded in three major ideologies: one cultural, focusing on black uniqueness; the second socioeconomic, in sync with African socialism of the time;

and the third political, with the twin objectives of national independence and pan-African unity (Toumson, 1998). Négritude's chief exponents disagree on the basis of black specificity while acknowledging its presence. For the Senegalese poet and ideologue Léopold Sédar Senghor, blacks are essentially close to nature and gifted with superior emotional abilities. Aimé Césaire, a native of the French Caribbean island of Martinique and négritude's other leading figure, spurned Senghor's biological determinism, preferring a cultural constructivist understanding of black identity. Both leaders, however, agreed on an anti-acculturationist agenda, arguing in favor of an intercultural dialogue between Africa and the West, as long as both would be able to preserve their distinct identities. In contrast to Créolité's celebration of a chaotic, heterogenous world culture where multiple histories coexist in a state of continuous mutual hybridization, the négritude movement rejected the hybridity thesis. In a famous talk at the first Congress of Black Writers, held in Paris in 1956, Césaire argued that "it is because a culture is not a simple juxtaposition of cultural traits that there could not be a hybrid culture." He then clarified: "I do not mean that people who are biologically hybrid would be incapable of founding a civilization. I do mean that the civilization that they would found would not be a civilization unless it is not hybrid" (quoted in Toumson, 1998, pp. 64–65, my translation). Interestingly, civilization here is invoked not in the French Enlightenment meaning of *civilisation*, a cosmopolitan, universalist, and material culture. Rather, Césaire's use of civilization is redolent of the German counter-enlightenment notion of *Kultur*, which encapsulates the unique and genial characteristics of the nation and focuses on inward, spiritual, and as such "pure" dimensions of national life. In Césaire's logic, a civilization cannot be hybrid, because mixture undermines national and cultural uniqueness.

Currently salient discourses of hybridity, with which Créolité is aligned, undermine more political discourses such as négritude by positioning themselves as discourses of openness and tolerance, casting the opposite perspective as provincial in its attachment to cultural distinctiveness. While négritude appeared in the second stage of the narrative of cultural encounters—colonialism presumably being the first—it is best understood from a dialectical, not chronological, perspective (Toumson, 1998). From Toumson's standpoint, négritude is the third moment of a dialectical process. Inversely, while sequentially Créolité came third, it should be relocated to the second stage of the historical dialectic of intercultural relations. In Toumson's view, the historical placement of the apolitical Créolité after the militant négritude masks the real opposition between them, and his adoption of a dialectical approach brings that tension to light.

Toumson's criticism of hybridity as an ambivalent and mythical discourse of power reflects a deep engagement with cultural mixture and therefore is qualitatively different from other critiques (Ahmad, 1995; Friedman, 1997). In highlighting négritude's and Créolité's commonality as two discourses of the dominated, Toumson underscores that négritude, claiming a radical cultural relativism, and Créolité, embracing a universalism predicated on cultural mixing, represent two sides of the hybridity discourse. Both négritude's glorification of the specific and Créolité's celebration of the diverse betray a preoccupation with ideologically defining a mixed, diverse world culture created out of a hodgepodge of particularistic ingredients. Toumson (1998) thus reaches the conclusion that "the ideology of hybridity is in effect ambivalent. Two problems are posed at the same time: that of the philosophical legitimating of cultural relativism, and that of the sociological rehabilitation of dominated cultures (p. 77, my translation). Nonetheless, Toumson sensibly recognizes that the value of hybridity as a discourse lies in its invalidation of the idea of total difference between cultures.

Criticism of hybridity reflects conceptual ambiguity, ideological differences, and various levels of tolerance of a ubiquitous and often misused trope. With the notable exception of Toumson (1998), whose thoughtful and provocative book explores the myriad dimensions of hybridity, the antihybridity backlash's emphasis on hybridity's problematic status rests on a priori dismissal at the expense of serious engagement. If hybridity is pervasive, as most scholars seem to agree, then we do need to call it as it is and develop conceptual tools to tackle its vexing ambiguity. Toumson (1998), and to a lesser extent, the late Said (1994) of *Culture and Imperialism*, demonstrate the value and possibility of a critical engagement with hybridity. In contrast, it is precisely by using the concept without rigorous theoretical grounding that we unleash hybridity's polysemic excesses and ripen it for various kinds of appropriation. Perhaps the most important foundation we can provide to uses of hybridity is the political and economic contexts that shape the variety of hybridities manifest in different cultural practices, heeding Said's call that "cultural forms are hybrid, mixed, impure, and the time has come in cultural analysis to reconnect their analysis with their actuality" (1994, p. 14).

The confusion and contention that surround hybridity make the reconnection Said advocates a daunting challenge. In the following chapters I explore various applications of hybridity, in order to illustrate how this trope works in actuality, and the role that communication processes play in the formation of hybridity. Chapter Four examines the utilization of the notion of hybridity in contemporary public discourse, and establishes a continuity with previous notions of cultural mixture as discourses of integration. Chapter Five explores hybridity's usefulness in studying the practices of the global television industry and in analyzing television texts that mix various cultural components. Chapter Six empirically analyzes hybridity as a local existential experience. The concluding Chapter Seven finally formulates the notion of *critical transculturalism* as a framework that enables analyses of the communication aspects of cultural mixture in their political and economic contexts.

4   Corporate Transculturalism

The issues and concerns of what constitute [North-South] ... relations occur within a "reality" whose content has for the most part been defined by the representational practices of the "first world."

—Roxanne Doty

Cross-cultural contact cashes in some cultures while others germinate.

—Tyler Cowen

Hooray for the hybrid. Hip-hip for the mongrel. Hallelujah for the global me.

—Pascal Zachary

COMPELLED BY the historical analysis of vocabularies of cultural mixture in the previous chapter, I now turn to contemporary representations of hybridity and address the following questions: Is there continuity between mestizaje, creolization, métissage, and transculturation in their historical contexts, and current characterizations of hybridity? What issues are incorporated and, conversely, what dimensions of hybridity already discussed in this book are omitted from present-day public discourse? To attend to these questions, I examine representations of hybridity in elite print media.[1] In agreement with the first epigraph's characterizations of representational practices in international relations, I set out to analyze how some public intellectuals (e.g., academics like Cowen and journalists like Zachary in the second and third epigraphs) use hybridity, and to explore how helpful these uses are in advancing our understanding of intercultural relations.

Understanding how much importance is given to power in intercultural relations is my primary objective as I consider how major U.S. media use the notion of hybridity. In this endeavor, critical discourse analysis is a suitable analytical approach. According to its leading proponent, Dutch scholar Teun van Dijk (1993), critical discourse analysis focuses on *"the role of discourse in the (re)production and challenge of dominance"* (p. 249, emphasis in original). Even as it recognizes that resistance to power plays an integral part in social relations, critical discourse analysis gives primacy to "top-down" uses of power, focusing on "elites and their discursive strategies for the maintenance of inequality" (p. 250). I use this methodology because its concern with social, as opposed to personal and interpersonal, uses of power is compatible with my approach to intercultural relations. Critical discourse analysis focuses on: (1) *access* to the means of discourse, such as the mass media; social, economic or political privilege; (2) *social cognitions*, defined as "[s]ocially shared representations of societal arrangements, groups and relations" (p. 257) that connect discourse to dominance; and (3) *discourse structures*, which refer to how a discourse is constructed. This methodology is particularly suited for the study of how elite media use hybridity since the "discursive (re)production of power results *from* social cognitions of the powerful, whereas the situated discourse structures result *in* social cognitions" (p. 259, emphasis in original). The forthcoming analysis will briefly address issues of access; then it will identify a variety of social cognitions that constitute hybridity as an increasingly pervasive discourse.

Database searches give a measure of how widespread a notion hybridity has become. A January 28, 2004, Lexis-Nexis search of "major newspapers" using the keywords "cultural hybridity," "cultural hybridization," and "hybrid culture" yielded 253 documents from the *New York Times, Washington Post, Christian-Science Monitor, Boston Globe, Denver Post, St. Louis Post-Dispatch, Newsday,* and other major dailies. A search of "magazines and journals" using the same keywords produced 66 additional documents from, among others, *Newsweek, U.S. News and World Report, Billboard, New Statesman, American Spectator, Weekly Standard,* and *Foreign Affairs.* Searches for "creolization," "cultural creolization," and "creole culture" located 375 items in major papers and 38 in magazines and journals; "transculturation," "transculture," and "transcultural" found 472 documents in major papers and 193 in magazines; "mixed culture," "blended culture," and "multiracial culture" turned up 425 hits in major papers. Finally, in what may be an indication of future usage, a Google search on January 28, 2004, using the keyword "cultural hybridity" listed around 24,100 items. Undoubtedly, the vocabulary of cultural mixture has entered the lexicon of public discourse. The following analysis of print-media uses of hybridity focuses on two distinct but related themes relevant to the topic of this book, namely the global impact of U.S. popular culture and the cultural dimensions of economic policies.

HYBRIDITY AND THE GLOBAL IMPACT OF U.S. POPULAR CULTURE

My examination of newspaper and magazine uses of hybridity in their coverage of the global influence of U.S. popular culture focuses on selected representative documents drawn from publications that cover the ideological spectrum, ranging from the *Utne Reader* to *American Enterprise,* and including the *New York Times, Washington Post, Economist,* and *Fortune.* Although most newspapers and magazines found in the Lexis-Nexis search are elite media, the analysis draws heavily on an "American Popular Culture Abroad" series of five articles that appeared in the *Washington Post* on October 25–27, 1998 (Farhi and Rosenfeld, 1998; Lancaster, 1998; Rosenfeld, 1998; Trueheart, 1998; Waxman, 1998). The articles were filed from a variety of locations such as Los Angeles, Kuala Lumpur, Paris, and Tehran, and credited numerous contributors to the stories from Tehran, Nairobi, Hong Kong, Beijing, New Delhi, Mexico City, London, Paris, Jerusalem, Bogota, Warsaw, Moscow, Berlin, Tokyo, and Toronto. In addition to these global credentials, the *Washington Post* is portrayed in a 1999 *Columbia Journalism Review* study as "the bible for coverage of national government and politics" ("America's Best," 1999). In the words of one media scholar: "The *Washington Post* is a newspaper with the potential for a disproportionately large impact on U.S. foreign policy. By virtue of its location and widespread influence, the *Post* is obligatory reading for the American and international diplomatic community. While it certainly hasn't dictated foreign policy, the newspaper's editorial page has helped guide both the agenda and focus on international initiatives" (Palmer, 1995, p. 144).

As an important site of elite discourse—whether through its global fleet of correspondents, or due to its status as the newspaper of record of the U.S. capital—the *Washington Post*'s utilization of hybridity will serve as the backbone of the upcoming analysis of media usages of hybridity. Whether mentioned literally, such as in the headline "Malaysians Create Hybrid Culture with American Imports" (Rosenfeld, 1998), or evoked indirectly, hybridity is used in the articles as a general characterization of intercultural relations between the United States and developing nations. This raises several questions: How is cultural globalization depicted? What social cognitions ground the articles' use of hybridity, and how are these cognitions formulated? Does public discourse account for power in the constitution of hybrid cultures? The analysis will find that the utilization of hybridity is based on a double negation of

(1a) the existence of cultural homogeneity and of (1b) Western cultural dominance. It will also show that the discourse of hybridity supports a double assertion of (2a) the notion of cultural counterflow into the West and (2b) globalization and free trade. Finally, print media use hybridity as a context where they assert (3) creative individualism and individual freedom.

HYBRIDITY AND THE ALLEGED MYTHS OF CULTURAL PURITY AND WESTERN CULTURAL DOMINANCE

Media accounts of global culture deny the notions of cultural homogeneity and Western cultural dominance by asserting the ubiquity of hybridity. "Nowhere is there more blending than in the United States," writes a *Washington Post* reporter in an article titled "The Trend to Blend." He continues: "We've melted the melting pot and become a pureed people. We toss races and ethnic backgrounds and ages and classes together into a combi-nation salad" (Weeks, 2002, p. C2). The Indian author Salman Rushdie is more emphatic when he poses a series of rhetorical questions in a *New York Times* column on European anti-Americanism: "[D]o cultures actually exist as separate, pure, defensible entities? Is not mélange, adulteration, impurity, pick'n'mix at the heart of the idea of the modern, and hasn't it been that way for most of this all-shook-up century? Doesn't the idea of pure cultures, in urgent need of being kept free from alien contamination, lead us inexorably toward apartheid, toward ethnic cleansing, toward the gas chamber?" (1999). The idea that all cultures are hybrid, as Chapters Two and Three have discussed, is clearly ascendant, and even nearly consensual, in intellectual and public discourse. However, as I have already argued, asserting hybridity as a sociocultural condition at large, disconnected from its political and economic contexts and from its constitutive processes, is conceptually untenable and ethically problematical. Also, setting hybridity in a polarized opposition to ethnic cleansing as Rushdie does, similar to Duboux's (1994) forced choice between *métissage* or *barbarie*, is rhetorically dubious and analytically limiting. Rather, our approach to hybridity should be framed by the type of hybridity put forward, the motivation for advancing it, its rhetorical topoi, and its material effects. It is therefore indicative, in the articles analyzed here, that the affirmation of hybridity as a pervasive condition at the national level is a springboard to utilize hybridity in the global realm. For example, in the aforementioned "Trend to Blend" article, the reporter moves from his discussion of hybridity in U.S. society to generalities seemingly plucked from the academic literature: "Call it globalization, call it imperialism," he writes, "but cultures, too, are commingling at an accelerated pace. There is a Burger King in Budapest. And Tex-Mex in Beijing" (Weeks, 2002, p. C2).

The leap from "all (national) cultures are hybrid" to "global culture is hybrid" paves the ground for the claim that "Western [often used to mean "American"] cultural dominance is inexistent." Take for instance the *Economist*, that bastion of British conservatism, whose probusiness articles consistently dismiss the existence of U.S. cultural dominance. A headline from that newspaper tells readers that the "global row" over American popular culture is "muddled" ("Culture Wars," 1998). Even if Hollywood studios reign over global screens and make approximately half their revenues overseas, readers are reminded of the customary story of Hollywood as a global cinematic mecca, drawing foreign stars like Chaplin, Murnau, and Hitchcock. The article also prompts its readers that Columbia Tri-Star and Fox, two leading studios, are not American-owned, a point also made elsewhere (for example, Huey, 1990). Conversely, and in spite of Hollywood's global success, we are reminded of the existence of vibrant national cinemas, like the Indian music film industry. "[T]he postmodern crazy quilt called Indian film music," according to a writer in the *Utne Reader*, "incorporates numerous Western sources (some of them quite corny) into a mix both global and distinctly Indian—and vastly more innovative than most American pop music" (Hermes, 1994, p. 20). Other reports, like a *New York Times* article titled "U.S. TV Shows Losing Potency around World" (Kapner, 2003), underscore the decreasing international prime-time presence of U.S. programs. "The shift," the reporter writes, "counters a longstanding assumption that TV shows produced in the United States would continue to overshadow locally produced shows from Singapore to Sicily."

CULTURAL COUNTERFLOW, FREE TRADE, AND GLOBALIZATION

While, strictly speaking, the global appeal of U.S. television may be declining, what is notable is how this decline is turned into one of several claims in favor of the notion of cultural counterflow. This rhetorical maneuver dislocates the issue of American television's international appeal from its initial context (the media industries) and deploys it in a broader argument in favor of global trade. According to another *Economist* editorial, "Pokémania v Globophobia" (1999): "The anti-globalists are . . .

wrong when they argue that conglomerates inevitably homogenize the ideas that they choose to hoover up. Some of the Pokemon have certainly had their names westernized . . . . But the little monsters still teach distinctively Japanese values about the importance of team-building and performing your duties. The only way to succeed at the game is to cooperate with others—and the easiest way to fail is to neglect to care for your charges." In a rhetoric typical of proglobalization views on culture, then, the preceding emphasizes the idea of "counterflow," or cultural forms emanating from Japan (Pokémon) and finding broad popularity in the West. As we will see in the next pages, the *Economist* selectively foregrounds high-profile examples of cultural products from Japan and the United Kingdom, themselves powerful economies, to emphasize the success of non-U.S. popular culture in the United States and to deny global U.S. cultural power.

Elsewhere, the notion of counterflow turns up indirectly in reference to the widely held idea that the global marketplace dictates U.S. studio practices. In this scenario, the flow of media products from the United States is subject to a "counterflow" of foreign audience tastes. Thus one *Washington Post* article, "Hollywood Tailors Its Movies to Sell in Foreign Markets" (Waxman, 1998), begins: "Most Americans know that our popular culture exerts a powerful influence across the globe, shaping attitudes, trends and styles. But the inverse—a more subtle effect—is also true: The worldwide hunger for US-made entertainment helps steer our own culture, by encouraging projects that will sell overseas and discouraging those that foreign audiences are thought to spurn" (p. A1). The article thus justifies the high number of violent action films churned out by Hollywood and reveals that ingredients for global box-office success are added to films. For instance, eight weeks before the film *Armageddon* (about an asteroid collision with Earth) opened, "Disney decided to add not only $3 million more in explosions, but also reaction-to-the-asteroid shots from Morocco and Paris" in order "to make sure the movie had more of an international feel to it," according to the head of Disney Studios (p. A1). An alternative interpretation could be that the film's internationally set reaction-to-the-asteroid shots cast the United States as the sole protector of the world, since in the movie no other country participated in the attempt to destroy the asteroid. The article's cosmopolitan surface, then, sits atop a latent paternalism.

The rhetoric of counterflow also serves as an entry point into a pro-free-trade, proglobalization argument, which oftentimes finds its expression in the dismissal of "protectionism." In the previously mentioned discussion of Indian film, Hermes (1994) writes that anti-Western rhetoric "frequently comes from a nation's cultural gatekeepers, who are seeking to preserve their power and control over economic resources" (p. 20). The author further construes this misguided elite that struggles for power at the national level as an obstacle to the unfettered flow of cultural commodities. In Hermes's view these national cadres are wrong, because "it's a mistake to underestimate the strength and integrity of local cultures." He proceeds: "[A]s the rich, *post-national creolizations* of the world suggest, there seems to be reason for optimism in the wake of globalism" (p. 20, my emphasis).

INDIVIDUAL CREATIVITY AND FREEDOM IN CULTURAL PRODUCTION AND CONSUMPTION

The motor of globalism, according to the articles under analysis, is the creativity and freedom of individual creators and consumers of popular culture. For example, the *Economist* editorial I cited earlier in this chapter argues that since both *Pokemon* and *Teletubbies* are not likely to endure, "why so many protectionists assume that the craze will be dreamed up by some faceless American corporation rather than by a Japanese bug-collector or a British welfare mother is getting more mysterious by the day ("Pokémania v Globophobia," 1999). In addition to criticizing antiglobalization discourse, this editorial shifts focus from the multinationals that control the global media and popular culture industry onto individual auteurs such as *Harry Potter* author J. K. Rowling—the "British welfare mother"—or *Pokémon* creator Satoshi Tajiri—the "Japanese bug collector" (ibid.). By displacing the issue from the social to the individual sphere, the editorial creates a hospitable space for the ideograph (see M. C. McGee, 1980) "individual creativity." In a further example, the magazine *American Enterprise* quoted a speaker at an American Enterprise Institute conference on global popular culture who approvingly commented on the ideological underpinnings of American culture: "The core of this ideology is uniquely insistent and far-reaching individualism—a view of the individual that gives unprecedented weight to his or her choices. Private property in the economic sphere, democracy and freedom from government control in the polity, the absence of rank, and more equality in the larger society: these are the distinguishing essential American values. All reflect pervasive underlying individualism" ("The Controversy," 1992, p. 79).[2] The view that free individuals operating in an unfettered marketplace—and not structures of ownership, production, distribution, and promotion—determine the success of cultural products, is also taken up by economist Tyler Cowen (2002a, b), who argues that globalization increases cultural diversity largely as a result of the creative power of individuals, and not "collectives." This view from economics is discussed subsequently in this chapter.

There is another expression of creative individualism that focuses on individual freedom during cultural reception—and not on individual creators of culture—which in the *Washington Post* series "American Popular Culture Abroad" is expressed in terms of consumer desire for U.S. technology and popular culture. U.S. technology, one article (Lancaster, 1998) suggests, is a fetish of Western modernity and creativity to which foreign audiences aspire, and which disables censorship in non-Western countries, rendering governments powerless against the Western cultural tide. In Iran, the cultural arch-nemesis of the United States and charter member of the "Axis of Evil," consumers have a "fascination with American movies" due to "Hollywood special-effects wizardry" (p. A1). In fact, "there is less to Iranian censorship than meets the eye. Despite stiff fines, satellite dishes are widely if discreetly used, and customs authorities are helpless against the flood of tapes, videocassettes and other illicit materials smuggled from abroad; one diplomat described an Iranian friend who boasted recently of having passed through the airport here with 35 CDs hidden in his clothing and bags" (ibid.). The dedication with which Iranian consumers seek U.S. cultural and media products underscores the argument that longing for Western popular culture is an irrepressible force that subverts even the most authoritarian governments, and suggests that, in the absence of cultural repression, Iranian and others would flock to U.S. popular culture.

Taken together, the notions that cultural homogeneity and Western cultural dominance are myths, that there is a cultural counterflow from the non-West to the West, that global free trade is beneficial to all participants in it, and that individual creativity and freedom explain global cultural success constitute a discourse whose central notion is hybridity. This discourse at once denies that the United States dominates global popular culture and asserts the irresistible power of U.S. popular culture on foreign audiences. It is to this apparent inconsistency—U.S. culture described as irresistible but not dominant—that the analysis now turns.

The position that Western technology and non-Western longing for U.S. popular culture sap authoritarian and protectionist actions is inconsistent with the stance that Western culture is not dominant worldwide.

The language used betrays unequal intercultural relations. The portrayal of U.S. popular culture as irresistibly attractive to foreign audiences in the *Washington Post* articles (Farhi and Rosenfeld, 1998; Lancaster, 1998; Rosenfeld, 1998; Trueheart, 1998; Waxman, 1998) is peppered with sexual language that casts U.S. popular culture as dominant in a masculinist frame. The first article's headline, "American Pop *Penetrates* Worldwide" (Farhi and Rosenfeld, 1998, my emphasis), sets the tone, and the article's authors write about "the *desire* to appear more American" (my emphasis) among Indian youth, who adopt one imported fad after another from the United States. Another article describes how Malaysia, "like much of the developing world . . . *embraces* American popular culture" and proceeds with the claim that in Malaysia "as elsewhere, *the love affair is fraught with turbulence and passion*, ambivalence and confusion" (Rosenfeld, 1998, my emphasis). Interviews with Malaysian artists and intellectuals highlight their concerns about sexual content in cultural imports from the United States, as indicated by a renowned Malaysian cartoonist when he said that people in his native village are no longer "*innocent*" (ibid., my emphasis) as a result of being exposed to U.S. popular culture through television. Likewise, a Malaysian advertising executive claims that to Malaysian censors "armpits are a no-no. No bare shoulders or backs. The *American influence they want to keep out is almost always sex*" (ibid., my emphasis). Sexual language is also present in other articles, one characterizing McDonald restaurants in non-U.S. locations as a "*pleasure zone*" (Trueheart, 1998, my emphasis), the other describing "*the lure of the forbidden fruit*" that has "grabbed younger Iranians by the lapels" (Lancaster, 1998, my emphasis).

The gendered language of manly conquest and seduction used to describe how foreign audiences relate to U.S. popular culture undermines claims that the United States is not dominant. This inconsistency perhaps stems from the fact that, as with mestizaje, créolité, and transculturation, there is tension in the contemporary hybridity discourse between the egalitarian pluralism it ostensibly conjures up and the inequalities inherent in intercultural relations. In the case of the four 1998 articles being analyzed, the discursive structure establishes a binary relation between U.S. popular culture and an aspiring non-West. The former sets global standards of taste and is clearly the engine driving the hybridity resulting from contact, while the latter is enthralled by the former's appeal and transformed into an eager but relatively passive and objectified hybrid. The paternalism at the heart of this relationship is manifest in interviews with the Malaysian elite, like the Malaysian rock star dubbed "the Bob Dylan of Malaysia," who claims that "our own people are very insecure about their music," or the head of the Malaysian Research Center, who acknowledges: "[W]e don't know what we want" (Rosenfeld, 1998).

According to another article, this confusion is remedied by Hollywood, which sets standards and helps foreign audiences develop more refined artistic tastes as a result of their exposure to American movies. As Sony Pictures Entertainment president John Calley is quoted saying: "[F]oreign moviegoers want to see anything that's good. They're like us. We have in some way Americanized much of the world; they've assimilated a lot of stuff" (Waxman, 1998). As a global benchmark, then, U.S. popular culture provides opportunities for audiences in developing countries to shed their allegedly unsophisticated tastes as they attempt to emulate the cultural sensibilities of American viewers.

In this discourse, the ostensible elevation of foreign audiences from immature viewership to sophisticated audiencehood sets up foreign audiences as culprits in racial conflict in the United States, as U.S. movie executives impute their propensity not to cast minority actors in major movies to the sensibilities of foreign audiences. In "Studios Say 'Ethnic' Films Are Not Popular Overseas," the reporter writes that "foreign distributors, according to . . . executives and producers, are less interested in investing in films that focus on women . . . and have almost no interest in movies that have African Americans or other minority casts and themes." The assumption that foreign audiences are racist and misogynist thus exonerates exclusionary casting practices. To its credit, the article describes the objections by minority actors in Hollywood to what they see as institutionalized racism, and mentions that independent movies with foreign funding are not subject to the same casting restrictions. Nonetheless, the reporter perfunctorily uses the euphemism "racial bias" in reference to the Hollywood studio system. The issue is expressed clearly in a quote by a Sony executive, who matter-of-factly states: "'We're cognizant of what does not work internationally. . . . Black baseball movies, period dramas about football, rap, inner-city films—most countries can't relate to that. Americana seems to be desired by international markets, but there comes a point when even they will resist and say, "We don't get it," and it's generally in that ethnic, inner-city, sports-driven region.' He paused. 'We can't give'em what they don't want.'" The last sentence's callous commercialism, expressed on the record by an industry leader, suggests that a notion of individual consumer freedom tainted by racial assumptions is entrenched among movie industry executives. This "white customer as king" cliché has major implications for minority actors. Whoopi Goldberg's film *Sister Act*, for example, was very popular abroad, writes the reporter, who nonetheless concludes that "[i]t's a question, largely, of mathematics. In Hollywood, cold calculations are made based on the projected international box office revenues." A "star power" list looms large over Hollywood casting routines, with Tom Cruise scoring a perfect 100, followed by Harrison Ford at 99, Mel Gibson at 98, etc. There are only two women in the top twenty positions, Jodie Foster at 94 and Julia Roberts at 92, and not a single ethnic minority is on the list (Waxman, 1998).

Does Hollywood really not cast minority actors because they are not popular with foreign audiences? Clearly, global markets are important to the U.S. media industry. However, most of the world's media markets are populated by a majority of people who share the ethnicity of U.S. minorities and immigrant groups, with the notable exception of Europe. It is probable that African, Asian, and Latin American viewers would be drawn to films and television programs that feature actors who share their ethnicity. More importantly, cultural assumptions about race and audience tastes affect the processes by which U.S. films and television programs are globally distributed (Havens, 2002). Distributors promote programs with "universal" themes that limit the market viability of blackness, namely "settings, situations and themes associated with middle-class family life in developed capitalist societies" (ibid., p. 386). The cultural viability of blackness as a selling mechanism is couched in a universalist rhetoric of whiteness primarily because the U.S. film and television industries have historically catered to a white middle-class audience, not because of foreign audience preferences. The sweeping changes that affected the television industry in the late 1980s and the 1990s—liberalization, new networks, growth of cable and satellite television—and the subsequent birth of what screen-studies scholar Michael Curtin (1999) called the postnetwork era, changed the hues of U.S. television. The belated recognition of the purchasing power of the African American middle class and the resulting desirability of African American television characters has led to the increased presence of "ethnic" or "multicultural" programs to attract the African American middle class. However, after a growth in media roles for women and minorities between 1992 and 1997, 1998 registered a decline in women and minorities' film and television roles ("Minority Roles," 1999). The 1999 Screen Actors Guild (SAG) survey found that in 1998, Asian/Pacific

Americans got more parts, while African Americans, Native Americans, and Latinos obtained fewer roles. Of the 56,700 acting parts covered by SAG contracts, African American roles made up 19 percent, and African American roles amounted to a total of 13.4 percent of all screen roles (ibid.). It is therefore probable that foreign audience preferences are not the only obstacle that affects minority participation in U.S. television and film.

The corporate rhetoric that uses foreign audience tastes to explain exclusionary casting decisions, in addition to the *Washington Post* article's inconsistent claim that U.S. popular culture is irresistible but not dominant (Lancaster, 1998), is based on an individualistic understanding of intercultural relations. In both cases, there is emphasis on the power of consumers to affect the global circulation of U.S. popular culture. Whether driven by the love of U.S. pop music to defy Iranian customs officials by smuggling forbidden CDs, or turned away by a U.S. movie because its hero is black, foreign viewers and listeners are cast as empowered and discriminating consumers whose engagement with U.S. popular culture is a catalyst of cultural hybridity. This discourse ignores broader structural considerations and articulates consumer empowerment with an optimistic message about globalization and cultural diversity. Whereas the foregoing analysis analyzed this theme in the press, more extensive treatments of hybridity in public discourse can be found in economist Tyler Cowen's *Creative Destruction: How Globalization Is Changing the World's Cultures* (2002a), and journalist G. Pascal Zachary's *The Global Me: New Cosmopolitans and the Competitive Edge: Picking Globalism's Winners and Losers* (2000). These two books articulate visions of what can be called the "cosmopolitan global economy" with the notion of hybridity at its center, which I examine next.

HYBRIDITY AND THE NEW COSMOPOLITAN GLOBAL ECONOMY

Economist Tyler Cowen (2002a) approaches global cultural exchange with what he calls a "gains of trade" model. From Cowen's perspective, individuals are rational actors who freely engage in intercultural transactions that they expect to "make them better off, to enrich their cultural lives, and to increase their menu of choice" (p. 12). The panoply of rhetorical ideographs that supports this thesis is strikingly similar to those discussed earlier in this chapter in my analysis of hybridity in the print media. First is the claim that all or most cultures are hybrid, which in *Creative Destruction* is unequivocal and direct: "Most Third World cultures," Cowen writes, "are fundamentally hybrid—synthetic products of multiple global influences, including from the West" (p. 7). In his article subtitled "The Idea that Globalization Will Produce a Bland McWorld Is a Myth" (Cowen, 2002b), hybridity is expatiated as a historically deep and geographically wide condition:

> For [third-world cultures], *creative destruction is nothing new*, and it is misleading to describe their cultures as "indigenous." ... The art of cultural synthesis has a long and honourable history, so to describe today's Third World culture makers as synthesizers is hardly to denigrate them. It is rather, the contrary emphasis on monoculture that is offensive in its implicit portrayal of non-Western artists as static, tradition-bound craftworkers, unable to embrace new influences. (p. A21, my emphasis)

The foregoing statement's accuracy, itself debatable, describes only part of non-Western cultural realities. Cowen (2002a) acknowledges that some cultures do suffer under globalization, what he describes as the "Tragedy of Cultural Loss." However, he conveniently writes that "[w]e cannot understand freedom without tragedy" (p. 47). The triumph of freedom is reduced to financial terms, as those of us who survive cultural loss "'cash in'" (p. 50) dying cultures, incorporating their energy and wisdom, thus becoming more hybrid.

The position that globalization does not cause homogenization is in *Creative Destruction* couched in the vocabulary of economic expertise and entails nothing less that a redefinition of diversity. Claiming that "diversity" is used as "a code word for a ... particularist ... anti-commercial or anti-American agenda" (Cowen, 2002a, p. 17) paves the way for an alternative formulation: "The common argument that globalization destroys diversity assumes a collectivist concept of diversity. This metric compares one society to another, or one country to another, instead of comparing one individual to another. ... By comparing the collectives and the aggregates, and by emphasizing geographic space, this standard begs the question of which kind of diversity matters" (pp. 129–130).

Diversity across different societies at a given time (diversity across space), Cowen argues, has no intrinsic value, because it freezes societies in a time period and limits options for consumers, in contrast to "intertemporal diversity" (p. 135) (diversity across time), which allows us to contemplate globalization-induced cultural change as a positive development because it "increases the menu of choice" (p. 135). For example, Cowen suggests, had the French opened their borders to new ideas and products, their present-day film industry would have been more competitive. Instead, he argues, they erected protectionist walls around their cinema industries, which motivated the creation of films that cater to bureaucrats and cultural elitists who make decisions on art subsidies, instead of addressing the popular masses whose patronage insures market viability. This system, Cowen contends, has created a vicious circle between the multiplying market failures of European films and their growing dependency on subsidies. In contrast, Cowen claims, market mechanisms explain American dominance of world cinema, as the lean and market-friendly U.S. system produces for a world of consumers, while the elitist and subsidized European cinemas produce for national critics and bureaucrats. The former thrives and enhances global diversity, the latter falter and wallow in so-called particularism. In a nutshell, according to Cowen, globalization and free trade are beneficial across the board, and those who claim otherwise are either misguided or self-serving.

A focus on individual consumers lies at the heart of market mechanisms, in Cowen's view (2002a). "If there is any contemporary ethos that is becoming predominant on a global scale," he writes, "it is an ideology of individualistic self-fulfillment, bred through democracy, relatively free markets, and modern commercial society" (p. 70). This atomistic view of cultural processes reaffirms the hybridity these processes spawn as an economic variable that focuses on individuals as customers and adds to an instrumentally defined diversity. Not surprisingly, Cowen recommends "a cautious embrace of multiculturalism as a guiding aesthetic principle and as a practical guide to policy" (p. 144). This version of multiculturalism is premised on individual choice, and not on Soviet-sounding "collectives."

Creative Destruction (Cowen, 2002a) received a warm reception among globalization-friendly critics, who diligently repeated its main principles: there are no pure cultures; American cultural dominance is inexistant; protectionism is misguided and its practitioners elitist; free markets benefit all; individual freedom and creativity are paramount, and so on. A *Wall Street Journal* review whose title, "An Invasion without Guns," contradicts its subtitle, "Cultural Imperialism Is a Red Herring in Today's Global Economy" (Henderson, 2002), fully embraces Cowen's book, rehearsing its antiprotectionist and protrade arguments. In the *Washington Times*, a reviewer hospitable to Cowen's argument insists that diversity increases as a result of cultural globalization, which is "a more creative way to go than the misguided cultural nostalgia peddled by the anti-globalization crowd" (Sands, 2002). A reviewer calls

Cowen's treatise "one of the most interesting books ever written on globalization" and his view of globalization "right on target" (Cantor, 2004). In the conclusion, this reviewer notes that *Creative Destruction* is "a vision of the triumph of cultural hybridity": "In particular, [Cowen] argues for the advantages of cultural hybridity, documenting how the clash of different cultures in the course of globalization often leads—not to annihilation of one by the other—but to the emergence of a synthesis of the two, and hence a higher cultural complexity" (ibid.). An interview in the libertarian *Reason* magazine (N. Gillespie, 2003) provides Cowen with the opportunity to belabor the ubiquity of cultural hybridity:

> *Reason*: Give an example that characterizes the sort of cultural exchange and hybridization that you discuss in *Creative Destruction*.
> Cowen: The first point to make is that *all* examples characterize it.... Just about anything you can find reflects a synthetic culture based on trade. It's really not even a question of degree. Virtually *everything* is a product of multiple cultures coming from very different places, and we should be acutely aware of that when we approach debates on globalization and nationalism and cultural protectionism.

In contrast with these friendly appraisals, two dissenting reviews by intellectual heavyweights agreed in their criticism of Cowen's *Creative Destruction* (2002a). Writing in the *New Republic*, the cultural anthropologist Clifford Geertz skewers Cowen for stylistic and substantive faults. The book, according to Geertz, mostly consists of "a stream of small examples and large pronouncements sewn together by insistence and reiteration" and uses one strategy throughout: "raise all objections in parodic form and then shoot them down with quips and instances." Cowen's narrow, economistic language, in Geertz's view, provides a mere apology for the way things are, as opposed to a critique. In that process, homogenization is recast as "universalization," and television "channel surfing" becomes "quality monitoring," semantically giving the detrimental aspects of trade an attractive luster. "For the neoliberal apologist," Geertz writes, "the real test comes in dispelling doubt as to the worth, on net, of the merely actual" (2003, p. 27). The political scientist Benjamin Barber states unequivocally what Geertz dances around: "the primary defect of [Cowen's] overall position," writes Barber in a *Los Angeles Times* review, "[is that it] ignores the role of power" (2003).

Whereas Cowen (2002a) arrives at the notion of hybridity by way of his central notions of individual freedom and unfettered markets, journalist Pascal Zachary (2000) focuses directly on the trope of hybridity in his book *The Global Me: New Cosmopolitans and the Competitive Edge:*

Picking Globalism's Winners and Losers, leading a reviewer to call the volume "a passionate diatribe for 'hybridity'" (Roush, 2000, p. 125). The oracular opening sets the book's tone:

> Diversity defines the health and wealth of nations in a new century. *Mighty is the mongrel.* The mixing of races, ethnic groups and nationalities—at home and abroad—is at a record level. *The hybrid is hip.* In a world of deepening connections, individuals, corporations and entire nations draw strength and personality from as near as their local neighborhood and as far away as a distant continent. *The impure, the mélange, the adulterated, the blemished, the rough, the black-and-blue, the mix-and-match*—these people are inheriting the earth. *Mixing is the new norm.* (p. ix, emphasis added)

"Mongrelization," Zachary proceeds, is suited to current world trends. This is because "[m]oney follows the mongrel," "[i]nnovation favors the mixed," and "[t]he adept handling of diversity is the secret of economic competitiveness and national vitality" (2000, p. xii). In chapter 3, flamboyantly titled "Mongrelize or Die!" Zachary takes up, again, the economic benefits of hybridity. He argues that hybridity is highly profitable, and counsels that "those who wish to profit from changing economic conditions must view *hybridity as their first and best option*" (p. 57, emphasis mine), because hybridity plays an important role in the initial stages of the entrepreneurial process. In entrepreneurial terms, creativity is associated with innovation, which leads to economic growth. He criticizes what he sees as a prevailing assumption in economics expressed by Columbia University economist Jagdish Bhagwati, who said that "if everyone's alike, of course you're better off economically" (cited in Zachary, 2000, p. 59), arguing that it stems from a "mechanistic view of human behavior" (p. 59).[3] Zachary (2000) also cites psychological research that finds that bicultural people are more flexible mentally, process knowledge in multiple ways, and have a greater tolerance for ambiguity. Based on these findings, Zachary depicts hybrids as misfits whose marginality and polyvalence spark creativity, expressed in "divergent thinking" (p. 58). To illustrate his argument, Zachary points to Silicon Valley, that legendary cradle of entrepreneurship and innovation. With its imported global talent, it is "a poster child for mongrelization, and the mixing of people is central to its success" (p. 64). In Zachary's view, Silicon Valley is a microcosm of the U.S. economy:

> All across the United States, hybridity pays off—big time—in higher-quality ideas, greater flexibility and tighter ties to places and peoples around the world. America offers the best example of what happens economically when an entire business class exploits hybridity. *The new*

economic paradigm, though still poorly understood, matches the skills and men-
talities of hybrids. It turns hybrids into a signal economic weapon. Because
the United States has more hybrids than anywhere else, it gets the biggest
bang from them. (p. 67, my emphasis)

Thus elevated to the status of linchpin of a new economic paradigm
extolled with military metaphors, hybridity is construed as a powerful
engine of economic growth in the United States, a competitive advantage
ignored by economists to their own and their national economies' detri-
ment. Zachary concludes that "in all the head scratching over how the
United States achieved such a virtuous economic cycle, leaving Europe
and Japan in the dust, hybridity remains the missing link" (p. 67). The
primary reason for U.S. economic superiority is that U.S. companies
have recognized the economic value of hybridity and have, according
to Zachary, consistently "exploit[ed] hybrid ideas because of the openness of U.S. society" (p. 69), even establishing entire strategies on the
culturally hybrid backgrounds of employees.[4]

Hybridity is thus presented as a meta-characteristic of capitalism.
On the one hand, it spawns creativity and stimulates innovation, since
["hybridity brings innovation; homogeneity brings stagnation"] (Zachary,
2000, p. xvii). On the other hand, it calls on clever macroeconomic policies to administer all this socioeconomic ferment. Zachary's enthusiasm
for things mixed slackens when he realizes that hybridity does not thrive
in all environments, but requires stability. For hybridity to fulfill its economic potential, it requires social and political stability. When these
are in place, Zachary writes, "hybrid societies trump monocultures"
(p. xvii), and he proposes a mathematical formula to explain his model
of hybridity (p. xvii)[5]:

HYBRIDITY + SOCIAL COHESION = NATIONAL POWER

Chiding (presumably economic) analysts for ignoring the determining role hybridity plays *"within* rich nations and competition *between*
them" (xviii, emphasis in original), Zachary concludes that hybridity's
potential—"national power" is presumably economic, and perhaps political, something the author leaves unexplained—can be reached only
in wealthy countries.

This credo is explored further in two chapters in *The Global Me,* one
that explains how Germany's homogeneity has slowed it down economically, the other that is devoted to the recent Irish economic miracle,
explained by Zachary (2000) in terms of hybridity. His line of thought
is: For as long as Ireland, one of the most homogenous countries in

Europe, lingered in uniformity, it remained economically backward. When Ireland opened its borders to immigrants and was hybridized as a result, the Irish economy boomed and continues to do so. Zachary reminds the reader that the 1848 potato famine triggered massive Irish emigration, which continued until the 1980s. Ireland's move out of Britain's orbit, first declared when Ireland joined the European Union in 1972, stimulated its economy by opening export markets for Irish products. Coupled with aggressive policies to entice investors and an open-door policy to recruit droves of highly qualified foreign workers, Zachary proceeds, Ireland had by the 1990s moved from being one of Europe's poorest countries, to being poised to join the wealthiest European nations. By the late 1990s, Ireland's economy was growing by a "torrid" 8 percent yearly, while the country welcomed a "torrent of immigrants" (p. 160).

Ireland, the title of the chapter indicates, is a case of "hybridity by design." As a small country, Ireland cannot assimilate all newcomers into its midst. Unlike Germany, it does not have the sheer population size and the government programs necessary to assimilate immigrants. This is what Zachary calls "small country advantage." As a small country without assimilation policies, Ireland is, in Zachary's view, fertile ground for thriving hyphenated identities. Furthermore, because it was once a net exporter of people, Ireland does not need strong cultural policy, because, in Zachary's view, the vast diaspora performs the function of preserving, albeit in adapted forms, Irish traditions. As a result, "Irishness as an identity has thrived for so long outside of its territorial home that a hybrid Ireland seems both just and inevitable" (Zachary, 2000, p. 161). When this historically and staunchly Catholic and overwhelmingly white country opened its doors to foreigners, it became hybrid and achieved impressive economic growth, even if "it was no longer obvious what it meant to be Irish" (p. 164). While problems persist, such as the hostility blacks still encounter in Ireland, Zachary sees a flowering Irish cosmopolitanism as an example for other small and perhaps homogenous countries.

From Corporate Multiculturalism to Corporate Transculturalism

Overall, the press received Zachary's position well, even though his impassioned tone and unsubtle style elicited some reservations, expressed by a reviewer in *Technology Review* who called *The Global Me* "a very long book that takes a fairly simple argument and hammers it home relentlessly" (Roush, 2000, p. 126). However, a reviewer for the *Boston Globe* calls Zachary's book "a stunning example of inventive reporting ... [that] confidently and clearly set out the dominant theme of the coming years" (Warsh, 2000, p. G1), and a writer for the online magazine *Salon* describes the book as "an unusual mélange—a lyrical political manifesto, a shrewd economic and business analysis and a finely-observed reportorial notebook" (Deutschman, 2000). In a more personal approach, a reviewer in the *Atlantic Monthly* who identifies himself as a "hybrid" concludes that Zachary's "account of the trials of multiracial, multinational identity is so good that I'll give it to my daughter when she starts asking the hard questions" (Pang, 2000, p. 120). The book also earned Zachary an interview on CNN International (Anderson, 2000), and speaking engagements at Washington, D.C., think tanks such as the probusiness American Enterprise Institute and the libertarian Cato Institute. Interestingly, Zachary joined none other than economist Tyler Cowen (and another guest) at a Cato Institute book forum titled "Mighty Is the Mongrel? Winning in the Global Economy" ("Mighty is," 2000). The discussion was dominated by now familiar themes of individual freedom, unfettered markets, and cultural hybridity.

The relevance of *The Global Me* (Zachary, 2000) for this book stems from its use of hybridity as the core concept, around which is built what I would term corporate transculturalism, a discourse in which fluid identities and porous cultural borders are depicted as growth engines in the service of a cosmopolitan capitalism. Hybridity is thus placed at the service of a neoliberal economic order that respects no borders and harbors no prejudice toward cultural and ethnic difference that can be harnessed for growth. This constitutes a rhetorical shift from corporate multiculturalism, where difference is tolerated and incorporated into the dominant framework, to corporate transculturalism, a profit-driven strategy that actively and systematically seeks to capitalize on cultural fusion and fluid identities. Albeit draped in hip terminology and fanned by authorial ardor, this discourse rests on shaky foundations. While Zachary's rhetoric can potentially give notions of diversity and hybridity wide exposure, four facets of this attempt to use hybridity to help corporations be more profitable bring to the fore how little this discourse advances our knowledge of cultural mixture in society. These include a reductionist understanding of hybridity, often confusing it with diversity or lapsing into bipolar equations; a functionalist recruitment of hybridity as an economic variable; the stipulation of social cohesion as a prerequisite for hybridity; and the strategic use of examples that support Zachary's line of reasoning (2002) while neglecting evidence countering it, even within his own examples.

[Zachary's binary logic muddles our ability to see hybridity as a fluid process.]His field of vision includes the "monoculture," a term he is obviously fond of and that he uses in reference to allegedly homogenous cultures such as Germany and old Ireland, and hybrid cultures such as the new Ireland and the United States (Zachary, 2000). He dismisses the former and rejoices at the latter, without recognizing gradations and variations within and between these countries. German urban centers such as Berlin are surely not monocultural; that city is rather vibrant, cosmopolitan, and diverse. Not all of America marches to the hybridity tune either. Students in one Georgia high school were holding white-only graduation proms as late as April 2003. Zachary's hybridity credo falls into the same trap that caught Edward T. Hall in the 1950s: the conflation of culture with nationality (Leeds-Hurwitz, 1990; Kraidy, 2003a). Thus, while ostensibly using "culture," as in "German culture" and "American culture," Zachary is really referring to Germany or the United States as nation-states. This undermines Zachary's point because (1) it reinscribes the nation-state as a powerful actor at a time when Zachary surreptitiously pleads for a weak state, and (2) it saps the analytical power of hybridity by placing it in a bipolar relationship with monoculture.[The value of the notion of hybridity resides in its avoidance of a binary model of intercultural relations in favor of a relational approach whose vectors are located on a continuum.]

Hybridity, in Zachary's vision, is a determining variable of what he refers to as an undefined "national power." This instrumental usage of the concept reduces cultural complexity to the algebra of economic growth. Nothing makes that point more forcefully than Zachary's counterintuitive formula in which hybridity added to a vaguely defined "social cohesion" produces national power: hybridity becomes a countable, therefore finite, component to be added and subtracted. This additive and summative use of hybridity betrays claims, which Zachary (2000) himself revels in, of dynamism and fluidity that mark the formation of hybrid identities. From a conceptual point of view, putting hybridity in such a mathematical formula muddles the complex processes that shape hybridity. In addition to these conceptual and epistemological frailties, Zachary's hybridity raises a political and ethical issue. His argument appropriates hybridity as a measuring device, as an ingredient in a bigger recipe whose ultimate tasters are the profit-driven multinational corporations. This lends credence to materialist critics of hybridity who, as we have seen in Chapter Three, have argued that hybridity-speak is an endorsement of the logic and aims of global capitalism, and is therefore politically retrogressive (for instance, Ahmad, 1995).

Zachary's vaguely articulated "social cohesion" also raises doubts about the applicability of his version of hybridity. What exactly does social cohesion entail? And doesn't this ideograph slide inevitably into a rhetoric of national unity enforcement, one that permits hybrids to thrive only as long as they do not challenge the status quo?[6] In Chapter Three I established that notions of cultural mixture have historically been deployed to neutralize ethnic and cultural difference that threatened prevailing power arrangements, the clearest example being the deployment of mestizaje as the ideology of nation-building in postcolonial Latin America, where it served the strategic purpose of severing ties to the Spanish Crown while consolidating the power of the descendants of the conquistadores. In the case of *The Global Me* (Zachary, 2000), does not the notion that the addition of hybridity and "social cohesion" equals "national power" suggest a similar rhetoric at play, one that tolerates ethnic and cultural differences to the extent that they can contribute to capitalist accumulation? I am not imputing to Zachary a pernicious intent, but these questions must be addressed if hybridity is to retain analytical value.

Finally, the case study of Ireland, which is central to Zachary's advocacy of hybridity as a goal of macroeconomic policy, raises questions that dull the effectiveness of his claims. As much as Ireland may have been depicted in the global popular imagination as a rural, backward, and homogenous nation until the 1990s, we can dispel this cliché, especially on the issue of cultural homogeneity. While Irish history and culture lie beyond the scope and interest of this book, there exists evidence to cast a reasonable doubt on Zachary's fervent embrace of Ireland as (in his view) a newly hybridized economic powerhouse. Ireland's history is replete with newcomers who were assimilated into the fabric of Irish society, stretching back to the Normans eight centuries ago. In the late nineteenth century, the Irish in fact identified with people of color such as the Indians, who shared with the Irish the experience of English domination (Longley and Kiberd, 2001). Also, since the Austro-Hungarian Empire, the Irish have had political and cultural exchanges with France, Spain, and Austria: "hybridity and heterogeneity," according to a writer in the *Irish Times* (P. Gillespie, 2002), "characterize Ireland's identities as well as those of other European nations" (p. 9). In fact, the same author claims that it is only in the early twentieth century that the emerging Irish state decided on a Catholic and Gaelic identity. Besides, Zachary's assessment of contemporary Ireland ignores recent experiences of Nigerian immigrants that indicate that racism among some Irish people, as with all national groups, is not a thing of the past (Longley and Kiberd, 2001), and glosses over the fact that a decisive proportion of immigrants to Ireland are middle- and upper-middle-class professionals. In other words, yesterday's Ireland, like most other countries, was already hybrid; and today's Ireland, like most other nations, despite having undergone significant changes, is no multicultural, postracist utopia.

CORPORATE TRANSCULTURALISM AND GLOBAL POPULAR CULTURE

Uses of hybridity by several authors (Cowen, 2002a; Farhi and Rosenfeld, 1998; Lancaster, 1998; Rosenfeld, 1998; Trueheart, 1998; Waxman, 1998; Zachary, 2000) rest on debatable assumptions. They depict hybridity as a consequence of creative reception practices by media audiences worldwide. Because of hybridity's conceptual ambiguity, and in light of the critique of hybidity elaborated in earlier pages, it is helpful at this stage to reformulate the central questions that animate this chapter: How is hybridity characterized, and how does this representation address global politico-economic and cultural relations?

The 1998 *Washington Post* articles construct a monolithic hybridity that lumps together nations as disparate as Brazil, Iran, Malaysia, Nigeria, and Poland, whose unabashed enthusiasm for U.S. popular culture is held as an indication of its superiority to local fare. Worldwide consumption of U.S. popular culture has spawned in these "cultures" a hybridity overtly heralded as a renewal of identity, but latently framed as a capitulation to a seductive Otherness. This hybridity is symptomatic of non-Western governments defeated by their citizens' desire for Western culture, and indicative of an economistic apology for casting decisions detrimental to minority actors by the U.S. film industry. At the same time, this rendition of hybridity involves an attempted semiotic closure of the meanings that global audiences give to U.S. popular culture. While global media conglomerates control production structures, program content, and distribution networks, two decades of research on audience behavior—as elaborated in Chapter Two—suggest that the processes and outcomes of cultural reception remain somewhat unpredictable. By not questioning the corporate argument that foreign audiences dictate content and are thus endowed with a contrived agency, the *Washington Post* articles miss an opportunity to address power in intercultural relations and celebrate a nonthreatening hybridity that forecloses the cultural reception process, effectively holding sway over the entire chain of signification between media institutions, texts, and audiences.

These articles and books on what I call "the cosmopolitan global economy" (Cowen, 2002a; Zachary, 2000) are symptomatic of a tendency in mainstream public discourse to enlist hybridity as a descriptive frame in international relations. The newspaper articles focus on the international impact of U.S. popular culture and its putative role in spawning hybrid cultural forms; the books emphasize hybridity as an economic energy stream to be leveraged by transnational corporations and exploited by individual consumers. The former focus on culture via politics and economics. The latter privilege economics, via a discussion of culture and politics. Both carry progressive potential, but both squander that promise by their strategic use of hybridity. Hybridity in contemporary public discourse is a metadescription of the global order that justifies the status quo of the early twenty-first century.

In this logic, the West and its core, the United States, are surreptitiously located at the center of the world. The exchanges that spawn hybrid cultures described in the "American Popular Culture Abroad" series (Farhi and Rosenfeld, 1998; Lancaster, 1998; Rosenfeld, 1998; Trueheart, 1998; Waxman, 1998) follow a U.S.-centric model, constructing a generic hybridity where cultures as different as Poland, Iran, Malaysia, Nigeria, and Brazil are lumped together as one big hospitable audience. The articles give the impression that there are no "horizontal" exchanges between, say, Iran and Malaysia, or Brazil and Nigeria. Rather, cultural interaction is presumed to occur only between the United States and Malaysia, the United States and Brazil, the United States and Iran, and the United States and Poland. This rhetoric positions the United States at the center of worldwide cultural exchange, and all other "hybrid" cultures in various peripheral positions. In this relationship, hybridity in the developing world is in effect the result of local powerlessness in relation to the charms of American popular culture. Indeed, that the articles define hybridity as symptomatic of the impotence of local governments to control the influx of foreign culture is a clear indication that their notion of hybridity is premised on a generalized—albeit selective—local capitulation to the West, rather than on a reinvigorating cultural renewal.

But we need not be preoccupied about the fate of hybrid cultures, at least if Zachary is to be believed. *The Global Me* (2000) is more ambitious than the *Washington Post*'s series because it articulates a normative argument in favor of hybridity as a macroeconomic and microeconomic policy. To countries and corporations alike, Zachary recommends: hybridize and you will profit. Scorning alleged monocultures like Germany and praising putative transcultures like Ireland, Zachary's celebration of hybridity ultimately founders under the weight of its own contradictions. What *The Global Me* proposes, albeit obliquely, is a full liberalization of national economies and state infrastructures, while its espousal of "social stability" as a condition for hybridity's market potential to be achieved betrays the libertarian tenet that the state's only legitimate function is to maintain order.

As a journalist, Zachary puts forth a *popular* version of hybridity, whereas as an economist, Cowen, in espousing a market-based cultural hybridity (2002a), articulates an *expert* version of hybridity in which the market and its laws of supply and demand are said to guarantee consumers a "broad menu of choice." Hybrid cultural forms that are attractive to the market will survive, while those that lack commercial value will die, which is just fine because other cultural products allegedly benefit and the range of choices remains broad. The cultures that die under globalization, in Cowen's economistic lingo, are simply "cashed in." The preponderant impression one leaves this literature with is that hybridity is not only natural and inevitable, but also supremely desirable for both the market and consumers.

This type of hybridity I call corporate transculturalism. In both its popular and expert versions, corporate transculturalism emphasizes cultural fluidity as a tool to make corporations more profitable, consumers more satisfied, and the world generally a better, more connected, and more vibrant place. However, as the raging debate on the alleged benefits and dangers of globalization confirms, representations of international and intercultural relations are by definition contested. In this environment of contention, hybridity may be better understood as a strategic rhetoric (Nakayama and Krizek, 1995).[7] Hybridity's ability to be many things at once imbues it with an aura of common sense. By advocating a power-free vision of intercultural relations supported by ideographs such as "consumer choice," "individual freedom," "free markets," and "free trade," corporate transculturalism uses hybridity strategically to highlight certain aspects of the global order and privileges a specific interpretive modality of that state of affairs, while at the same time discarding other elements that do not fit its strategic vision. This rhetoric, as I will elaborate in Chapter Seven, compels me to conceive of hybridity as the cultural logic of globalization, and to propose *critical* transculturalism as a framework whose main concern is human agency, not corporate profitability. An examination of the political economy of mediated hybridity, carried out in the following chapter, is a prerequisite to such a framework.

5   The Cultural and Political Economies of Hybrid Media Texts

The visibility of mimicry is always produced at the site of interdiction.
—Homi Bhabha

THE HISTORY of broadcasting before the satellite era is one of national systems in which different political outlooks and cultural policies engendered alternate functions for electronic mass communication: broadcasting was a tool of development in much of the non-Western world, a public service in Western Europe, an instrument of direct propaganda under authoritarian regimes, or a commercial enterprise in the United States and elsewhere. National considerations shaped the broadcasting operations inspired by these various media philosophies. Considered an important national asset, broadcasting was harnessed to promote social stability, foster economic development, and consolidate national unity. In addition to national political and socioeconomic factors, the limitations of available technology restricted the expansion of media activities to the confines of the nation-state. National considerations were therefore paramount in determining the agenda, policies, and content of electronic media.

A closer examination, however, suggests that broadcasting's presumed national scope is in effect an ideal type, not a technically accurate description of actual media operations. Since most broadcast signals travel in concentric circles and most countries are not circular in shape, signal spillover has been historically pervasive. Southern Norwegians can watch Swedish television over the air, and denizens of the eastern Mediterranean receive terrestrial signals of varying quality from Egyptian and Greek television stations during hot and humid summer nights. Some countries' public broadcasters, such as Japan's NHK, have committed extraordinary technical and financial assets to achieve universal national coverage of an insular territory that presents enormous physical challenges. It is also evident that many countries have used their national media for transnational influence: in the United States, television has been regarded as a global strategic asset since the emergence of the free flow doctrine during Woodrow Wilson's presidency, and later formulated as policy by Federal Communications Commission head Newton Minow (see Blanchard, 1986; Curtin, 1993). Nasser's Egypt harnessed radio as a redoubtably effective tool for pan-Arab mobilization, compelling the Saudi royal family to develop its own broadcasting operations. Last, cooperation agreements between governments to exchange programming have been a recurring phenomenon, indicating that national media systems are not hermetically sealed entities.

In the last two decades, information technologies have overcome many restraints on terrestrial broadcasting. The advent of geo-stationary satellites, whose orbit is calculated to follow Earth's movements in order to keep the coverage area, or footprint, constant has decreased the technical laboriousness and financial cost of television coverage. Global information networks have mitigated time and space restrictions, albeit selectively and asymmetrically. Faster, less costly, and more efficient information and transportation technologies have made it easier for companies and governments separated by oceans or landmass to cooperate on media ventures. The growing international regime of free trade and decreased government intervention has triggered some of these changes and exacerbated others, as states de facto relinquish the principle of prior consent and cope with a global system based on the free flow precept. These circumstances have inexorably pushed television's transnational and global expansion.

If technology made the transnational expansion of television possible, the neoliberal momentum that peaked in the late 1990s turned television into a largely deterritorialized, global industry. The deregulation of media and telecommunications has entailed the withdrawal of the state as an active manager of national broadcasting, and the concomitant rise in importance of the multinational corporations that now control much of world media activities. These corporations themselves restructured to embrace a post-Fordist modus operandi, as public and national media systems worldwide were thrust into a liberalization frenzy of privatizations, mergers, acquisitions, and vertical and horizontal integration. This transformation became ostensible in the 1990s, as world television screens filled up with internationalized programs, including talk and game shows, reality television, and music videos.

Transnational post-Fordist practices are the undertow of these industry trends. As an economic paradigm, post-Fordism focuses on procedures such outsourcing, subcontracting, multidivisional competition and collaboration, and joint ventures, caused by a decentralized accumulation of capital. British film and television scholar Michael Wayne argues that political economists of the media have ignored or dismissed post-Fordism because it implies that capitalism's affinity to create monopolies has been at least partly set back. Wayne (2003) argues that post-Fordism is characterized by a "discrepancy between the real [economic] relations and their appearance forms" (p. 84), where industry consolidation is masked by the superficial appearance of pluralism and competition. These practices are "transnational," following Danish media scholar Preben Sepstrup (1990), for whom transnationalization is a primarily economic process which drives sociocultural change.

Another post-Fordist postulate is a belief in regional markets as a counterbalance to the power of global market forces (Wayne, 2003). There is indeed a process of regionalization going on in tandem with media globalization. While the giant conglomerates—Time Warner, Bertelsmann, the News Corporation, Sony, and so on—lead globally, companies such as Televisa and TV Azteca in Mexico and Rede Globo in Brazil continue to strengthen their positions in and beyond Latin America. In the much discussed pan-Arab satellite television industry, dominant companies are emerging amidst a trend toward specialization and consolidation. The privately owned Lebanese Broadcasting Corporation and the Saudi-owned, London-published, Arabic-language daily *al-Hayat* merged newsgathering operations in 2002, and the rise of al-Jazeera in the post–September 11 era has stimulated competitors such as Al-Arabiya and others. In the meantime, U.S. cable company CNBC launched an Arabic service in June 2003, purporting to bring the wonders of personal finance to the nearly three hundred million Arabs in the region and the few million Arabs in North America and Western Europe. The size of this regional audience, in addition to the wealth of Persian Gulf consumers and the demographic youth of the entire area, will undoubtedly continue to attract global players in the near future.

These developments explain why television programs are increasingly hybrid, embedded with signs and symbols with transregional appeal, and executed in line with the imperative of market expansion. It is important to note that since most emerging regional media spheres are commercial, modeled largely in line with U.S. production, promotion, and financing standards, cultural dissimilarities within geocultural regions often require extra production and marketing expenses, which by necessity embed regional processes in global media operations.

Liberalization and consolidation have also triggered a race to the bottom as media companies strive to reach increasingly larger audiences without incurring proportionally higher costs. One result has been that television programs are increasingly designed to appeal to worldwide audiences, a strategy with considerable advantages. Logistically simpler than coproduction, creatively less restrictive than format adaptation, and economically less onerous than both coproduction and format adaptation, program internationalization now pervades television news and entertainment alike, categories that are themselves increasingly blurred. The Cable News Network (CNN) and Music Television (MTV) are textbook cases, the former in news and the latter in entertainment. CNN launched *CNN World Report* in 1987, a unique program that showcased reports on various countries sent in English by local reporters working for local stations. Two presenters in CNN studios introduced the reports, but other than that CNN had no direct production involvement in the content of the program. In the early twenty-first century, executives at CNN International are talking about "de-Americanizing content," according to Chris Cramer, head of CNN International ("The One," 2003, p. 73). Between 1996 and 2001, the percentage of American content on CNN International was reduced from 70 percent to 8 percent, although how to clearly define what is American is arduous, and the most direct definition is content that deals with U.S. issues. Music Television's localization—which in reality means internationalization—strategy relies on segmenting international audiences according to linguistic, cultural parameters in their national or regional contexts. This is conducted through featuring the work of some local artists, hiring local VJs (video jockeys) to host programs, and overall sensitivity to the cultural specificities of the country or region in which MTV operates. Between 2001 and 2003, MTV launched fourteen new channels, including MTV Romania and MTV Indonesia. The total number of worldwide MTV stations stood at twenty-eight in 2003. An MTV executive has even claimed that "[w]e don't even call it an adaptation of American content: it's local content creation. The American thing is irrelevant" ("The One," 2003, p. 73). Becoming more local is, for CNN and MTV, the surest way to become more international.

Another result of global media liberalization is the proliferation of lower-cost, high-impact genres such as the variety show, the talk show—in both its low-brow and high-brow variations—and more importantly, the now ubiquitous reality genre and its many subtypes. These genres have in common an absence or minimal presence of highly paid talent, low-cost studio or outdoor production, and a tendency toward the raw, bizarre, and sensational. In this environment program-format adaptations and coproductions are increasingly common; the former entail the adaptation to local parameters of tastes and style of a popular program format gleaned from a different culture, whereas the latter involve a partnership between several companies based in multiple countries.

MULTINATIONAL PARTNERSHIPS AND CULTURAL HYBRIDITY: THE GROWTH OF COPRODUCTIONS

Coproductions give companies several advantages. Canadian media economists McFadyen, Hoskins, and Finn (1998) include as incentives for entering into coproduction agreements "pooling financial resources," "access to foreign government incentives and subsidies," "access to partner's market," "access to third-country market," "access to particular project initiated by partner," "cultural goals," "desired foreign locations," "cheaper inputs in partner's country," and learning new marketing, production, and management strategies from the partner. These benefits outweigh drawbacks such as "coordination costs," "loss of control over cultural specificity," and "opportunistic behaviour by the foreign partner."

Joining forces allows companies to share equipment, technical staff and know-how, and shooting locations. These benefits, in turn, expand potential sources of funding, including government subsidies and tax breaks, and also spread the risk, so that different entities share the burden of a potential commercial failure. Reducing risk is also related to the bigger markets reached by companies that enter into coproduction arrangements: if a television program or movie fails in a national or regional market somewhere, commercial success in a different market will make up for the losses. These considerable financial, technical, and market incentives have triggered a significant worldwide increase in coproductions. Between 1950 and 1994, there were at least sixty-six bilateral coproduction treaties (P. W. Taylor, 1995), and more than two thousand coproductions took place between 1978 and 1995 (Television Business International, cited in Miller et al., 2001, p. 85). Television documentaries and dramas accounted for the majority of coproductions, and film ventures for the remaining 21 percent (ibid.).

There is a distinction between "equity coproductions" and "treaty coproductions" (Miller et al., 2001, p. 84). Equity coproductions constitute a strategic and temporary partnership between two or more companies, driven by the search for maximal profits and usually not eligible for treaty status. As purely commercial joint ventures, equity coproductions do not directly involve issues of cultural policy and national identity. Many equity coproductions have included European and Japanese companies contributing to the financing of Hollywood movies. In contrast, treaty coproductions are formal partnerships concluded under the auspices of national governments. This type of coproduction customarily involves artists, technicians, financiers, and the more-or-less active participation of government officials from two or more countries. As a consequence, treaty coproductions are formal affairs that fall in the realm of international relations and involve issues of national identity and cultural policy. Most treaty coproductions come about in the European Union. According to *Screen Digest*, in 1998, out of a total of a 183 movies produced in France, Europe's largest film producer, 81, or 44 percent, were coproductions. The figures were lower for Italy, Germany, and Britain: 14 percent, or 13 out of 92 Italian films; 22 percent, or 11 out of 50 German films; and 28 percent, or 24 out of 87 British movies, were coproduced. Interestingly, that year's figure was significantly lower for the United States, where only 15, or 9 films out of a total of 661, were coproductions (cited in Miller et al., 2001), in contrast to the 1978–1995 period when 14 percent of U.S. television shows were coproduced. This figure during the same time period is 16 percent for France and the United Kingdom, 10 percent for Germany, and 7 percent for Canada (Brown, 1995, cited in ibid., p. 86). While the benefits of coproductions to companies are by now clear, why are governments taking such an interest?

Striving to capitalize on the globalization of media productions, national and regional governments have aggressively pursued and fostered coproductions in order to boost exports and broaden financial investment in television and film productions. The United Kingdom is a case in point. In the 1990s the then ruling Conservatives decided that the cultural industries had to take advantage of "tremendous export opportunities in a rapidly expanding international market" (Barnett and Curry, 1994, p. 221, cited in Freedman, 2001, p. 3). One of the major obstacles to British and other television-export strategy is the documented prime-time domination of local productions in most domestic markets worldwide. In the United Kingdom itself, for example, *Coronation Street* remains the most popular television program. Despite this recognition, British government support of television exports continued with the rise to power of New Labour. By the late 1990s, Tony Blair's Third Way politics explicitly incorporated free trade in global media products (Blair, 1998). Greg Dyke, who was the chief executive officer of private media conglomerate Pearson before becoming head of the

British Broadcasting Corporation, enthusiastically advocated a British strategy for competing in the global television industry. Dyke had made Pearson a world leader in buying, adapting, and selling program formats. "The trick is," he said, "can you globalize and make it local?" (Baker, 1997, cited in Freedman, 2001, p. 4).

In addition to audience preferences for local programs, the entanglement of national and global considerations is another obstacle to television exportation. This snag had been a source of controversy since the 1994 publication of a white paper on the BBC, *Serving the Nation, Competing Worldwide*, which advocated a focus on selling BBC programs worldwide. In an interview with British media researcher Des Freedman in 1997, Harry Reeves, then head of general broadcasting policy, declared international television commerce to be "very high on the list of policy objectives" and not to pose a fundamental contradiction of the BBC's national public service mandate (Freedman, 2001). In this context, the Department of Culture, Media, and Sport (DCMS) commissioned a report to explore areas of improvement in British television exports. The report, *Building a Global Audience: British Television in Overseas Markets* (Graham, 1999), found that the United Kingdom suffered from a substantive deficit in television trade, and that British dramatic productions were too slow, dark, or serious, which hindered their global competitiveness, while British comedy was internationally successful. The report recommended increased liberalization of the domestic British market.

The British example demonstrates the changing relationship between the state and media institutions, in which the mass media are increasingly treated in economic—contra social, cultural, or educational—terms, frequently the media's own economic terms. From regulator and arbiter, the state has become promoter and cheerleader. The role of government institutions increasingly resembles that of the impresario: they scout opportunities, expedite deals, and reap a portion of the proceeds. Using a mix of financial incentives and cultural appeals, they facilitate access to new markets and coordinate pecuniary transnational partnerships. Even in program-format adaptations, as the next section will demonstrate, the state plays a role.

FROM *TELETUBBIES* TO *TELE CHOBIS*: THE UNBEARABLE LIGHTNESS OF TELEVISION PROGRAMS

The widespread popularity of reality television in the late 1990s accelerated a transnational process of program-format adaptation that goes back to the pretelevision radio era. Australian media researcher

Albert Moran (1998) has documented that adaptation as historically pervasive, and current trends indicate that it is poised to increase as the television industry continues to globalize. Like coproduction, format adaptation helps companies reduce risk and uncertainty, in this case by working with a format with demonstrated success. However, formats might not be popular across cultural boundaries. According to Moran: "a television format is that set of invariable elements in a program out of which the variable elements of an individual episode are produced" (1998, p. 13), which means that unlike coproductions, where a program's intellectual property is jointly owned by the partners, the legal ramifications of format adaptation are tricky, and involve the three legal instruments of copyright, breach of confidence, and passing off (Mummery, 1966, cited in ibid., p. 15).

L'affaire Tele Chobis demonstrates the problems that can arise in program-format adaptation and the ill-defined space between adaptation and plagiarism. In the fall of 1999, the leading Mexican network, Televisa, began airing the British and globally popular *Teletubbies*. During the previous summer, marketing executives from Itsy Bitsy Entertainment, the exclusive North American distributors of *Teletubbies*, had been prowling Latin American countries promoting their flagship program. Initially, TV Azteca, Mexico's second-rated television network, was interested and entered into contract negotiations to purchase *Teletubbies*. TV Azteca executives changed their minds when Itsy Bitsy insisted that *Teletubbies* must be broadcast without commercials. While advertising before and after the airing of *Teletubbies* was acceptable, the condition that no advertisements appear during *Teletubbies* broadcasts was nonnegotiable and thus a contract breaker. Televisa, on the other hand, agreed to broadcast *Teletubbies* commercial free and as a result purchased the program from Itsy Bitsy. The reaction of TV Azteca executives was swift and surprising: they created a copycat program, which they called *Tele Chobis*. An exploration of the design, promotion, and distribution of *Teletubbies*, followed by an examination of the structural forces and cultural specificities that have shaped *Tele Chobis*, provides a rare vista of the active links that exist between media systems and textuality, and helps us understand the political economy of hybridity.

Anne Wood, a former schoolteacher and founder of Ragdoll Productions Ltd. of Buckinghamshire, U.K., created the original *Teletubbies* with her partner, Andy Davenport, a speech therapist. Since its launch by the British Broadcasting Corporation in 1997, this program has been a watershed event in children's television akin to globally successful classics such as *Sesame Street*. Wildly popular and reaching dozens of countries, it has triggered references to the four "tubbies"—Tinky Winky, Dipsy, Laa Laa, and Po—as the Fab Four, a clear intertextual nod to Beatlemania. It is also routinely controversial, especially in the United States, where a slightly modified version is broadcast by PBS, attracting detractors and supporters from the medical community, religious leadership, and the gay press alike.[1] A typical episode features the four Teletubbies, chubby humanoids dressed in gaudy colors who live in an imaginary space of green nature and friendly animals. They sing, dance, and communicate in a verbal code replete with infantile giggles and playful body movements. The same everyday life and household objects appear with regularity during each episode, and simple stories are repeated several times. The Teletubbies also have screens in their bellies, used to show footage of real children.

An aggressive and wide-ranging marketing campaign centered on successful synergistic deals propelled *Teletubbies* to household-name status. In December 1998, QVC Inc., the world's leading "electronic retailer," broadcast a special Teletubbies program, promoting the newly released home videos "Here Come the Teletubbies" and "Dance with the Teletubbies"; a music CD, "*Teletubbies* the Album"; *Teletubbies* bean-bag characters; and myriad gadgets and accessories ("Teletubby Mania," 1998, December 28). Less than a week later, Ragdoll and Itsy Bitsy announced a deal with Microsoft to create ActiMate Interactive Teletubbies ("Tinky Winky," 1999, January 6). Two months later, FAO Schwarz New York hosted an "International Teletubbies Celebration" to launch the ActiMate Interactive Teletubbies ("International Teletubbies," 1999). In the same year, Burger King's *Teletubbies* promotional campaign was so successful that the fast-food chain found its fifty million finger-puppet Teletubbies depleted within less than a month (Morgan, 1999).

These synergistic retailing agreements have made the juvenile quartet ubiquitous in Western popular culture and highly popular worldwide, triggering a wave of imitation. The Mexican *Tele Chobis* is not the only *Teletubbies* copycat. In March 1999, Ragdoll Productions Ltd. and New York–based Itsy Bitsy Entertainment Company filed a lawsuit in U.S. federal court in Manhattan against Wal-Mart Stores Inc. alleging unauthorized copying. Wal-Mart had been selling Bubbly Chubbies, Teletubbies look-alikes that shared shelf space with the original Teletubbies ("Teletubbies declare," 1999). Wal-Mart argued that the supplier of Bubbly Chubbies had produced a legal opinion by the law firm Buchanan Ingersoll stating that the Bubbly Chubbies "did not infringe upon any trademarks or copyrights" ("Walmart had," 1999). Less than two months after the lawsuit was filed, Wal-Mart agreed to remove from its shelves and destroy the remaining stock of Bubbly Chubbies, ending the legal feud between Wal-Mart and Itsy Bitsy, who continued legal action against the unidentified manufacturer of the Bubbly Chubbies ("Wal-Mart to destroy," 1999).

Publicity for *Teletubbies* also came via the U.S. culture wars. The February 1999 issue of *National Liberty Journal*, edited and published by the Reverend Jerry Falwell, former leader of the Moral Majority, carried the headline "Parents Alert: Tinky Winky Comes Out of the Closet" with an article alleging that purple Tinky Winky was a gay character, and that the "subtle depictions" of gay identity were intentional. Falwell reportedly said: "As a Christian I feel that role modeling the gay lifestyle is damaging to the moral lives of children" (Reed, 1999). This triggered a firestorm of controversy in the U.S. and international media. Across the Atlantic, the BBC sniffed: "the Teletubbies have made the Rev. Falwell, chancellor of Liberty University in Lynchburg, Virginia, hot under the collar" ("Gay Tinky," 1999). The BBC's official response that "Tinky Winky is simply a sweet, technological baby with a magic bag" (ibid.) seemed to be shared by the press and the public alike. The *Washington Post* asked: "Can Mr. Falwell believe that just because Tinky Winky is purple, has a triangle antenna on top of his head and carries a handbag that he's a gay role model for our toddlers? Even Laa Laa, Dipsy and Po must be shaking their heads in disbelief" ("Subliminal Messages?" 1999).

Inevitably, the debate became highly politicized. A February 1999 resolution was introduced at the city council in Berkeley, California, backing the Teletubbies and condemning Falwell's views, leading Ken Viselman, head of Itsy Bitsy Entertainment, to call for leaving politics out of *Teletubbies*. About Tinky Winky, Viselman said: "He's not gay. He's not straight. He's just a character in a children's series. I think that we should just let the Teletubbies go and play in Teletubbyland and not try to define them" ("Calif. Resolution," 1999).[2] A few days later, the March edition of *National Liberty Journal* carried a front-page Falwell article in which he wrote: "Until the recent media explosion accused me of 'outing' Tinky Winky as being gay, I had never heard of this sweet looking character. I certainly have never criticized Tinky Winky in any way" ("Falwell Denies," 1999). However, the conservative reverend stood by his warning about the conjectural dangers of homosexuality (ibid.). Needless to say, this controversy added to the already strong visibility of the program.

The Mexican adaptation, *Tele Chobis*, retained *Teletubbies'* basic structure, but offered variations in terms of the leading characters, the story lines, and the overall content. Instead of Tinky Winky, Dipsy, Laa Laa, and Po, Azteca's copycat featured Nita, Toso, Ton, and Tis. Nita wears green, Toso yellow, Ton blue, and Tis dark pink. Both programs are set in a garden populated with rabbits and replete with toys: the Teletubbies play on a seemingly placeless green hill and live in a bunker under that hill; the Tele Chobis live in a house inside the trunk of a big talking tree that overshadows what looks like a pastoral garden. Like *Teletubbies*, *Tele Chobis* unfolds in the two spaces of nature and technology (see the analysis of *Teletubbies* in Lemish and Tidhar, 2001), the former represented by the garden, the latter by the nine screens on the wall of the *Tele Chobis* house in the tree. *Teletubbies* and *Tele Chobis* episodes both focus on a limited number of issues and repeat information about them, in addition to circuitous story lines that revisit issues several times during each episode. Also, each installment of both programs includes several familiar objects. For *Teletubbies* these comprise a tittering baby face framed in a sun, a hat, a purse, and a vacuum cleaner. In *Tele Chobis* these encompass the commentators Champi and Ñon (*champiñon* is Spanish for "mushroom"), a sheriff's badge, animals, and the big talking tree. In all these aspects, the similarities between the original and the copycat are straightforward.

Differences between *Teletubbies* and *Tele Chobis* reflect the intended audience. Whereas *Teletubbies* was conceived as a culturally "neutral" text that could be sold across national and cultural borders, *Tele Chobis* was intended for Mexican children. This is manifest in the different placements of real-life children in the two programs. In the British original, sequences of older children appear on screens in the tubbies' abdominal areas, monitors intentionally designed as instruments of localization: different buyers of the program have the ability to insert culturally relevant material in those screens. In contrast, the Mexican copycat incorporates real children in the narrative through parallel editing and montage sequences. One final difference: whereas *Teletubbies* is touted as the only program to have targeted children under the age of two, *Tele Chobis* cast a wider net to include what is probably a two-to-eight age bracket. Unlike the nonlinguistic blabbering of Tinky Winky, Dipsy, Laa Laa, and Po, the Tele Chobis Nita, Toso, Ton, and Tis speak a Mexican-accented Spanish. More importantly, because *Teletubbies* was designed as a "universal" text while *Tele Chobis* was created for the domestic Mexican market from the original and now global format, the latter exhibits a cultural hybridity that is marked, the ensuing analysis will demonstrate, by incongruent scenes and costumes, a diversity of objects from a variety of geographical and cultural locations, and a hodgepodge of commercials and public service announcements for Mexican and American products and programs.

An episode of *Tele Chobis* ran an hour with six commercial breaks, three to four minutes (six to eight commercials) each. Typical advertisers—oddly, not all targeting children—included clothing companies, technical colleges, computer support, snacks and candy, and Mexican federal government public service announcements on public health, sexual hygiene, the environment, and social development. For example, episode 4, which aired in March 1999, began with the Tele Chobis singing under the talking tree where they live. Then a rapid montage sequence featured the Tele Chobis dancing and walking on waterside alleys, alternating with shots of farm animals. After that, we see Nita, the Tele Chobi dressed in green, waking up in a room inside the tree trunk filled with television monitors, tall glass panels with water bubbles, a yellow cupboard, and a big clock above the door. Nita feels lonely and seeks consolation by talking to the tree. The other three Tele Chobis are then seen having a picnic next to the water, with trees painted white about two feet high. The episode's theme is loneliness, explored in the context of children who are left at home to their own devices. We see testimonies from several real children between the ages of six and three saying what they like to do when they are home alone, one of them a brown-skinned, black-haired boy wearing an NBA T-shirt. Then the Tele Chobis are seen, interspersed with shots of children in gardens and at school, dancing to a song whose lyrics focus on loneliness. Cedar and cypress trees can be glimpsed in some shots, with green mountains reminiscent of *Teletubbies*, but most shots are taken in front of the large tree trunk that serves as the Tele Chobis' abode.

The first break carried advertisements for *Aventuras de Doug* (a Disney cartoon), Hecali clothing, Expertus computer services; public service announcement for the Comisión Nacional de Derechos Humanos (National Human Rights Commission) and La Clave (the telecommunications ministry, promoting new phone services); and finally a promotional preview for the broadcast of an ice-hockey game between Ottawa and Dallas. After the break we are back to the picnic, and a phone number appears on the screen with an invitation for children to call and share their favorite surprise. Nita, Toso, Ton, and Tis initiate a waterside dance, dressed in snow hats, scarves, and earmuffs. After a brief intervention by Champi and Ñon, two tree-perched boorish animal commentators, the scene changes and Ton, the Tele Chobi in blue, comes in dressed as a U.S. sheriff, dancing to a tune of imitation U.S. country-western music. The others have red scarves around their necks, cowboy style, one green, the second dark pink, and the third yellow. The background is interspersed with typically Mexican maguey cacti, and the music shifts from Western line dance to Norteño (Northern Mexican) music, and then settles into a hybrid mix of the two genres. After the dance, the Tele Chobis hug Nita, who tells Ton, Toso, and Tis how lonely he felt waking up without them. After the second commercial break ("Presumed Guilty," a soap opera; Marinela chocolate cakes; environmental and public health PSAs; Elektra electronic appliances store; and a promotional preview for *Los Simpsons*), one's imagination and doing what one likes are introduced by voice-over as palliatives to loneliness, with a children's soccer game providing visuals for a ragtime tune. After the third commercial break, colored balloons cross the screen upward and the Mexican copycat quartet is seen dancing to Norteñas, whose rhythm is enhanced by fluid camera movements and parallel editing of children dancing to the same tune in a school yard.

The hybridity of *Tele Chobis* is manifest on two fronts. First, the set includes many markers of Mexicanness. Unlike their English counterparts, whose abdominal screens project footage of children, in *Tele Chobis* scenes of real children are intrinsically part of the program's structure, which belies *Tele Chobis'* intended national audience. Indeed, markers of Mexicanness are many, the first of which is the use of spoken Mexican Spanish. Second, maguey cacti, whose pulp is the raw material of the quintessentially Mexican pulque or tequila, are prominently featured in the program, often in close-ups. Other markers include the monarch butterflies, identified with the Mexican state of Michoacan, a major resting area for these Monarcas on their seasonal peregrinations, and increasingly associated with Mexico as a country. There is also the Guacamaya parrot, found in Mexico's tropical areas. Also, Norteño music tunes underscore the Mexican identity of *Tele Chobis*. Finally, many of the outdoor scenes are shot in ex-haciendas, whose late colonial architecture is also closely associated with Mexico. These visual and aural markers—most of them naturalistic and therefore highly localized—stamp *Tele Chobis* with Mexicanness, a hybrid identity grafted onto an original and innovative text, product of the imagination of a British schoolteacher and promoted by a U.S. entertainment company.

There is, however, a second, more complex embodiment of hybridity. *Tele Chobis'* odd mixture of icons, signs, and objects underscores a radical intertextuality where foreign cultural elements collide and fuse. NBA T-shirts, country-western music, sheriffs' badges, and promotions for U.S. shows like *The Simpsons* and myriad Disney productions, point to the preponderance of U.S. popular culture as a provider of content and as a source of dialogical connections. Earmuffs, scarves, and wool balaclavas worn by the Tele Chobis while promenading or dancing outdoors are also emblematic of a hibernal northern ethos incongruent with *Tele Chobis'* Mexicanness. The iconic mushrooms, balloons, Jeeps, and other items that swirl vertically across the screen throughout each episode increase the atmosphere of radical cultural diversity characteristic of the show. The carnivalesque nature of the program comes in full focus in a scene where Nita, Toso, Ton, and Tis are dressed like medieval entertainers, in a mise-en-scène that transforms their exaggerated baby faces, protuberant cheeks, and dark-lined eyes into monstrous features.

In keeping in mind the show's intended infantile and juvenile audience, these menacing facial traits are neutralized, as the Tele Chobis use them to scare away insects, especially a bee that is harassing a frightened Toso. At that moment, the voice-over of the tree conveniently intervenes to remind children that insects are good for us and should not be harmed, and a song *"Abejas, Hormigas"* (Bees, Ants), praises the lives of insects and the benefits of insects to humans and the environment. When a butterfly finally lands on Ton's arm, the four humanoids are fascinated and fully converted to friendliness toward insects.

This positive pedagogical turn notwithstanding, the visual monstrosity of that scene, centered on the characters' physical appearance, is symptomatic of a radical cultural openness, a carnival aesthetic. As film scholars Ella Shohat and Robert Stam (1994) write, following Bakhtin: "carnival embraces an anticlassical aesthetic that rejects formal harmony and unity in favor of the asymmetrical, the heterogeneous, the oxymoronic, the miscegenated . . . . In the carnival aesthetic, everything is pregnant with its opposite, within an alternative logic of permanent contradiction and non-exclusive opposites that transgresses the monologic true-or-false thinking typical of a certain kind of positivist rationalism" (p. 302). Indeed, *Tele Chobis* carries the cross-fertilized debris of variegated cultural influences and aesthetic styles. It may have been a copy of *Teletubbies* from the perspective of modern copyright—an issue I will address shortly—which is why the program was pulled off the air within a few weeks of its first broadcast. To the cultural critic, however, more than a violation of intellectual property laws, it is a rich text replete with signs and symbols whose intertextual tie-ins subvert the laws of genre as the text itself undermines the copyright regime. *Tele Chobis* is therefore an ideal hybrid text, reminiscent of mythological fables, where aesthetic conventions and artistic practices are subverted, where the monstrous cohabitates with the sublime and the universal with the particular, and where the hybridization of cultural forms is not merely an aesthetic attribute of the text, but actually constitutes its texture and pervades its identity.

Tele Chobis can thus be interpreted as a modern version of the fable of ancient mythology. According to Serge Gruzinski, a French anthropological historian of Mexico and author of the ingenious *La pensée métisse* (Gruzinki, 1999), the fable as a genre exhibits "an indifference to geographical and historical markers" (p. 145, my translation) and a propinquity to embrace disorder and mixtures. Therefore, Gruzinski concludes, the fable is an ideal framework for hybrid cultural forms. As a radically open semiotic system, the fable is a creative space where, Gruzinski wrote in reference to colonial-era Indian paintings in Puebla and Ixmiquilpan, "a centauress can flirt with a Mexican monkey under the eyes of a Spanish cleric" (p. 149).[3] Reeling from Spanish colonial control, native Mexican artists during the Conquista used the fable and grotesque art to effectively subvert colonial aesthetic conventions, a subversion made possible by the fable's intrinsic tendency toward the foreign, the fabulous, and the fantastic. In sharp contrast with sacred art, where colonial church surveillance would be intense and the borders of the iconographic canon heavily policed, the grotesque arts gave free reign to the imaginative and seditious expressiveness of local artists. Thus Gruzinski demonstrates that the Indian painters of Puebla and Ixmiquilpan appropriated a form, the grotesques, originally conceived in Renaissance Italy, in addition to a native cultural content to create hybrid images that playfully undermined colonial aesthetics. Gruzinski sees the same phenomenon at work in contemporary creations such as Peter Greenaway's *Prospero's Books*, where hybridization "opens the way for all kinds of appropriations: it pokes fun at ordinary logics, scrambles the laws of plausibility, of space and time, ignores the laws of gravity, foils representational conventions" (p. 156).

Arguing for a linear historical correspondence between native Mexican painters of the colonial era, aesthetic innovations in Renaissance Italy, Peter Greenaway's dramatic creations, and *Tele Chobis* would be imprudent. However, as products of a world increasingly characterized by cross-cultural interpenetration, texts from these different periods offer more than simple intertextual traces. Like the fable, children's television offers an extremely flexible creative environment, where the form itself, whether through animated or acted imaginary characters, is a creation, and the content is allowed license (in the use of language, colors, forms, sound, etc.) that would not be tolerated in most other television and film genres (see Kraidy, 1998b, for a treatment of this issue in children's animated film). With its placeless green fields, outlandish characters, invented nonlanguage, and heteroclite content, the original *Teletubbies* embodies this conspicuous openness perhaps more than does any other program for children. As a hybrid offshoot of the already hybrid *Teletubbies*, *Tele Chobis* thrusts this radical dialogism into new territory, where intertexts jostle in a seemingly random dance of push-and-pull of discordant icons, discrepant musics, dissonant fashions, and incongruous characters.

Unlike hybrid colonial painting, however, which as Gruzinski (1999) evinced, survived and prospered under colonial strictures, the textual excess incarnated in *Tele Chobis* was curbed by the prevailing system of reference and power. Today's global copyright regime, it turns out, is more successful than the colonial Spanish church in bringing overflowing creative energy back into the fold of the permissible. Whereas Indian Mexican painters indulged in aesthetic subversion, the threat of legal action by the U.S. Itsy Bitsy Entertainment and British Ragdoll Productions brought the Mexican *Tele Chobis* to a quick end: as mentioned earlier, the program was taken off the air a few weeks after it was first broadcast. This was facilitated by an environment of stricter intellectual property–law enforcement by Mexican authorities in the wake of the North American Free Trade Agreement (NAFTA), and a transitional period for the Mexican cultural and media sectors.

The *Tele Chobis* affair occurred at a time of fundamental changes in the Mexican audiovisual industries, triggered by their increased integration in global media markets (Lomelí, 2003) and increasing competition between Televisa, the leading media company, and TV Azteca, the creator of *Tele Chobis* and second in Mexican audience ratings. The background of these changes was the liberal economic drive initiated during the Miguel de la Madrid presidency (1982–1988) and culminating in NAFTA. This trend continued after NAFTA, so that by 2000, Mexico had entered twenty-seven free trade agreements ("México en el Mundo," 2000, cited in Sánchez-Ruiz, 2001). In the 1990s, both Televisa and TV Azteca embarked on ambitious global expansion plans. Televisa, which had expanded into the U.S. market in the 1970s and mid-1980s (Sánchez-Ruiz, 2001), in the 1990s pursued a vigorous international strategy to "create a greater dependency on Televisa programming among foreign broadcasters" (Paxman and Saragoza, 2001). The world's leading Spanish-speaking media company also underwent restructuring, cutting costs by U.S. $175 million in 1997 and 1998 ("Televisa Mexico," 1999), which caused its shares to rise by 10 percent ("Mexico's Televisa," 1999).

TV Azteca was privatized during trade negotiations that led to NAFTA, and it was purchased in 1993 for U.S. $643 million ("TV Azteca and Canal," 1998). Its soon-to-be broadened operations consisted of Azteca 7 and Azteca 13, two national stations. In 1997, the company expanded swiftly, issuing U.S. $425 million in publicly traded bonds in February, and going through an initial public offering of over 20 percent of capital stock in August, also grabbing 32 percent of the U.S. $1.4 billion Mexican advertising market, rising to 36 percent in the first quarter of 1998 (ibid.). This, in addition to several domestic joint ventures and foreign media acquisitions, established TV Azteca as a serious competitor to Televisa. Notably, TV Azteca's joint venture with CNI Canal 40 television gave it access to nearly 100 percent of the Mexico City metropolitan area's 22 million television viewers ("TV Azteca and Canal," 1998). The deal entailed TV Azteca's purchase of 10 percent of Canal 40 shares, giving TV Azteca wider exposure by adding a third channel to its lineup, and providing Canal 40 with content from Azteca's production studios. In late 1998, TV Azteca clinched an exclusive free TV-licensing agreement with Disney for its "Kids and Young Adults" Canal 7 ("TV Azteca Signs," 1998), where *Tele Chobis* was broadcast with commercials for various Disney products. TV Azteca's growth led it to announce that it would raise its advertising rates by 40 percent starting in January 1999 (Barrera, 1998). That same month, TV Azteca became embroiled in a dispute with the Chilean government over the way it managed its acquisition of 75 percent of Chile's Channel 4 television, and faced allegations that it did not comply with Chilean law that mandated top executive positions in television stations to be occupied by Chilean nationals ("TV Azteca Denies," 1999). Nonetheless, TV Azteca's shares rose 10 percent in December 1999 ("Mexico's TV," 1999). Since then, TV Azteca has maintained its number two position, in effect sharing duopolistic control of the Mexican media market with leader Televisa.[4]

Predictably, media liberalization in Mexico involved legal changes. The Mexican Federal Copyright Law (FCL), officially published on December 23, 1996, became effective in March 1997, repealing the 1963 Federal Copyright Law. In the new law, television and broadcasting copyrights are recognized, but "ideas," "formulas," and "concepts" are not legally protected ("Highlights of," 1998). A few years earlier, the Law of Cinematography of 1992 repealed a 1941 law requiring that 50 percent of movies be nationally made. According to the 1992 law, this proportion was to be reduced to 30 percent in 1993, and by five more percentiles yearly until it was down to 10 percent by the end of 1997. The cable television industry was also deregulated to allow up to 49 percent non-Mexican ownership (Sánchez-Ruiz, 2001).

These technological and regulatory changes, coupled with increasing autonomy from government intervention, put enormous pressure on Mexican media companies to provide commercially attractive content. In addition to global expansion and joint ventures elaborated previously, heightened competition led to programming that clashed with prevailing social values, such as talk shows inspired by the "trash" talk-show genre in the United States (LaFranchi, 2000). It was in this environment that TV Azteca created and launched *Tele Chobis*, after deciding that it could neither afford to purchase *Teletubbies* for commercial-free broadcasting, nor let Televisa's acquisition of *Teletubbies* broadcast rights for Mexico go unchallenged. TV Azteca thus resorted to program mimicry, running afoul of intellectual property laws, literally illustrating Homi Bhabha's claim in this chapter's epigraph that "the visibility of mimicry is always produced at the site of interdiction" (1994, p. 89). The *Tele Chobis* story consequently embodies a crossroads of historical, economic, technological, and cultural forces, all of which contributed, at different levels and with various intensities, to the creation of a hybrid, transcultural text.

The hybridity of media texts is explained by the media's transnational political economy. Post-Fordist practices and systemic forces account for the fact that hybrid media texts reflect industry imperatives for targeting several markets at once with the same program or, alternatively, are symptoms of commercially motivated "borrowing." In the absence of the present global structure where interlocking regulatory, financial, political, and cultural forces drive a race to reach the highest number of people for the lowest cost and the minimum amount of risk, therefore entailing creative productions that cross and fuse cultural differences, hybridity would likely not be as pervasive in media texts worldwide. However, as the dissection of the Mexican copycat *Tele Chobis* has shown, both the raison d'être and the kiss of death of hybrid television programs are to be found in political-economic arrangements, which in this case included a Mexican industry in transition, embedded in the

North American Free Trade Agreement and the international copyright regime. Granted, media texts, even before the acceleration of the sector's globalization, have always sought and found inspiration in each other, as the example of Hong Kong I used in Chapter One demonstrates, but the contemporary phenomenon of media programs that carry composite aesthetics and fused cultural elements, in both its breadth and depth, is a product of neoliberalization. Hybrid media texts have the intertextual traces of an increasingly standardized global media industry where successful formats are adapted ad infinitum, hybridized to cater to the proclivities of one audience after another, but always remaining firmly grounded in the same commercial logic where hybrid texts are instruments finely tuned in pursuit of profit.

6   Structure, Reception, and Identity

On Arab-Western Dialogism

I, too, have ropes around my neck. I have them to this day, pulling me this way and that, East and West, the nooses tightening, commanding, choose, choose. I buck, I snort, I whinny, I rear, I kick. Ropes, I do not choose between you. Lassoes, lariats, I choose neither of you, and both. Do you hear? I refuse to choose.

—Salman Rushdie

MODERN LEBANON is a bundle of paradoxes. Relations between its numerous confessions have ebbed and flowed between peaceful coexistence and violent conflict.[1] Mirroring these changes, public discourse in the West and the Arab region has alternately extolled Lebanon as the "Gateway to the Orient" or the "Paris of the East" (in the 1950s and 1960s) and denounced the mayhem of "Lebanonization" and the "orgy of violence" during the 1974–1990 war. Lebanon's political system is at once ostensibly democratic and subject to neofeudalist networks of patronage. Also, despite being one of the smallest nation-states, Lebanon's national identity has been contested under myriad banners, secular and religious, progressive and reactionary. Finally, the delicate interconfessional demographic balance and precarious political equilibrium have historically made Lebanon vulnerable to both endogenous and exogenous forces, including internal strife, the Arab-Israeli conflict, Cold War superpower rivalry, and Syrian claims over Lebanon. These quandaries have ensnared Lebanon in a permanent identity crisis, leading to occasional flare-ups that culminated with the 1974–1990 war.

The Maronites have until recently played a major role in Lebanon's convoluted politics. Maronites adhere to religious teachings that developed in the fourth and fifth centuries around Saint Maron, spiritual leader of a group of monks in the valley of the Orontes River in present-day Syria (Valognes, 1994, p. 370). At Maron's death around 410 A.D., his followers institutionalized his doctrine, and effectively started the Maronite confession, which became a branch of Catholicism. Due to persecution by other Christian groups and later by Muslims, Maronites moved to the Lebanese mountains, a relatively safe homeland they shared for centuries with other ethnic minorities like the Druze and Shiite Muslims. When the Ottoman Empire collapsed in the wake of World War I, strong relations with the French, who controlled Lebanon under a League of Nations mandate, and demographic preponderance in the Lebanese mountains helped the Maronites occupy a leading position in the Lebanese polity, consolidated in the 1950s with U.S. assistance against pan-Arab forces. Maronite clout was reflected in the unwritten but nonetheless binding 1943 National Pact, which stipulated "an independent Lebanon with an Arab face" (*wajh arabi*) but nonetheless open to Western civilization, and notably reserved the Lebanese presidency for a Maronite. Some Maronite leaders at times maintained a neutral stance in the Arab-Israeli conflict, which alienated many Lebanese Muslims and some Christians and contributed to Lebanon's descent into protracted violent conflict in the 1970s.

The balance of political power shifted away from the Maronites in postwar Lebanon. During the war, some predominantly Maronite factions occasionally allied themselves with Israel and Iraq, which in addition to inter-Maronite fighting in the late 1980s considerably weakened the community's bargaining power in negotiations toward a postwar settlement. In 1989, with U.S. blessing and Saudi sponsorship, the Document of National Understanding, better known as the Ta'if Agreement, put an official end to military conflict. Ta'if's core focused on reforming institutions and on national reconciliation, and the text of the document officially settled Lebanon's identity dilemma by asserting that "Lebanon is Arab in belonging and identity." Among other amendments to the 1926 Lebanese Constitution, the Ta'if Agreement shifted the seat of executive power from the presidency of the Republic, a position by tradition reserved for a Maronite, to the Council of Ministers, customarily headed by a Sunnite Muslim, effectively sapping the institutional bases of Maronite political power. Fifteen years after Ta'if, in a postwar environment of economic depression, political subservience to Syria, rampant politico-economic corruption, and rising confessional tensions, the Maronite community is undergoing an internal crisis experienced by its youth in an environment of media proliferation.[2]

This chapter explores cultural reception by Maronite youth in the postwar Lebanese media landscape as a case study of the role of mediated communication in the dynamics of cultural hybridity. I focus on the Maronites, and not on any of the other Lebanese confessions, because of

the peculiar role of the Maronite community in modern Lebanese politics I have just summarized, and also for the practical reason that this is
the Lebanese community to which I have a high level of access, which
has enabled me to probe locally sensitive and controversial issues at a
time when the wounds of the war have not yet healed. My local empirical focus is not conceived as a counterpoint to globalization, but as a
site of existential and epistemological engagement with a local-to-global
continuum culturally manifested in terms of hybridity. I therefore posit
locality in all its complexity and explore how local manifestations of hybridity are best analyzed and what importance communication practices
have in their constitution. What are the structural and ideological forces
that bear upon local cultural hybridity? Does global culture loom larger
than regional and national culture over Maronite cultural reception, and
what roles do these different realms play in hybrid Maronite identity?
As I address these questions, a critical objective is to situate empirical
audience data within the political economy of Lebanese media.

   This chapter draws on field research conducted mostly in the districts
of Kisirwan and Matn, located to the north and east of Beirut, between
1992 and 2004, including dozens of in-depth interviews and a total of
sixteen discontinuous months of fieldwork. I make significant use of
data obtained during a three-month research trip in the summer of 1993
in the form of fifty open-ended multipage questionnaires, each con-
taining ten self-reflexive (one-page) essays about media consumption
and cultural identity, in addition to extensive field notes over a period
exceeding ten years. Informed by these initial data, since 1994 I have
conducted dozens of interviews with viewers, television directors and
producers, journalists, and academics, the latest during four months
of continuous fieldwork in Lebanon between March and August 2004.
My objective has been an in-depth understanding of what it means to
have a hybrid cultural identity on an everyday basis. To achieve a grasp
of hybridity as an existential experience, my analysis will focus on ten
relatively sophisticated, mostly middle-class participants, five male and
five female, referred to by pseudonyms, with each of whom I conducted
several in-depth interviews and participant observation over a period
of three years. Finally, my study draws on selected television programs
and songs and other texts from among hundreds of hours of television
and music that I have collected in Lebanon over the last decade.

   As a Christian community in a predominantly Muslim Middle East,
the Maronites may not appear to be the best case study of media-related
hybrid identity, because they seem to have been always already hybrid,

a factor that marginalizes the role of communication in the formation of hybridity. This view, however, rests on the assumptions that (1) there are hybrid cultures and nonhybrid cultures, and that (2) Maronite identity is stable across history. In contrast, as I have already discussed in Chapter Three and further elaborate in Chapter Seven, I consider cultural mixture to be pervasive and focus on hybridity as a matter of degree, direction, and implication. In other words, I am not concerned with the question of whether a culture is hybrid, because I believe that all cultures are to some extent hybrid but that in each case hybridity requires a firm grounding in its particular context. My interest rather lies in the historical, sociopolitical, economic, and discursive contexts where *local hybridities* take shape. In this case, hybridity is not an essential historical characteristic of Maronite identity, but neither is it merely a result of contemporary foreign media consumption. As I briefly explain, hybrid Maronite identity has developed within a field of interacting and often contingent local and extralocal forces. Consequently, I argue against a primordial understanding and advocate instead a relational approach to Maronite identity, in whose contemporary dynamics media and communication play an active role.

Unfortunately, an essentialist comprehension of identity is manifest in some historians' obsessive quest for the Maronites' "true" origins. Some scholars suggest that the Maronites are the descendants of "the worshippers of Adonis and Astarte," "Assyrians who emerged from Mesopotamia" (Melia, 1986, p. 154). Another theory claims that the Maronites are the descendants of an Arab Bedouin population, the Nabateans, who settled in the Levant during the pre-Christian era (Valognes, 1994, p. 369). A third theory, based on the work of the historian Theophanes, presents the Maronites as the heirs of an Anatolian or Iranian population, the Mardaites, who were allegedly militarily used by the Byzantines against the Arabs because of the Mardaites' outstanding fighting skills (Melia, 1986, p. 158; Nisan, 1992, p. 171; Valognes, 1994, p. 369). According to the fourth and last theory, the Maronites descend from the Phoenicians, a claim held by some Maronite (and other Christian Lebanese) intellectuals as a key building block of their identity, which some scholars dispute (Salibi, 1988; Tabar, 1994; Valognes, 1994), and others support (Gemayel, 1984a, b; Melia, 1986; Nisan, 1992). Chabry and Chabry (1987), among others (Melia, 1986; Nisan, 1992; Tabar, 1994; Valognes, 1994), argue that Maronite claims of a Phoenician heritage are not unfounded (p. 55), because the ethnic makeup of the Maronites is a mixture of Mardaite, Greco-Phoenician, Aramean,

Franc, Armenian, and Arab elements (p. 305). In spite of this mixed origin, the Maronites are said to have maintained a presumably unchanging identity—fiercely autonomous from both Muslims and other Christians—and remained "untamed in their ways of living and thinking" (Melia, 1986, p. 159; see also Nisan, 1992, p. 171).

The Phoenician-roots theory parallels the belief among Copts in Egypt and Nestorians in Iraq, both Christian communities, that they have respectively Pharaonic and ancient Assyrian roots. Whether the Maronites' ancestors were Phoenician or not is beyond the interest and scope of this book, as the emphasis is on the lived experience of present-day identity and its connection to a remembered past, not to the putatively "objective" trajectory of recorded history. All identities draw on mythical pasts as they evolve historically. In this case my research demonstrates that Maronite youth are themselves ambivalent toward the debate on Maronite origins. As much as some clung to a cultural identity distinct from that of the Arabs, only very few among them exhibited a complete rejection of Arab identity or an unconditional acceptance of Phoenician roots. Constant references by interviewees to cultural "blending" and "mixing" clearly put hybridity, and not teleological authenticity, at the heart of their everyday experience of identity. Clearly in this case, oral history is ambivalent toward recorded history.

The inter-Christian relationship between the Maronites and the West, portrayed in the written historiography as a constitutive factor in a pro-Western Maronite identity, did in fact not necessarily entail identification with the West and hostility toward Muslims. For example, in 1182 one of the earliest Maronite-European contacts created controversy within the Maronite community, when some Maronite archers joined the Crusaders while others took the Muslims' side and fought against the European conquerors (Valognes, 1994, p. 371). In fact, it was not until the nineteenth century that religious feeling became the dominant component of Maronite identity, when the "culture of sectarianism" (Makdissi, 2000) emerged in an entanglement of military, diplomatic, and religious forces between the Ottoman Empire, the European powers, and the communities of Mount Lebanon, the traditional Maronite homeland that was enlarged to form the modern state of Lebanon. As the Lebanese-born historian Ussama Makdissi explained:

> The story [of sectarianism] begins ... when local Lebanese society was opened, and indeed opened itself, to Ottoman and European discourses of reform that made religion the site of a colonial encounter between a self-styled "Christian" West and what it saw as its perennial adversary, an

"Islamic" Ottoman empire. This encounter profoundly altered the meaning of religion in the multiconfessional society of Mount Lebanon because
it emphasized sectarian identity as the only viable marker of political
reform and the only authentic basis for political claims. The story is of
the symbiosis between indigenous traditions and practices—in which
religion was enmeshed in complex social and political relations—and
Ottoman modernization, which became paramount in reshaping the
political self-definition of each community along religious lines. (2000,
p. 1)

Indeed, under pressure from the European powers in the mid–
nineteenth century, Ottoman authorities launched the reforms known as
tanzimat, which institutionalized religious differences among imperial
subjects, including various communities in Mount Lebanon. Before the
tanzimat, the central marker of difference in Lebanese society was social
class. Feudal lords of all confessions ruled over commoners of all confessions, many villages were mixed, and religion did not play the most
important role in social relations. The advent of Ottoman reform led
to a series of fragmentations and realignments that in 1861 resulted in
violent conflict between Maronite and Druze villagers. It was then that
Lebanese sectarianism was born. "Sectarianism," Makdissi thus argues,
"is a *modern* story" (p. 2, my emphasis).

The most violent episode of that "story" unfolded during the 1974–
1990 war in Lebanon, facilitated by Lebanon's already mentioned precarious political equilibrium, triggered by the influx of armed Palestinians
into Lebanon, fanned by the ideological forces of the Arab-Israeli conflict and the Cold War, and fueled by the sectarian sentiment now deeply
entrenched in Lebanon's social structure. The most important aspect of
the conflict as far as this study is concerned is the wartime proliferation
of privately owned media. Feuding confessional factions established
unlicensed radio and television stations as mouthpieces, culminating in
the early to mid-1990s with more than fifty television and a hundred
radio stations (Kraidy, 1998a). I now turn to events triggered by media
proliferation that constitute the politico-economic context of Maronite
media reception.

HISTORY AND STRUCTURE OF THE LEBANESE MEDIA

Lebanon's experience with the mass media is uniquely complex (Boulos,
1995; Boyd, 1991; Harik, 1994; Kraidy, 1998a, 1999b, 2000, 2001). Lebanon
can be said to have one of the freest media systems and one of the highest

literacy rates in the Arab world, although recent developments indicate increased state repression of the media (Kraidy, 2002d). In wartime the Lebanese had access to dozens of mass media with conflicting ideological allegiances and diverse content in Arabic, French, English, and Armenian. In 1995, more than fifty terrestrial television stations and more than a hundred radio stations catered to Lebanon's estimated three million inhabitants, who lived in a country of 10, 452 square kilometers, or 4,105 square miles, only twice the size of the U.S. state of Delaware! To this day, sharing screen space with local fare are U.S. sitcoms and police shows, British comedy, French drama, German documentaries, Egyptian soap operas, and dubbed Mexican telenovelas (Kraidy, 1998a, 2003a). The growth of pan-Arab satellite services in the 1990s exponentially expanded television content, accessible at a low cost. There are no licensing fees and subscription fees are rare, so that the only expense for the Lebanese viewer is the cost of the television set and the electricity to power it. In a postwar environment where the state has more pressing concerns than enforcing intellectual property and television subscription rights, private neighborhood cable networks constitute a peculiar phenomenon. Enterprising citizens pay satellite subscription fees and establish their cable network that in some cases includes hundreds of subscribers, or even upward of a thousand. While illegal, these businesses are ubiquitous in Lebanon and promote their services through home-printed flyers and word of mouth. By late 2002, many households linked to such a network were enjoying in excess of eighty channels, including all the Arab satellite channels, some Indian networks, and the major U.S. and European cable and satellite channels. Choices have ranged from Al-Manar to ESPN to Canal Plus. This "package" typically costs around U.S. $10 per month.

This all began in 1985 when the Lebanese Forces, a Christian wartime militia and later a political party, launched the Lebanese Broadcasting Corporation (LBC), Lebanon's and the Arab world's first privately owned and continuously running commercial television station. Conceived as both a profit-making company and an instrument of propaganda, LBC's inaugural grid relied heavily on imported—mostly pirated—programs such as British comedy, French drama, and U.S. sitcoms and soap operas. I personally remember the excitement generated by the launch of LBC in the mid-1980s. As teenagers confined indoors by indiscriminate shelling and bombing, we were glued to the television set, watching *The Benny Hill Show*, *Zora La Rousse*, *Santa Barbara*, and *The Cosby Show*, hoping the next electrical power blackout would wait till the end of the program. These programs were decisively more attractive than state-operated Télé-Liban's stodgy diet of older U.S. police series, German documentaries, French vaudeville theatre, and the occasional local dramatic series. I also recall quite vividly the growing popularity of LBC's local game shows, a format "adapted" by LBC director Simon Asmar from U.S. and European originals, where participants won consumer goods from the programs' sponsors, ranging from brand-new French or Japanese cars to the winner's weight in soap from the local Procter and Gamble agent. Numerous other stations followed, whose stripes mirrored Lebanon's plural polity: religious and secular, national and local, Communist and probusiness, Christian and Muslim, Arabist and Lebanist. In this media cacophony, LBC played a pioneering role in introducing U.S.-style commercial television and mediated consumerism to the Middle East several years before other Lebanese terrestrial stations and half a decade before it was emulated by the now illustrious pan-Arab satellite television industry (Kraidy, 2002b).

The rise of private commercial broadcasting occurred at the expense of Télé-Liban, the national station co-owned by the state and private interests. Created in 1956 and on the air since 1959, Télé-Liban's fortunes have ebbed and flowed with Lebanon's political mis/fortunes (Boulos, 1996; Kraidy, 1998a). It was the only television witness of Lebanon's golden era in the 1960s and early 1979s, when Télé-Liban explored how to operate a national television in a pluralistic nation. In this creative laboratory, dramatic productions eschewed characters with names that were clearly Christian or Muslim, such as Joseph or Muhammed, opting instead for neutral Arabic names, such as Ghassan and Ziad. In the golden years of the 1960s and the first half of the 1970s, several dramatic series such as *Ad-Dunia Hayk* (That's life) and *Abou Melhem* (the name of the elderly protagonist) explored interconfessional coexistence and traditional methods of conflict resolution. Like all state institutions, Télé-Liban was weakened by the eruption of the war in the mid-1970s, and its scattered studios were claimed by the militias on the ground. As a result, in the 1980s Télé-Liban was unable to compete with LBC's pirated programming and went through a protracted decline precipitated by political interference, rolling ownership of the private shares, and technical deficiencies (Kraidy, 1999b; 2001).

In 1994, Lebanese authorities passed the Audio-Visual Media Law (AVML), the first legislation of its kind in the Arab region. It revoked Télé-Liban's legal monopoly over broadcasting without proposing a viable solution for the ailing station, and at the same time legalized private broadcasting (Kraidy, 1998a). In 1996 all Lebanese television stations were forced to close, except four licensed under the auspices of the 1994 AVML. LBC, which was awarded a license after a reshuffling of its board of shareholders to include influential politicians, remains Lebanon's leading station. Murr Television (MTV), opened in 1991, belonged to the brother of the then deputy prime minister, and was initially oriented toward entertainment programming, foregoing a news department for the first three or four years of its existence. Since 1997, when government officials attempted to ban an interview with an exiled opposition figure, MTV had become the increasingly strident voice of the opposition, leading to its permanent shutdown on September 4, 2002 (Kraidy, 2002d). At the time of its forced closure, I was told by Lebanese media sources that MTV was beginning to rival LBC's domestic audience ratings, due largely to its oppositional stance toward the regime. Future Television (FTV), affiliated with Prime Minister Rafik al-Hariri, has a probusiness, pro-Saudi message, in line with Hariri's neoliberal economic agenda. The National Broadcasting Network (NBN), controlled by Speaker of the Council of Deputies Nabih Berri, is the smallest of the stations and does not really compete at the national level. NBN was initially the butt of jokes (its acronym was derided as "No Broadcasting Network") because it secured a license before the station existed, and the station has followed a niche approach that focuses on cultural and current affairs programming. Later, during a ministerial reshuffle in which Hariri temporarily lost the premiership, two religious stations, Télé-Lumière, affiliated with the Maronite clergy, and Al-Manar, owned by Hizbullah, the Islamic Shiite formation that leads anti-Israeli guerilla resistance in South Lebanon, were also allowed to continue broadcasting, and a license was awarded to New Television, owned by Tahseen Khayyat, a Sunnite businessman and archnemesis of Hariri.

The four initial stations obtained their licenses largely according to confessional considerations, in line with Lebanon's consociationalist political system, where resources of all kinds are distributed under a strict formula of "confessional balance" rather than according to merit or competence: LBC was the Maronite Christian station, FTV the Sunnite Muslim station, NBN the Shiite Muslim station, and MTV a Greek Orthodox Christian station, in which the Druze community was rumored to have some influence. MTV was less confessionally typed than the other stations, because its owner and the Greek Orthodox community in Lebanon did not have a unified and predictably confessional political discourse. Consequently, MTV and Télé-Liban could have become television stations with a national discourse that transcended confessional affiliations and loyalties (see Kraidy, 2000). Unfortunately, this potential was squandered, as MTV became increasingly associated with the mostly Christian opposition, while Télé-Liban was appropriated by some leading politicians who did not own television stations and, as I noted earlier, was eventually stripped of most of its resources and compelled in 2002 to rebroadcast old series from the 1960s and 1970s to maintain a prime-time presence.

Clearly, the decline of Télé-Liban and its original mandate to create programs meaningful to Lebanon's plural publics constitutes a loss for which the private stations, with their narrower political and commercial imperatives, cannot compensate. The broad structural context that shapes media consumption rests on the assumption that media ownership corresponds to audience preferences along confessional lines— hence the presupposition that young Maronites would primarily watch LBC, whose programming caters to their social and ideological proclivities, an assumption that I will now scrutinize. Following Abu-Lughod's (1999) observation that rigorous research requires that we "interrelate [the] various modes of the social life of television" (p. 114), I now ask: How do the affective links that young Maronites establish with media texts relate to the political economy of the Lebanese media? In other words, how do the dynamics of cultural hybridity relate to media texts and structures?[3] These questions are addressed in several stages, beginning with an exploration of Maronite historical memory, followed by an analysis of how young Maronites relate their media consumption to their sense of self and community, and finally situating consumption practices in their broad sociopolitical context.

HISTORY, MEMORY, IDENTITY

Collective memory, more than official recorded history, plays a crucial role in shaping the self-image of nations and communities. Inasmuch as the past is the remembered, "and not merely the recorded, past" (Lukacs, 1994, p. 32), it is often invoked by social groups for the purpose of self-construction, since "identity is formed at the unstable point where the . . . stories of subjectivity meet the narratives of history" (Hall, 1993, p. 153). From this perspective, it is important to explore how young Maronites incorporate their remembered past in their present sense of identity, and the role media consumption plays in that process—hence my presumption that questionnaires and interviews with young Maronites about their media consumption and cultural identity would probably elicit comments about history.

Indeed, the diversity of Lebanon's historical heritage was a recurring theme in this study. In a clear hint to the Phoenician-origins theory, a young man earnestly told me that "being Lebanese is being committed to an idea, a concept, a history... [that] is six thousand years old," and others wrote in their questionnaire answers that their country "belonged to an old and glorious civilization." Another participant rehearsed Lebanon's much-vaunted status: "We are the link between East and West. And we have been like that for a long time, throughout our history. This is the true aspect of civilization: one keeps one's own customs and traditions but also tries to enrich these traditions and customs by adding foreign aspects to them. This is the true meaning of civilization." Probing their perceptions of Maronite, and not just Lebanese, identity elicited different answers, ranging from the self-righteous to the outwardly critical. Serge, a twenty-two-year-old engineering student at the public Lebanese University with a rural, working-class, and conservative background, argued that "[v]ery few groups can claim to be the authentic Lebanese who came here before all the others. All were persecuted minorities who took refuge in Lebanon: the Maronites, the Armenians. There were some other people, maybe of Phoenician origins, a fact we cannot assert, because the Phoenicians lived in Lebanon so long ago. They lived in Phoenician city-states such as Tyre and Byblos." Other respondents went further, questioning the premise of the Maronite-origin debate. Peter, a twenty-four-year-old middle-class medical student at the Lebanese University who lives in a northern outer suburb of Beirut, spoke of a "historical lapsus" that makes it difficult for the Maronites to "determine our ascendance." He continues: "Lebanon has been repeatedly invaded, a lot of mixing. Genetically, we cannot trace our Phoenician roots. What about all the blond-haired Lebanese? These cannot be of purely Phoenician origin." Others offered similar statements, such as Serge, who said: "I am neither Arab nor Phoenician. The blending which occurred throughout history does not allow me to choose one." These representative responses reveal an ambivalent stance on the issue of Phoenician heritage: On one hand, participants do not wholeheartedly embrace Phoenician roots; on the other, they do not reject them but refer to a "mixing" and "blending" that occurred throughout history. This tacit acknowledgment of the Phoenician factor is a far cry from its mythical importance suggested in the historiography discussed earlier in this chapter.

Criticizing the Lebanese social structure, which recognizes individuals as members of a confession rather than as citizens, virtually all persons I interviewed readily conflated Maronite and Lebanese identities: "You go and ask other Muslims and they will tell you that Lebanon is merely a piece of an Arab nation," said Fouad, a twenty-seven-year-old restaurant manager with a college degree in philosophy, thus conflating Arab nationalism and Islam. Arab nationalism, which calls for a pan-Arab nation from Morocco to Iraq, is one of several political ideologies to have laid claim to Lebanon (see Firro, 2003; Khalaf, 2002; Salibi, 1988; Zamir, 2000). Other such ideologies include Syrian nationalism (or Syrianism), which calls for the unification of Lebanon, Syria, and parts of historic Palestine into Greater Syria; the Christian-tinged Lebanese nationalism or Lebanism (see Phares, 1995), which advocates an independent and fully sovereign Lebanon; and Islamism, in both Shiite and Sunnite versions. Fouad proceeded to argue that Maronites, because of their attachment to Lebanese "folklore and cultural heritage," are more committed to Lebanon than are other confessions, a view held by some Maronite nationalists who believe themselves to be more loyal to Lebanon (a more accurate view would be that different communities may be more or less loyal to different visions of Lebanon). In contrast, Antoun questioned the assumption that the Maronites are the "authentic population" that constitutes "the essence of Lebanon." Nonetheless, many respondents followed Fouad's perspective with numerous examples that illustrate what they perceive to be the Maronites' greater pride in Lebanese identity, implying a nearly complete overlap of Maronite and Lebanese identities. The chapter now continues with an exploration of contemporary expressions of the equivalence between Maronite and Lebanese identities in the remembered past.

"THE WEST" AND "ARABS" AS DIALOGICAL COUNTERPOINTS

Young Maronites perceived two competing discourses, modernity and tradition, that they saw constructed by the mass media. Sweepingly identified as "the West" and "the Arabs," these two discourses functioned not as a dichotomy, but rather as dialogical counterpoints, a notion I borrow from Said (1994) to refer to discursive variations that create a space where the central theme is elaborated. An overriding concern among young Maronites was their inability and unwillingness to exclusively belong to one or the other of what they perceived as two irreconcilable worldviews. This double-voiced posture embodies a cultural version of Bakhtin's definition of linguistic hybridization as "a mixture of two social languages within the limit of a single utterance, an encounter ... between two different ... consciousnesses, separated from one another by an epoch, by social differentiation or by some other factor" (Bakhtin, 1981, p. 358).

Simultaneously identifying with Western and Arab cultures and rejecting parts of both of them, young Maronites embody hybridity in that they live simultaneously on two sides of a symbolic fault line without full allegiance to either, a position verbalized by Peter, the twenty-four-year-old medical student I interviewed in a fast-food restaurant overlooking the Mediterranean Sea: "In some things, we resemble Arabs. In other things, we resemble Europeans. Nothing makes you distinct as a [Maronite] Lebanese .... Food? You have falafel and you have hamburger. Where is Lebanon? You go to a shop and you ... get a creative mixture of the hamburger and the falafel; ... they put humus inside of a hamburger or some blend of that sort. Sometimes ... you begin to see this mélange becoming homogenous, you start finding an identity ... but ... we are confused. From the time I was born, I haven't been able to find an identity.... Who are we?" Peter's ambivalence is typical, his colorful metaphors notwithstanding (perhaps they were inspired by the sights and smells of the setting): struggling to position themselves vis-à-vis two worldviews, young Maronites used the terms "Maronite" and "Lebanese" interchangeably, expressing their vision of Lebanon as a hybrid culture. Most readily acknowledged themselves as Arabs or "similar to Arabs" because they spoke Arabic and lived in the Arab world and embraced values such as hospitality and social compassion that they perceived as typically Arab, but most also declined to identify with strong social and religious conservatism, authoritarianism, and anti-Western attitudes that they associated with Arab societies. Simultaneously, young Maronites identified with Western commitments to individual freedom and civil liberties but criticized Western individualism and sexual mores. Elham, a twenty-five-year-old video artist who worked for a local advertising agency, and her friend Karine, twenty-three, who worked at a local television production house, told me that in Lebanon "a lot of people are confused" about their identity because, in Karine's words, "we want to be Westerners but are bound by Eastern values." Says Elham: "We are Arabs by virtue of language and geographic location. At the same time, I do not have the Arab [value] ... of conservatism. I *fit in Western culture* better. At the same time, I have some Arab facets to my identity. I blend both, I keep both and enjoy both at the same time. This is what is so special about being Lebanese" (emphasis mine). Identifying the Arab world with tradition and the West with modernity, young Maronites uttered both discourses through the cultural matrices that permeate their use of media and popular culture.

The Arabs and Tradition

Arab societies are traditional in the sense that they tend to emphasize the community and the family, rather than the individual, as the core social unit. Young Maronites related to nuclear family values, social compassion, and hospitality associated with Arab society but spurned other Arab values they perceived as socially, culturally, and politically conservative, because of strict interpretations of Islam and autocratic regimes. Respondents opted for a partial acceptance of Arab norms intermixed with a selective embrace of Western values, expressed by Marianne, a twenty-one-year-old advertising major at a private university, who volunteered, rather defensively: "I want to keep my Eastern values, like hospitality and morals, but add to them Western values, like the love for freedom and knowledge. Is that a crime? I want to have both because I am Lebanese." To young Maronites, Arab television reflects Arab values. In their view, Egyptian soap operas epitomize Arab television because of their popularity in Arab societies. In interviews, they referred to the portrayal in Egyptian serials of Arab society and its parental and political authoritarianism, social conservatism, and religious restrictions. Female viewers who I interviewed believed Egyptian television drama's depiction of Arab society to be accurate. This led them to set themselves apart from Arab social norms while acknowledging that these norms were partly their own. Rima, a twenty-two-year-old working-class woman from a rural area in the Bekaa Valley who came to the Beirut area to study law at the public Lebanese University, said that as a Maronite "I can wear a mini skirt when I want," adding that her parents usually granted her permission to stay out late, and concluding with a blunt reference to a Muslim practice: "I do not wear a veil. I am free."[4] This view was echoed in many conversations with other young women, represented by Karine, twenty-three, who felt "freer than other women in the [Arab] region. In a way, I am as free as women in the United States and Europe, but here I have to work at it," which meant, in her words, to "keep [her life] somewhat private and hidden." This last statement underscores how relative that freedom is in reality.

Males I spoke with were less concerned with matters of individual dress and behavior—clearly, men are subject to fewer restrictions in patriarchal Arab societies, and this includes Lebanon—and more interested in broader issues. For example, Peter said that he liked Egyptian movies and television series that "go in depth into Egyptian society" and treat some of the serious problems in it such as "corruption, injustice, and inefficiency." These productions "explain why the bus never arrives on time and why accidents happen, because drivers are not qualified . . . and mechanics . . . incompetent." In that statement, Peter utters a hegemonic reading that uses Egyptian television drama as a metonymy of perceived Arab backwardness in opposition to the putative technical competence of Western modernity.

Others echoed this understanding and associated Arab productions with Latin American telenovelas. These typically Mexican but sometimes Colombian or Venezuelan serials, dubbed in Arabic by Lebanese actors, have been a popular genre in Lebanon since the late eighties and have become part of an informal cultural "industry" that includes clothing, music, gossip, and popular jokes. Ever since the first telenovela, *Corazón de Piedra* (Heart of Stone), was broadcast in the late 1980s, the Lebanese have simply referred to these serials as "Mexicans." For programmers, they are a low-cost alternative to expensive local production. In addition, dubbing telenovelas in Arabic opens lucrative possibilities for exporting them to the rest of the Arab world. The popularity of telenovelas has meant good audience ratings and, in turn, big advertising revenues. However, the fact that these Latin American serials were put in the same category with Egyptian soap operas was at first surprising. Geographically, Mexico is, according to the European-centric mapping vision, in the West. Culturally, also due to Spanish colonialism, Mexico belongs to the West, albeit in a peculiarly hybrid fashion, as discussed in Chapters Three and Four. Interestingly, young Maronite viewers placed Mexican telenovelas within the "Arab" generic category. A typical telenovela story line, according to Maha, a twenty-five-year-old middle-class female who works at a cultural center, who spoke derisively, unfolds like this: "He loves her but she loves his brother, but his brother loves her mother, who cannot get over the fact that her husband is fooling around with her best friend, who is still her best friend although she is sleeping with her best friend's husband."

Viewers found both Egyptian and Latin American serials to be highly melodramatic, even histrionic. In what is perhaps an expression of an educated middle-class sensibility, they claimed that the screen theatrics would have been acceptable to them if the acting had been good, but according to virtually all those I interviewed, both Egyptian soaps and Latin American telenovelas displayed poor acting. Watching a Colombian telenovela while conversing in Karine's house, Elham derided the characters because they kept "crying, howling, and whining." Whereas Maha criticized the artificially convoluted plots and the lack of verisimilitude in telenovelas, other viewers indicated that they were unable to identify with the "very remote" and "irrelevant" characters and experiences in Mexican and Egyptian serials. After subsequent interpretation, I concluded that telenovelas were being evaluated in comparison to slick U.S. television production values that epitomized a normative Western "look" against which other television programs were judged (see James, 1995, for a similar finding among Hungarians). This explains why Maronite viewers relegated telenovelas to the non-Western, Arab category, in a discursive elaboration of two genres that is itself a hybridizing act that expresses a synthetic aesthetic.

The West and Modernity

Associating modernity with the West, Maronite viewers described the latter as a locus of individual freedom and "love for knowledge," two aspects that they associated with what they saw as a typically Maronite "openness to other cultures." Delving into this issue, I learned that "the outside" and "other cultures," although denotatively all-encompassing, had a more limited connotation that referred to "the West." "It is a good thing that Francophonie is alive and well in Lebanon," Fouad told me; he cast the space of Francophonie, a strong cultural presence in the Maronite community because of historical ties with France, as a marker of openness to the West. Prodded further, he said that openness to the West according to him was "better than wearing a veil and not seeing beyond a couple of meters." Besides its obviously stereotypical tenor, this statement reveals an opposition between the West (here represented by the Francophone cultural space) and the Islam invoked by the reference to the veil. Fouad declined to adopt Francophonie as his own identity but nonetheless preferred it to the symbolic field conveyed by the veil, which in his opinion conjured up short-sightedness and social strictures. Several—but not all—respondents expressed similar hegemonic views about the veil, underscoring that hybridity is pervaded with processes of making Others. This selective incorporation of Arab and Western icons contributes to the hybridity of Maronite identity but at the same time is suspicious of alternative engagements with markers of Arab and Western identities. Far from reflecting a radical openness, then, hybridity follows politicized rules of inclusion and exclusion.

U.S. productions loomed large in the media habits of my respondents who noted the ideology of individual freedom, in their view especially visible in *The Cosby Show* and *Beverly Hills 90210*. The latter program was appealing to some of my mostly middle-class respondents, who were nonetheless cognizant of the show's characters' upper-class status. In addition, female viewers emphasized that they did not experience as much personal and sexual freedom as *90210* depicts. Also popular was *The Cosby Show*, broadcast by LBC during Sunday prime time until the early 1990s, whose fans told me they often watched it with their families. Marianne told me how she occasionally "exploited" *The Cosby Show* to extract more social freedom from her parents: she would discuss the relationship between the parents in *The Cosby Show* and their daughters, arguing that despite the Huxtables' social conservatism, they allowed their daughters to go out on dates because they trusted them. At age sixteen, she said, she was attracted to a young man with whom she wanted to attend a party. At the time, her parents did not let her stay out later than ten o'clock in the evening, which was a problem since the party was to start at nine o'clock on a Friday night. *The Cosby Show* episode broadcast the Sunday before the party provided Marianne with an effective negotiating tool. As she told me: "Denise [one of the Cosby daughters, played by actress Lisa Bonet] was not yet eighteen years old, and she wanted to go out with a young man to his prom party. Her parents were hesitant, but after a long discussion, they allowed her to go, as long as she promised to come back before one o'clock in the morning." After watching the show with her family, Marianne argued to her parents that her situation was very similar to Denise's, and as a result, she told me, she was allowed to attend the party. Marianne keenly believed that *The Cosby Show* helped ease parental restrictions.

In contrast to a generally favorable reception of *The Cosby Show*, viewers criticized "many" U.S. movies and television programs for gratuitous violence and "cheap, purely commercial, sexual scenes" (Elham, Maha), or for portraying "excessive promiscuity between teenagers" (Serge, Rima). However, Adib, a twenty-three-year-old dentistry student, argued that such scenes were "okay because, to an extent, they [reflected] real life," and others simply recognized that some movies—*Basic Instinct* was cited by a few—effectively used sexuality for dramatic and aesthetic values. There is a subtle variation between genders here, with males more eager to claim acceptance of sexual content, reflecting a society where gender roles remain traditional. When I probed my respondents about their own social and sexual life, they said they enjoyed less freedom than the American youth they saw on television but believed they endured fewer restrictions than other Arab youth, thus positioning themselves, again, between the "Western" and "Arab" counterpoints.

When asked about his interest in U.S. television, Antoun, one of the more conservative persons I encountered in my fieldwork, launched a diatribe against MTV's *Beavis and Butthead*. "In my opinion," he told me vehemently, "*Beavis and Butthead* is . . . mental pornography," more pernicious than real porn because it is a cartoon. He proceeded to explain: "If you understand the dialogue between Beavis and Butthead, [you will see that] it is worse than porno, in many ways. They are anti-social, they are against everything, they are against all values. They have that destructive impulse, they like to break everything, violate all existing norms and rules. They show contempt for values such as family and respect for teachers." Antoun offered his own interpretation of the antiteacher attitude glorified in *Beavis and Butthead*, speculating that it might have been influenced by Pink Floyd's *The Wall*. The British rock band Pink Floyd was popular among Lebanese youth in the 1980s and into the early 1990s, especially their hit double album *The Wall*. Antoun in effect used one Western text to interpret another. Even though he voiced harsh criticism of *Beavis and Butthead*, he asserted that Pink Floyd played some of the best music he had ever heard, and that the artistic talent of the band was undeniable. This comparison suggests a hierarchical scheme by which Antoun classified Western cultural texts and indicates that Maronite youth did not view Western culture as a monolith. Antoun argued that *Beavis and Butthead* is at odds with "Lebanese values," thus underscoring what he saw as lower moral standards in the West, but he immediately praised Western values of "knowledge and culture," which he then proceeded to claim as his own while avowing a difference with "self-isolated" Arabs, hence the hybrid identity between the categories of "West" and "Arabs." Dominated by television consumption, this process of hybrid identity construction entailed three aspects: propinquity toward consuming ostensibly hybrid texts, quotidian acts of mimicry, and cultural nomadism.

THE LURE OF HYBRID TEXTS

The view that everyday consumption of media and popular culture is a meaning-making activity has become conventional. Indeed, some field

interlocutors expressed a predilection for ostensibly hybrid literature—
betraying their socio-educational level and perhaps a desire to impress
me with their erudition—and then moved on to television and music.
Fouad said that he "love[d] and identified with border-crossing writ-
ers," living "between two or more worlds" and "perpetually looking
for an identity of their own," such as Yugoslav-born Milan Kundera and
Moroccan-born Tahar Ben Jalloun, novelists living and writing in France.
Maha, Adib, Peter, and others favored Lebanese-French author Amin
Maalouf, and to a lesser extent members of the anticolonial négritude formation discussed in Chapter Three. Other respondents admired Salman
Rushdie as a typical "in-between" writer, which in light of the *Satanic
Verses* controversy and the outrage among Muslims worldwide is an
ostensible act of self-differentiation from Muslims. But at the same time,
many Maronites criticized *Satanic Verses* for its offending content to
Muslims, thus assuming the ambivalence symptomatic of hybridity. On
yet another level, the claim to have read Rushdie's book—which I could
ascertain with only a handful of respondents—banned in Lebanon for
years after its publication, reflects cultural "poaching." In regard to television, comments about the lure of hybrid texts were more elaborate.

Since its inception, Lebanese television has relied on inexpensive
Egyptian, French, and U.S. dramatic productions, and the few locally
produced dramas were about rural life or historical events. Breaking
with that tradition, *The Storm Blows Twice*, a 1994 *Télé-Liban* series, was a
daring treatment of contemporary Lebanese society, depicting what one
viewer described as "that tearing apart between Western and Eastern
values" with characters, including women, struggling to balance competing priorities: family and career, conservative social norms and individual freedoms, and so on. The 178-episode series questioned religious
restrictions, broke social taboos, and explicitly tackled controversial issues such as premarital and extramarital sex and the professional and
private lives of divorced women. The series included bedroom scenes,
adulterous relationships, daring social statements, and edgy dialogue.
Unusually risqué in the Arab environment, the program aired during
prime time on Wednesdays and was remarkably popular with Maronite
viewers.

The Storm Blows Twice's stylistic choices enact social and cultural
hybridity, described by Serge as a "refreshing" portrayal of "a mixed
cultural reality." In one of our many conversations, for example,
Fouad described the characters' wardrobes as "a mixture of classical . . .
clothing with avant-garde fashion." The show's production style was

characterized by fluid camera movements, dynamic editing, high-quality acting, and overall sophisticated creative execution, giving it a "Western" veneer. Ironically, the series was stylistically similar to the Latin American telenovelas that some young Maronites denigrated, which suggests that content was more important than form. Indeed, other viewers praised the series' "realistic" and "sincere" depiction of Lebanese society more than its attractive production values. For example, Peter, the medical student with a proclivity for culinary metaphors, said that *The Storm Blows Twice* "carried a chunk of the problems of Lebanese society and its anxieties," and Hala, whose house I often visited, elaborated a gender-conscious reading: "It is the life of a woman who got divorced. You know, in Lebanon, *divorce is taboo*. A woman who divorces is regarded negatively. Anyway, she lived around twenty years with her husband, tolerating him.... She cooks for him and pampers him. But whenever he feels like it, he fools around with other women" (speaker's emphasis). Divorce is socially frowned upon and legally very difficult in Lebanon, because like marriage, birth, and death, divorce falls under the jurisdiction of religious authorities. Because marriage is outside the prerogatives of the state—the exclusive domain of the church or mosque—civil marriage is legally nonexistent. In the Maronite community, where conservative Catholic values dominate, divorce is virtually impossible, and even when couples with compelling reasons such as physical abuse or nonconsummation of the union are granted permission to separate, they sometimes remain legally wed. This system is so entrenched that even the then president of the Republic Elias Hrawi failed in 1998 to legalize civil marriage, as a result of a concerted opposition campaign spearheaded by Christian and Muslim clergymen. Male and female viewers alike admired *The Storm Blows Twice*'s strong female characters and criticized the womanizing of some male characters. Respondents supported the show's position that divorce should gain more acceptance without, however, becoming "too easy"—that is, as in the West—and praised the writer and director for their unconventional treatment of gender roles and relations. In that context, both male and female viewers mentioned that the show brought into focus the social challenges faced by Lebanese women who combine family and work.

In sync with my respondents' affective engagement with the locally produced *The Storm Blows Twice*, their musical preferences gravitated toward Lebanon's most celebrated family of musicians, composers, and singers, the Rahbanis: brothers Elias and Mansour; the key figure, Assi; his wife, Fairuz; and son, Ziad. The popularity of the songs and music of the Rahbanis, identified by respondents as "typically Lebanese," is a peculiar exception to the preponderance of television in Maronite media consumption. The Rahbanis enjoy a mythical status in Lebanese culture, carried by Fairuz's voice to the Arab world and Western concert halls such as Bercy in Paris and the Royal Festival Hall in London. The Rahbanis' composition blends Lebanese folk melodies with classical Arabic and modern Western music, and Fairuz sings mostly in colloquial Lebanese Arabic. Their music is seen as a mixture of Western and Eastern influences, which to the young people I spoke with signaled "typically Lebanese." *All* of them claimed to be unabashed fans of Fairuz.

Especially popular was Ziad Rahbani, Fairuz's and Assi's son, musician, composer, singer, actor, writer, director, satirist, and leftist social critic. During one of my interviews with Peter, he described Ziad's music as "pluralistic" but a "harmonious mélange" and described Ziad's so-called Oriental jazz as "the greatest music ever." Similarly, Elham described the music as "a unique mixture of . . . conflicting cultural legacies," and Fouad and Antoun agreed with Peter that Ziad's music was "influenced by so many musical currents, but . . . [was] different from all of them," unwittingly underscoring hybridity's dual centripetal and assimilationist thrusts. In Fouad's words: "You cannot [clearly] discern different structural musical elements in his music. You cannot say this part is jazz, this other Arabic. It is a unique and innovative blend. Just like his father was influenced by classical music but never let it dominate his music, Ziad is very subtle in mixing differences. Others have been trying to blend Western and Eastern music, but the result is artificial. It has no genius and no creativity."[5]

In contrast to Fouad's technical musical dissection, Elham expressed a more emotional connection to Ziad's songs:

> Ziad Rahbani makes great music. I love straddling two cultures [she said this sentence in French and her exact words were "à cheval entre deux cultures"]. He . . . mixed jazz with Eastern music. He mixed blues guitar scales with the *taqassim* [Arabic scales] of the *oud* [a traditional Arab instrument]. He mixed Charlie Parker with Sayyed Darwish . . . . He rendered "Round Midnight" with the *oud* and the *qanoun* [another Arab stringed instrument]. The result is unique, special. *It is not Western, but not Arab either. It is more Lebanese than anything else. It is in between. It is more Lebanese than the cedar.* (emphasis mine)

Beyond their artistic accomplishments, the emphatically reiterated assertion that Fairuz and Ziad were "typically Lebanese" due to culturally "mixing" and "blending" underscored the gravitational pull of hybrid texts on this audience. The juxtaposition with the cedar is unequivocal: since the cedar (*cedrus libani*) is the quintessential symbol of Lebanon, the comparison posited Ziad (in addition to Fairuz) as a paramount cultural text that elicited unconditional identification from *all* my respondents. In Fouad's exalted words: "Fairuz and the Rahbanis sing us! They sing Lebanon at its best. They sing Lebanon the mixture, Lebanon the mélange, Lebanon East and West and neither of them, Lebanon Christian and Muslim and both of them, Lebanon the in-between." Western popular culture served tactical purposes such as using *The Cosby Show* to be able to attend a party or invoking Pink Floyd and *Beavis and Butthead* to criticize Western values. In contrast, the music of the Rahbanis was of a more enduring value, as it encapsulated what respondents claimed was the truest expression of their hybrid identity. This selective engagement with local and foreign popular culture carries implications for how cross-cultural media consumption is conceptualized, to be discussed shortly.

THE ENACTMENT OF HYBRIDITY THROUGH MIMICRY

In the early stages of this project, it occurred to me that Maronite youth mimicked snapshots of Western lifestyles, an impression validated by subsequent observation and in-depth interviews in which several unsolicited remarks about the issue clearly implicated the mass media. For example, Antoun claimed that "the social life of the Maronites has a very non-Lebanese face. They like to live the European way, or the American way. Maybe because of all these programs on television, maybe because they travel a lot. . . . They brought different lifestyles with them or got them from television." When I pressed him for an example, Antoun invoked the "torn jeans fashion," which he imputed to the influence of Music Television (MTV).[6] Peter brought up the same example when he spoke of a "tremendous phenomenon of imitation of everything Western, particularly from the United States," and said that fads took "phenomenal proportions" among Maronite youth, who "snatched up [the fads] rapidly, as if . . . waiting for something new to swallow in order *to fill an unbearable void*" (emphasis mine). Invoking this "urge to imitate," Serge confirmed what I had repeatedly observed when he told me how English phrases from *Beverly Hills 90210* became "leitmotifs, repeated over and over again: the word 'man' [as a greeting device], for instance. Also 'Hi, guys,' 'I've had it,' and others." Serge concluded that *90210* had become a cult series in Lebanon because "young people really 'identified' with that bright picture of happy shiny boys and girls."

The pervasiveness of social mimicry notwithstanding, respondents candidly said that imitation occurred mostly at the superficial level of appearances rather than in mentalities and actions. Said Peter: "They see *Beverly Hills 90210*, they start imitating it. Although the lifestyle of the people in the program is different. I don't know if at A.U.B. [the American University of Beirut] it is like that, but at the Lebanese University where I study we have different relationships with our professors than in *90210*."

Antoun went further, criticizing young Maronites who "pretend to be what they are not. They only pretend. They look Western and everything, but they have the same old archaic mentality. They just dress like that *to provoke*... and imitate, rather than *live their freedom*. Just to provoke and imitate;... we are fake" (my emphasis). In other words, this is a phenomenon of simulation. "[T]o dissimulate," wrote Baudrillard (1983), "is to feign not to have what one has," while "to simulate is to feign to have what one has not" (p. 5). According to Baudrillard, simulation means concealment of the nonexistence of something; in other words, it is the display of a simulacrum, a copy with no original. Young Maronites' adoption of simulative tactics reflects a lack in their cultural identity wherein simulated action masks the absence of a clearly defined, organic identity. Thus, mimicking Western popular culture serves to symbolically fill a void. Elham explained, first in Arabic: "We have a fragmented identity lost between two or three languages, between different worldviews. This leads to a crisis. An identity crisis." She carried on in French, using the same metaphor she used when talking about Fairuz: "Nous sommes à cheval entre deux cultures [We straddle two cultures]." Then she proceeded in Arabic: "We do not really have an identity; the stronger your feeling of not having an identity, the more you want to *pretend* to have one" (emphasis mine).

Hybridizing acts of mimicry and simulation were thus key to Maronite youth identities. Simulation, because "it is simulacrum and it undergoes a metamorphosis into signs and is invented on the basis of signs" (Baudrillard, 1987b, p. 59), serves to hide that a void exists and to project the impression that the emptiness does not exist. As such, simulation helps young Maronites navigate a cultural realm that irrevocably slipped into hybridity. According to Baudrillard (1987a), resorting to simulation is a manifestation of deterritorialization, which is "no longer an exile at all...[but rather] a deprivation of meaning and territory" (p. 50). Nomadic everyday life tactics underscore that lack of meaning and territory.

CULTURAL CHAMELEONS: HYBRIDITY'S NOMADIC EXPRESSIONS

Various competing identities living cheek-by-jowl in Lebanon compel young Maronites to resort to expressions of identity that can be called no-madic, since they move between and adapt to different sociocultural set-tings. In formulating her "politics of nomadic identity," political philoso-pher Chantal Mouffe (1994) contends that identity is relational, which in the case of the Maronites is expressed in the "Arab" and "Western" dialogical counterpoints. For example, Peter expressed his reluctance to identify himself as an Arab when he is among Westerners because of his weariness of being associated with Western stereotypes of Arabs and Muslims. Antoun elaborated this context-bound nomadism: "Some-times, yes. I am an Arab, but only sometimes. It depends. If a Christian asks me 'Are you Arab?' I will say yes. If a Muslim asks me the same question, my answer will be no. Why? Because if you are a Christian in an Arab country, you lose your rights and freedom.... You are a second-class citizen. I am against that." This sweeping statement underscores the insecurity felt by a member of a minority whose nomadic behavior is both empowering and defensive. In that sense Maronites are cultural chameleons.

Etymologically, the term "nomad" stems from the Greek *nomos*, meaning "an occupied space without limits," and the Greek *nemo*, which means "to pasture" (Laroche, 1947, cited in Deleuze, 1994, p. 309). Thus, a nomad is someone who lives in an open space, without restrictions. Furthermore, "pasture" connotes a temporary sojourn in a particular location, which the nomad leaves after having used what that place had to offer. The term "nomad" does not necessarily imply physical move-ment from one place to another. In *Nomadology: The War Machine* (1986), French philosophers Gilles Deleuze and Félix Guattari explicate differ-ences between nomads and migrants: "The nomad is not at all the same as the migrant; for the migrant goes principally from one point to an-other, even if the second point is uncertain, unforeseen and not very well localized. But the nomad only goes from point to point as a conse-quence and as a factual necessity: in principle, points for him are relays along a trajectory" (p. 50). Conflating Maronite and Lebanese identities,

Fouad suggested that nomadic expressions of identity reflected the fact that the Lebanese "*roam . . . in search of several identities . . .* [because] there is no clear Lebanese identity" (emphasis mine). He then lamented the fluidity of Lebanese identity: "It is impossible to paint a portrait and point to it and say, 'This is the Lebanese.' It is the *Lebbedeh* [traditional headdress] and the *Sherwal* [traditional pants] now, the jeans and the T-shirt some other time, and [smiling facetiously] maybe the [Indian] sari at some other occasion. The Lebanese cannot find himself in what is around him. This mixture of all sorts of very different things is really pushed to the extreme among the Lebanese." Fouad thus argued that circuitous practices of self-definition resulted from the absence of a holistic identity and reflected the peripatetic trajectory of synthetic cultural identities, a distinction—between holistic and synthetic—I expatiate on in Chapter Seven.

BEYOND CULTURAL PROXIMITY? TEXTS, AUDIENCES, INSTITUTIONS

After the exposé on the structure of Lebanese media and the analysis of Maronite media consumption, it is now useful to ask: What connections exist between Maronite youth identities and the systemic aspects of the Lebanese media? Does the resonance between hybrid domestic television programs and popular music—described as "typically Lebanese"—on one hand, and an existential experience of cultural hybridity on the other hand, constitute an example of what Straubhaar (1991) and others have called "cultural proximity"? Or is there something more to be read in the fact that the two most popular texts among young Maronites are not compatible, as will be explicated next, with the ideological orientation usually ascribed to the Maronite community?

What appears to be a lack of compatibility between audiences and texts is noteworthy in the case of the Rahbanis. While my respondents lumped the Rahbanis as one cultural text, Ziad Rahbani's vision of Lebanon is markedly different from his parents'. The musicals created and executed by Assi and Fairuz were lavish folkloric celebrations of the history and culture of a Lebanon basking in glory that became central events at the International Baalbeck Festival in the 1950s and 1960s, putting Lebanon on the global cultural map. In sharp contrast to this patriotic romanticism, Ziad's plays and songs in the 1970s and 1980s, in which he often parodies his parents' creations, convey a mixture of disappointment and cynicism, rendered in the biting sarcasm that is Ziad's trademark. In the elder Rahbanis' productions, the Arabic spoken is a Lebanese lingua franca that reflects Lebanon's pride as a unified, sovereign, and beautiful nation. Ziad's plays and songs, however, are heteroglossic reflections of Lebanon's fractured ethnic and class landscape, as enacted by the different accents of his actors: a working-class *Bastawi* accent mixes with a middle-class spoken Lebanese peppered with French, in addition to broken, gender-confused Arabic spoken by Armenian characters. While his parents were not politically active beyond composing and singing both for Lebanon and, in a more limited fashion, the Palestinian cause, Ziad Rahbani, himself a Maronite, is a known leftist activist who lived in predominantly Muslim West Beirut during the war.

Ziad's take on Lebanon's descent into chaos is expressed in his song *"Oum Fout Naam"* (Get Up and Go to Sleep), in which he asks a putative Lebanese interlocutor to dream that Lebanon has become a country. The song's disappointment at the fragmentation of Lebanese polity has a powerful resonance, albeit ironic, with Lebanese youth. Ziad fully exploits the polysemy of the Arabic language, in which words for the mathematical operations addition, subtraction, and division also mean, respectively, unity, posing (or propounding, an idea or a problem), and (sociopolitical) division, to express the breaking apart of Lebanese society. Ziad's bitterness about the war is also clear when he sings about a youngster who shuts down a neighborhood, a reference to the (sometimes juvenile) armed thugs, domestic and foreign, who terrorized the Lebanese population during the war.

In contrast, Fairuz has declared an undying love for her homeland in the song *Bhebbak Ya Loubnan* (I love you, O Lebanon). Where Ziad sees evidence of irredeemable fragmentation, Fairuz sees wartime destruction as an opportunity for rebirth. That young Maronites perceived both Ziad and Fairuz as embodying Lebanon's character reflects ambivalence about its identity. On one hand, there is the romantic view of Lebanon, replete with epithets such as "green," "beautiful," "proud," sung indefatigably by Fairuz, which is counterbalanced on the other hand with a harsher but more realistic acknowledgment of Lebanon's predicament, rendered in Ziad's acerbic but, at bottom, melancholy songs. There is an uncanny parallelism between the two repertoires and the metaphors used for Lebanon, from "Paris of the Orient" and "Switzerland of the East" in its glory days to "Precarious Republic" and "Improbable Nation" during conflict.[7]

As with the Rahbani musical oeuvre, viewer interpretation of the television drama *The Storm Blows Twice* is trapped in a paradox. On one hand, the series elaborates a secular, conspicuously progressive ideology, but on the other hand it is popular with members of a community often labeled socially conservative and politically Christian. What does this contradiction suggest about the dynamics between audiences and media content in a pluralistic, multiconfessional country like Lebanon? *The Storm Blows Twice* was produced by Télé-Liban at a time when the hybrid state-private station was attempting to become a public television in the European, mostly French tradition. Under the leadership of then director Fouad Naim, Télé-Liban initiated an ambitious plan to become a public, national television, headlined by the slogan "The Nation's Imagination." As a dramatic series that addresses social issues between and beyond Lebanon's confessional dynamics, *The Storm Blows Twice* can be read as one of the main components of that agenda and is in some ways reminiscent of the 1960s and early 1970s, when Télé-Liban productions like *Ad-Dunia Hayk* and *Abou Melhem* explored Lebanon's identity as a small, pluralistic, fragile democracy.

As carriers of different worldviews that articulate a hybrid positionality, Ziad Rahbani's work and *The Storm Blows Twice* take a predominant cultural position in the Lebanese mediascape. On the surface, they appear to be textbook examples of "local" productions whose cultural "proximity" makes them popular with Lebanese audiences. However, the local—identified as "typically Lebanese"—character of these texts is ontologically dubious. In global media research, the "local" often connotes cultural authenticity, the expression of local identity in its historical and cultural dimensions. This notion of the local as unadulterated is fundamental to the concept of cultural proximity, whose premise is that audiences tend to prefer local productions because they are proximate to their life experiences. The idea of cultural proximity can be traced back to the U.S. Foreign Service Institute in the 1940s, where anthropologist and cross-cultural trainer Edward T. Hall emphasized proxemics, or use of personal space, as an important dimension of cross-cultural communication (Leeds-Hurwitz, 1990). For Hall, culture consisted of stable, observable, and therefore predictable patterns of behavior. This use of proximity risks reducing culture to the idea of tradition, understood as a set of practices performed in a locale with relatively clear spatial demarcations and embodied in a local identity assumed to be unaffected or barely affected by historical change.

A closer reading, however, suggests that rather than being "local"—in other words, being typed with a distinct and particularistic cultural belonging—*The Storm Blows Twice* and Rahbani songs in fact carry inherent contradictions. The hybridity that stems from the fusion of different cultural forms suggests that proximity need not necessarily be understood in terms of being spatially near a relatively distinct cultural sphere. Rather, it may be useful to complement the idea of cultural proximity with the notion of social relevance in reference to an existential experience—in this case the Maronites'—that lacks a clearly defined identity because of cultural polyvalence. I use the adjective "social" deliberately to establish a distinction from cultural studies scholar John Fiske's (1988) definition of relevance as when "[t]he viewer makes meanings and pleasures from television that are relevant to his or her social allegiances at the moment of viewing" (p. 247). In Fiske's view, relevance occurs in a "moment of semiosis," which comes to be "when social allegiances and discursive practices are personified and held in *relative stability on a point of relevance*" (p. 247, emphasis mine). In contrast, the notion of social relevance that I am proposing shifts emphasis from the atomistic links between media texts and personal identities to the communal aspects of media consumption in its socio-politico-economic context. Whereas "cultural proximity" assumes a synchronic predictability of cultural patterns, "social relevance" in my opinion reflects a diachronic and therefore more dynamic understanding of collective identities.

Like Ziad Rahbani's music and plays, *The Storm Blows Twice* can be read as carrying a message that attempts to transcend confessional sensibilities. However, this is not an ideology-free national/ist discourse, but rather a recasting of Syrian Nationalist ideology, which advocates the unification of Lebanon, Syria, parts of historic Palestine, and other Arab countries into Greater Syria, geographically extending "from the Taurus river to the North to the Suez Canal in the South, and from the Mediterranean to the Syrian desert" (Zamir, 2000, p. 234). In fact, the series' writer, Choukry Anis Fakhoury, comes from a prominent Lebanese family of writers and journalists known for their Syrian Nationalist political beliefs.[8] This is one of the reasons why *The Storm Blows Twice* was criticized in some Maronite circles for carrying a pro–Syrian Nationalist political message. In this context, the concept of "storm" is highly symbolic, since the National Syrian Party's symbol is the *zawbaa* (which in Arabic means "whirlwind"), a jagged, thunderbolt-like star that connotes revolutionary political action. Other signs can be read in that direction, such as a party leader referred to as the *zaim*, or chief, the nickname given by his followers to Antoun Saadeh, the founder and chief ideologue of Syrian nationalism.

The admiration for *The Storm Blows Twice* expressed by young Maronites, whose mainstream political leaders have historically advocated a Lebanese nationalism antagonistic to Syrian Nationalist ideology, raises important questions about the relationship between, on one hand, audience interpretations and, on the other hand, the political economy of Lebanese television. As discussed earlier in this chapter, broadcasting licenses were awarded according to Lebanon's consociational political system. The philosophy that underscores this allocation of media holds that each station will cater to its community, so LBC would have a Christian, predominantly Maronite audience, Future TV a Sunnite following, and NBN Shiite viewers. While I do not purport to generalize from a study of admittedly limited scope, this chapter nonetheless suggests that the Lebanese state's approach to media policy may not correspond to Lebanese audience realities—hence this study's broader implications for media policy in confessionally diverse societies.

The persistence of the confessional formula in the Lebanese polity is a formidable challenge to the establishment of a national public television station, as Télé-Liban's demise poignantly demonstrates. The carving up of the audience on confessional lines by the political elite who negotiated and passed the 1994 Audio-Visual Media Law ensures the continuing networks of political patronage that constitute the power base of Lebanon's political leaders (see Khalaf, 1987). More importantly, it virtually guarantees that television will not contribute, as it should, to a national public discourse whose existence is essential for Lebanon to move into sustainable civil peace. Now that militia rule has been replaced by Pax Syriana—a Lebanese security state under Syrian control—the Lebanese media and political landscape, once pluralistic, is turning monochromatic. The state apparatus exercises a large degree of control over media institutions through indirect and, increasingly, direct pressure. In 2004, a growing—and imposed—homogenization of political discourse is palpable in television newscasts and talk shows.

In the current situation, privately owned television stations are unable to contribute to building and strengthening a sense of national citizenship that over time could mitigate the political influence of confessional identities. However, the experience of a segment of Maronite youth with *The Storm Blows Twice* intimates that the right programs will lead audience segments to "move" out of their traditionally predictable confessional lines. The popularity of a text with a decidedly secular message does not constitute a decisive crossing of confessional boundaries; nonetheless, it is ripe with potential, especially if it indicates, as I think it does, that the Maronite community itself is not monolithic but rather is diverse across generational and ideological lines.

Historical precedents of programming strategies that aim to cross the Lebanese confessional divide do exist. Since the 1980s, Maronite-owned LBC has scheduled special programming during the Muslim holy month of Ramadan, such as Egyptian *Fawazir Ramadan*, or Ramadan quiz shows, and Arabic dramas, in order to attract Muslim audiences. A more intriguing example of "crossover" programming is the serial drama on the Virgin Mary, an Iranian production, which Al-Manar, Hizbullah's station, aired during Ramadan in 2002. Driving on Lebanon's coastal highway during Ramadan in November 2002, I was struck by the numerous billboards that promoted this series in predominantly Christian East Beirut and elsewhere.[9]

Media Reception and Hybridity

In this chapter I presented an empirical case study of the lived experience of hybridity in order to understand the role of mediated communication in the constitution and maintenance of hybridity as an existential condition. Three concluding insights are in order.

First, the finding that young Maronites gravitate toward cultural texts that do not cater to traditional Maronite ideology demonstrates that media reception can, in some cases, "subvert" the politico-economic context in which it occurs. Even as the structure of Lebanon's media serves the interests of the elites by consolidating their power over their communities, the data suggest that when presented with well-crafted programs, viewers will gravitate toward cultural productions that oppose the dominant particularistic ideology of their confessional group. As British media political economist Graham Murdock aptly wrote: "although arenas circumscribe options for action, they do not dictate them. There is always a repertoire of choices" (1995, p. 92). A propensity to cross confessional lines, however, will remain fragile in a system whose raison d'être has been hijacked by a deeply rooted political confessionalism. Notably, as I elaborate on in Chapter Seven, structural changes must take place in the Lebanese media system if television is to contribute to the growth of interconfessional dialogue beyond narrow commercial considerations dictated by the small size of the Lebanese audience.[10] Nonetheless, the existence of audience "confessional crossover" indicates that communication practices that constitute hybridity do not always reproduce politico-economic power arrangements.

[Second, this chapter provided empirical data that shows that young Maronites drew on a variety of texts, many outside their ascribed cultural space, to articulate their hybrid identities, but that the communicative constitution of hybridity, even as it subverts the broader sociopolitical context, is subject to forces of exclusion and inclusion that sometimes reflect confessional politics.] In drawing on several sources, respondents related to selected media texts, and their interpretations of these texts drew boundaries of identity and otherness. For instance, Egyptian soap operas and Latin American telenovelas were dismissed for poor production qualities but also for perceived cultural irrelevance. Moreover, comments about the Muslim veil by at least one respondent reinscribe a hegemonic Western reading of this Muslim practice. While strong "media effects" were not found, this case study nonetheless suggests that the contrapuntal interpretation of media texts to articulate hybrid identities is haunted by a hegemonic echo.[11]

Third, hybridity must be understood in its historical depth. In the context of cultural consumption, elements are selectively unearthed from the remembered past and integrated in an unstable present to make better sense of that present. Young interlocutors framed their personal narratives about identity in a historical context where they acknowledged multiple historical trajectories and cultural realities. They invoked different histories and appropriated myriad cultural bits and pieces to make sense of their present-day identity, a phenomenon that, as already discussed, casts doubt on the validity of a broadly defined notion of cultural proximity. Conversely, the present is also projected onto the past, insofar as the experience of a hybrid identity makes it imperative to construct a past that justifies the current state of affairs. In effect, communicative practices such as media consumption activate a process where the past and the present are used to mutually make sense of each other, highlighting the point I made, pace Makdissi (2000), early in this chapter that confessional identities are contingent and best understood as historically constructed relations, not as ahistorical, primordial essences. The historical haggle over Maronite origins was of marginal interest to a Maronite youth concerned more with grappling with its current-day hybridity than with teleological, mythical, and ultimately irrelevant origins. Hybrid identity is in effect, as illustrated by the protagonist of *East, West* (Rushdie, 1994) in this chapter's epigraph, a refusal, or perhaps an inability, to make definitive identity choices. As the past is rearticulated in the present and the present is projected onto the past in an affective economy animated by media texts, it is clear that hybridity is not a negation of identity; rather, it is its quotidian, vicarious, and inevitable condition.

7   Hybridity without Guarantees
Toward Critical Transculturalism

Cultural experience or indeed every cultural form is radically, quintessentially hybrid, and if it has been the practice in the West since Immanuel Kant to isolate cultural and aesthetic realms from the worldly domain, it is now time to rejoin them.

—Edward Said, *Culture and Imperialism*

THE CLAIM that hybridity is symptomatic of resistance to globalization is troublesome, and the less forceful assertion that cultural mixture reflects the lightness of globalization's hand is misguided. Hybridity as a characteristic of culture is compatible with globalization because it helps globalization rule, as Stuart Hall once put it, through a variety of local capitals. Hybridity entails that traces of other cultures exist in every culture, thus offering foreign media and marketers transcultural wedges for forging affective links between their commodities and local communities. As a discourse of intercultural relations, hybridity conjures up an active exchange that leads to the mutual transformation of both sides. Mainstream public discourse frames this exchange as benign and beneficial. The sheer repetition of the word "hybridity" in hundreds of media outlets and dozens of academic disciplines gives hybridity an aura of legitimacy and hides its inherent contradictions as it mystifies globalization's material effects. Hybridity, then, is not just amenable to globalization. It is the cultural logic of globalization.

As the cultural logic of globalization, hybridity is not posthegemonic. By now this book has substantiated the claim that hybridity does not implicate the relenting of inequality. Whether in Lebanese television reception, in Mexican television production, or in U.S. journalistic discourse, unequal intercultural relations shape most aspects of cultural mixture. In many instances there are causal links between politico-economic power and cultural hybridity. This, however, does not mean that hybridity is tantamount to an effect of dominance. The processes and outcomes of hybridity are too convoluted to be explained by an always already

148

direct politico-economic causality. Consequently, in order to understand the complex and active links between hybridity and power, we need to move beyond commonplace models of domination and resistance. Critical transculturalism is designed to help us accomplish this task in international communication.

A reiteration of this book's cardinal argument is in order before we put forward the framework of critical transculturalism. The congregation of postcultural imperialism approaches to international communication and culture, which first emerged under the banner of audience activity and can now be identified by the cultural pluralism or cultural globalization rubrics, have been either unwilling or unable to focus at once on the *discursive and textual* aspects of international communication while at the same time emphasizing *material structure*. The move from the monoculture of imperialism approaches to the multiculture of pluralism perspectives will remain incomplete until it considers structure and meaning in tandem in the current global transculture. The corporate view of this transculture elaborated in Chapter Four should be replaced with a critical and humanistic vision. It is with that objective in mind that I now propose critical transculturalism.

[Critical transculturalism is a framework that focuses on power in intercultural relations by integrating both agency and structure in international communication analysis.]The following is critical transculturalism in a nutshell, visually captured in Table 1. Critical transculturalism takes a synthetic view of culture, unlike cultural imperialism's holistic premise and cultural pluralism's view of culture as a merely pluralistic entity. Whereas in cultural imperialism agency is located in the global structure of capitalism, and in cultural pluralism agency is found in local individuals or communities studied contextually, critical transculturalism considers that social practice, acting translocally and intercontextually, is the site of agency. In terms of the relation between structure and agency, cultural imperialism sees it as a dialectical determination of the latter by the former, and cultural pluralism as a dialogical interaction between the two, whereas critical transculturalism conceives it as a lopsided articulation in which the dialogical aspects of communication must be analyzed concurrently with its dialectical dimensions. Finally, whereas cultural imperialism focuses on the production and distribution stages of the media communication process, and cultural pluralism emphasizes message/text and reception, critical transculturalism takes a more integrative approach that considers the active links between production, text, and reception in the moment of cultural

Table 1   Critical Transculturalism in Comparative Perspective

	Cultural Imperialism	Cultural Pluralism	Critical Transculturalism
Conception of Culture	Holistic	Pluralistic	Synthetic
Conception of global culture	Monoculture	Multiculture	Transculture
Central trope	Dominance	Resistance and/or adaptation	Hybridity
Site of agency	Structure	Individuals and/or community	Social practice
Scope of agency	Global	Local and contextual	Translocal and intercontextual
Empirical focus	Material/ Institutional	Discursive and/or textual	Material and discursive and textual
Relation between structure and agency (process)	Dialectical	Dialogical	Dialectical and dialogical
Relation between structure and agency (outcome)	Determination	Interaction and intertextuality	Articulation (lopsided)
Media focus	Production and distribution	Reception and text/message	Production, text, and reception reproduction
Relation of state to external forces	Too weak	Too strong	Mediator/ Referee

reproduction. In the following pages I emphasize the differences between cultural imperialism, cultural pluralism, and critical transculturalism.[1]

In contrast to multiculturalism's reference to the coexistence of plural cultures (or cocultures), transculturalism characterizes a mixture of several cultures. The former establishes boundaries of recognition and institutionalization between cultures; the latter underscores the fluidity of these boundaries. When the Chicago Cultural Studies Group (1992) coined the term "corporate multiculturalism," it was referring to the "great danger [that] lies in thinking that [U.S.] multiculturalism could be exported multiculturally" (p. 550). Along the same lines, Chapter

Four explored the rhetorical claims of a corporate transculturalism elaborated in (mostly) U.S. public discourse, including its advocacy of free trade, individual consumerism, and reduction of culture to economic variables. No wonder, then, that the discourses of globalization and corporate transculturalism are so compatible. "[S]o convinced are people that global capitalism is relentlessly opposed to local cultures and diverse identities," Zachary (2000) writes, "that they fail to realize that among the most vigorous proponents of mongrelization are the world's biggest, richest, most profit-hungry corporations" (xx). Indeed! The shift in public discourse from multiculturalism to transculturalism, from the recognition of cultural difference to the celebration of cultural fusion, is at its core economic.

Critical transculturalism reclaims the notion of hybridity from doctrinaire free marketeers. It redefines cultural fusion as a social issue with human implications, from its earlier definition as an economic matter with commercial implications. People's identities may be refracted through individual consumption, cultural and otherwise, but consumption alone is not tantamount to being. Hybridity theory, and cultural theory at large, cannot consider people merely as individuals who constantly recreate themselves by way of consumption. Rather, agency must be grasped in terms of people's ability to accomplish things in the world they inhabit. If culture represents the meanings, ways of action, and ways to evaluate the value of actions in a society, and if cultural hybridity entails a change in those meanings and actions, then attention ought to be paid to hybridity's ability or inability to empower social groups to have influence over the course of their lives. Ultimately, then, the value of a theory of hybridity resides in the extent to which it emphasizes human agency.

Critical transculturalism emphasizes the relation between hybridity and agency. The former is its conceptual core and the latter its central concern. This framework focuses on the links that communication processes create between power and meaning in the context of cultural transformation, and with the material and discursive consequences of these links. Whereas structure is the site of agency in the cultural imperialism thesis, and agency is located in the individual/community for the cultural pluralism perspective, in critical transculturalism agency is sited in social practices. By "practices" I mean, following Stuart Hall, "how a structure is actively *reproduced*" (1985, p. 103, my emphasis). Understood as practices, communication processes harnessed to express different kinds of hybridity serve to reproduce social, political, and

economic structures. When hybridity is posited as a naturally occurring and globally desirable condition in public discourse, it reproduces
the prevailing global order. Even the hybridity articulated by Maronite
youth who themselves see it as an empowering identity can be perceived to be hegemonic by other Lebanese confessions. This brings us
to the issues of volition and intention: whether hybridity is self-asserted
or ascribed will determine to a large degree its relation to agency.

In this regard, Bakhtin's distinction between intentional and organic
hybridity in language can be usefully applied to culture. Intentional
hybridity, characteristic of, for example, the novel, is the result of an
artistic intention and stylistic organization. It is therefore "a *semantic*
hybrid ... not ... in the abstract ... but rather a *semantics that is concrete
and social*" (Bakhtin, 1981, p. 360, emphasis in original). In contrast, organic hybridity is "unintentional, unconscious hybridization" (p. 358)
that occurs and changes historically when several languages—and, for
our purposes, cultures—enter into contact: "The image of a language
conceived as an intentional hybrid is first of all a conscious hybrid (as
distinct from a historical, organic, obscure language hybrid); an intentional hybrid is precisely the perception of one language by another language, its illumination by another linguistic consciousness. An image
of language may be structured only from the point of view of another
language, which is taken as the norm" (p. 359). Intentional hybridity
is therefore primarily a communicative phenomenon. Its intentional-
ity increases the possibility that it will become a process of othering,
where identities are projected by powerful social agents onto others
who are less powerful. The necessity of translation, of rendering meaning cross-culturally, raises the issue of who controls the means of translation. Communication is central in the formation of hybridities because
it strengthens the agency of those with the means to translate and name
the world, while weakening the agency of other participants. In other
words, whether hybridity is self-described or ascribed by others is primarily a communicative process. The means and ability to communicate
are therefore an important determinant of agency in intercultural relations that form the crucible of hybridity.

Based on the central relation between hybridity and agency, critical transculturalism has three foundational pillars: a conception of
culture as synthetic, an emphasis on the translocal and intercontextual links between hybridity and agency, and a commitment to an
epistemology with multiple methodologies—discursive, textual, and
empirical.

Critical transculturalism advocates doing away with the view that cultures are stable and autonomous units, because the holistic view of culture is an obstacle to a critical approach to international communication. Though notable scholars have advanced a nonholistic view of culture (Appadurai, 1996; Bakhtin, 1981; Benhabib, 2002; Hannerz, 1992; Marcus, 1998), social analysis and conventional wisdom still reinscribe what Benhabib called the "reductionist sociology of culture" (2002, p. 4). This approach presupposes that (1) cultures are homogenous units, (2) culture is congruent with nationality or an ethnic group within a nationality, and (3) cultures are for the most part separate from each other and interactions between them are epiphenomenal. While studies conducted from the cultural imperialism perspective adhered to these premises to varying degrees and focused on intercultural power differences, research done under the cultural pluralism/globalization umbrella rejected the holistic view of culture but for the most part neglected power. Indeed, cultural holism explains what I believe to be the fatal flaw of "cultural imperialism," namely the equivalence between politico-economic dominance and cultural homogeneity (Kraidy, 2004). This assumption has been challenged, if only indirectly, for example, in postcolonial criticism and even—as discussed in Chapter Two—within the critical political economy tradition itself. However, the tendency to equate homogeneity with dominance, rooted as it is in the conflation of culture with its political economy, has empowered opponents of critical approaches to international communication to associate hybridity with pluralism and resistance. To reclaim power as a major and legitimate focus of research, it is important to view cultures as synthetic entities whose hybrid components are shaped by structural and discursive forces. Critical transculturalism differs from both cultural imperialism and cultural pluralism in that it rejects what anthropologist George Marcus called the "fiction of the whole" (1998, p. 33) but at the same time emphasizes that intercultural relations are unequal. In order to understand the intricate entanglement of structural and discursive elements in relations between cultures, we shall revisit our conception of the local.

SHIFTING GEERTZ: THE LOCAL IS NOT WHAT IT USED TO BE

When Clifford Geertz (1983) wrote that "the shapes of knowledge are always ineluctably local, indivisible from their instruments and their encasements" (p. 4), he was explicitly stating an implicit tradition in anthropology to treat the local as an autonomous site, sometimes recognizing but rarely dissecting the local's enmeshment in supralocal networks. In the two decades since Geertz's pronouncement, social scientists have focused on "the local" as a conceptual issue (see, for example, D. Miller, 1995; Mirsepassi, Basu, and Weaver, 2003; Rosenau, 2003), especially as the opposite of "the global" in globalization theory. In international communication, where the local/global dichotomy has become pervasive, the local is treated as the site of meaning construction, power struggles, and social action, ranging from an individualistic emphasis on "resistance" to a focus on social aspects of communication, for example, in research on alternative media.[2]

Rather than consider the local and the global as opposites, it may be more helpful to think of them as mutually constitutive, a perspective advanced in terms of "glocalization" (Kraidy, 2003b; Robertson, 1994), "interpenetrated globalization" (Braman, 1996), or "distant proximities" (Rosenau, 2003). However, it is Appadurai's claim that local knowledge is "not only local in itself but, even more important, for itself" (1996, p. 181) that enables a productive contrast to the Geertzian view on the local. The local knowledge envisioned by Geertz was, as his definition quoted earlier demonstrates, "local in itself." In other words, its locality was primarily empirical. Local knowledge "for itself" à la Appadurai, however, foregrounds the political nature and uses of local knowledge. (Chapter Three offers historical examples of how local knowledge of cultural and racial mixtures was local for itself.) Locality, then, is not naturally formed, waiting for the anthropologist to interpret it. Rather, locality is shaped by myriad forces, including the people who inhabit it and the anthropologist or media scholar who studies it.

This is not a radical constructivist proposition. The local is primarily although not exclusively a physical reality in nature and matter. The insight that local knowledge is also "for itself" fills a major gap in the Geertzian "culture-as-text" legacy, namely its relative neglect of material power. In this regard, it is important to stress that the exercise of power in the realm of the local is not the exclusive prerogative of the global. The local itself is often the scene of power struggles between local actors, who are themselves embedded in larger external networks. In other words, the local is at once a site of empowerment and marginalization. This point is overshadowed by the recurrence of romantic views of the local, alternately defined as "a residual category overtaken by development . . . [or] a haven of resistance against globalization" (Haugerud, 2003, p. 61). This view elides the fact that the local itself is pervaded with power and inequality, a fact with troublesome implications for those studies in communication and cultural studies that glorify local cultural hybridity as resistance.

Critical transculturalism, then, considers that (1) the local is intricately involved in supralocal relations and that (2) exogenous and endogenous circuits of power pervade the local. For these two reasons, I prefer to conceive of locality in terms of translocality (Kraidy and Murphy, 2003). A translocal approach focuses on connections between several local social spaces, exploring hitherto neglected local-to-local links. A translocal approach reformulates Galtung's "wheel model" (1971) of cultural imperialism, where the hub and rim are metaphors for, respectively, the center and periphery, by shifting the focus of research on connections between several points on the rim of the wheel, without predetermining that such connections must necessarily spring from the hub and through the spokes. This suggests an alternative approach to hybridity than, for example, the one spun in the *Washington Post* articles analyzed in Chapter Four, where various countries' hybridity is a function of their relation with U.S. popular culture, positing the United States at the center of cultural exchanges and all other cultures in various peripheral positions.[3] In contrast to this hub-through-spokes-to-rim model, a translocal perspective calls for an analysis of how these different nations' hybrid cultures are shaped by their mutual interaction, in addition to their links with the West. While there is a risk of overemphasizing these local-to-local connections, lapsing into another romanticization of the local that would obscure supralocal power plays, a translocal perspective, at least analytically, allows us to remove the West from the center of intercultural relations. International communication research would benefit greatly from more emphasis on local-to-local, "East-to-East," or "South-to-South" interactions and exchanges. The objective of this decentering is not to deflect attention from Western power, but to pave the way for the construction of alternative perspectives on hybridity and locality that are not confined to global-to-local links that reinscribe dependency. Thinking of international communication and hybridity in terms of translocality, then, keeps issues of power high on the agenda.[4]

The consideration of hybridity in tandem with power is perhaps best captured by the term "intercontextuality," (Appadurai, 1996), which allows us to understand text and context to be mutually constitutive. As used here, "context" does not refer merely to a natural environment or a social setting where practices are put in motion and texts find their interpretative frames. Rather, I employ "context" as a constitutive and constituting force in the sense elaborated by critical communication scholar Jennifer Daryl Slack (1996) when she wrote that "context is not something *out there, within which practices occur or which influences the development of practices*. Rather, *identities, practices, and effects generally, constitute the very context with which they are practices, identities or effects*" (p. 125, emphasis in original). Using the notion of intercontextuality, we can maintain that hybridity is always already permeated with power, without, however, arguing in favor of a generalized hegemonic outcome. In other words, while most hybridities tend to be structured in dominance, the resulting hybrid forms and identities are not always and not necessarily reflective of total dominance. Critical transculturalism views the relationship between structure and agency in terms of a lopsided articulation. Articulation, according to Stuart Hall (1986), "is both a way of understanding how ideological elements come, under certain conditions, to cohere together in a discourse, and a way of asking how they do or do not become articulated, at specific conjunctures, to certain political subjects" (p. 53).[5] Our attention, then, needs to be redirected from debating the political and theoretical usefulness of hybridity, to analyzing how structures and discourses operate in a variety of contexts to shape different hybridities, and how, in turn, hybrid cultural forms—as we have seen, for example, with *Tele Chobis* in Chapter Five—reflect at once the presence of hegemony and its limitations.

While some, perhaps the most powerful, politico-economic structures are global, it may be helpful to pay more attention to the role of the state as a regulator of communication processes that shape hybridity. Critical transculturalism, as mentioned earlier, considers social practice as the site of agency whose scope is both translocal and intercontextual. The state, even as its economic prerogatives have been frittered away under globalization, retains most of its political, legal, regulatory, and military power. In these domains, the national state mediates between not only the global and the local, but also the local and other locals. It is therefore helpful to reappraise the role of the state in international communication, and to explore the implications of this role for the issue of cultural hybridity.

POLICY MATTERS: HYBRIDITY AND THE STATE

It is widely agreed that globalization challenges the Westphalian nation-state from "above" and facilitates internal dynamics that challenge the state from "below," leading to the conclusion that the nation-state may be a threatened form of political organization. However, many advocates of globalization depict the state as a problem to be solved, an argument in different versions, from liberal economics to "cultural globalization," in both public and scholarly settings. Criticism of the state is present both in academic discussions of cultural globalization (as discussed in Chapter Two) and in public discourse (as analyzed in Chapter Four), or both, for example, in free flow views hostile to the New World Information and Communication Order, analyzed in Chapter Two. Contra these depictions of the state as bureaucratic, protectionist, and authoritarian, which reflect the views of transnational capital, it may be productive to contemplate a positive role for the state.

Recently, perhaps as a reaction to globalization's hostility to the state, the nation-state has emerged as an explicit theoretical and empirical concern in international communication (Braman, 2002; Curran and Park, 2000; Morris and Waisbord, 2001). States have always been preoccupied with the mass media because electronic signals ignore territorial borders and breach sovereignty. The state's role has traditionally been that of a protector of the nation, but, as discussed in Chapter Five in regard to British television exports, states have increasingly been acting as mediators between national spheres and global processes. In the international system, however, most states speak for their nation as a unified cultural entity, even when national diversity is acknowledged, based on the faulty holistic premise discussed earlier in this chapter. My advocacy for a renewed local knowledge leads me to focus beyond the state's mediating role between the national and the global and consider the state's role in administering the local, in all its diversity, within the national space. The local, that always already hybrid realm, is where relations between political, social, cultural, and economic forces take concrete forms in people's lives. And in terms of media, the links analyzed in Chapter Six between audience perceptions and media policy in Lebanon indicate that hybrid cultural identities have important implications for media policy. I will therefore conclude with some normative reflections on hybridity as a locus of interaction between the national and the local.

Situating hybridity in fields of power as I have striven to do brings to the surface the tension between cultural politics of recognition and social demands for distribution, a tension that reflects the materialist-idealist divide and that is inherent between the local and the national. In many academic and intellectual quarters, these two visions—recognition and redistribution of justice—have had a conflictual relationship, the former associated with the New Left and the latter with the Old Left, the first with "cultural studies" and the second with "political economy," recognition with discourse or representation and redistribution with material resource allocation. To many, this competition has been asymmetrical, with the notion of recognition ascending at the expense of the redistributionist view, as captured by political theorist Nancy Fraser (1997): "Claims for the recognition of group difference have become increasingly salient in the recent period, at times eclipsing claims for social equality.... Empirically, of course, we have seen the rise of "identity politics," the decentering of class, and, until very recently, the corresponding decline of social democracy. More deeply, however, we are witnessing an apparent shift in the political imaginary, especially the way in which justice is imagined.... The result is a decoupling of cultural politics from social politics and the relative eclipse of the latter by the former" (p. 2).

With its simultaneous emphasis on the material and discursive aspects of hybridity, critical transculturalism aims to recouple cultural and social politics. Cultural research and criticism concerned with social justice examines how socioeconomic structures enable, hinder, or even cripple individual and social agency. For example, by "creating" a multiracial option, the 2000 U.S. Census undoubtedly encouraged people who believed they fit in one of the older categories to see themselves in terms of this hybrid identity. In other words, the institutionalization of a category by the state legitimizes it in the eyes of individuals and groups, thus enhancing its appeal for people whose mixed identity predisposes them to select the multiracial identity. From a critical transculturalism perspective, however, the fact that structure and ideas are reciprocally formative entails no necessary outcome. As we saw in Chapter Six, Maronite youth gravitated toward television content that is theoretically counter to the political sentiment prevalent in their community. Whether this "subversive" consumptive behavior coalesces in real action at the social or political level; whether, to put it differently, segments of Maronite youth enact real social agency; and whether, in an extrapolation beyond the scope of this book, other Lebanese communities do the same and initiate an indirect dialogue stimulated by media content, depends to a major extent on the state.

States must devise competent media and cultural policies for hybridity to act as a progressive political reality that mitigates tension, averts conflict, and enhances representative democracy. These policies must coordinate public and private interests without systematically privileging the latter. In the United States, for example, with the exception of public broadcasting, the primacy of commercial interests in broadcasting is clear, and this logic permeates both how the system works and how it is engaged by social movements. Negative media representations of minorities, for instance, are not monitored or sanctioned by the state; rather, activist groups address stereotypical media depictions by organizing commercial boycotts. Because media corporations recognize the rising purchasing power of certain groups, they often accommodate their demands, whether these are ethnic groups, such as African Americans and Hispanics, or more recently the gay community.

The situation is different in less commercial media environments. In Latin America, states tend to follow a preservationist approach to culture, and cultural policy thus concentrates on traditional folk art and crafts and elite plastic arts. In the past, media and popular culture were neglected by policy, and when included, they were treated according to the same "preservation of culture" logic, an approach now giving way to market considerations in the wake of economic liberalization (García-Canclini, 1995/2001). In western Europe and Canada, on the other hand, commercial considerations have overshadowed public broadcasting ideals, but well-enshrined social democratic values and the laws these values have inspired have arguably worked against too rapid a change and mitigated the impact of liberalization.

In the Arab world, the media are caught between the exacting demands of markets and the repressive tendency of states. Lebanon, its freewheeling economy and relatively free civil society notwithstanding, is no exception to this combination of laisser-faire media economics combined with authoritarian state control over content. This tension is mediated by a system of political patronage and partitioning of media and other resources perhaps best captured by the phrase "oligarchical capitalism," in which media resources are distributed along sectarian lines and controlled by the elite of each confession. This system, as explained in Chapter Six, devolves power and control to the confessional level, so that leading politicians in each group have a monopoly over public expression. Instead of enhancing the prospects of constructive dialogue between communities, this rigid structure concentrates the ability to communicate in the hands of unaccountable political leaders. Therefore, oligarchical media capitalism hardens pluralism into enclavism where recognition and redistribution are perfectly (at least in theory) aligned under elite control, and it preempts hybrid identities from developing into progressive political energy.

An alternative policy must be imagined, at least from a normative, if not yet practicable, point of view. In the United States, where public

advocacy and electoral campaigns are largely determined by the financial means of the contestants, and where ethnic minorities are increasingly targeted as cultural-economic enclaves or electoral enclaves (when
justified by population size as in the case of Latinos), public discourse
could benefit from a more vigorous regulatory policy. The establishment of public financing of elections, for instance, could help ethnic
minorities reclaim a sense of agency that is less dependent on financial
power they do not have. It could also help bring about a true diversity
of opinion by helping third parties reach critical mass. Throughout the
Western world, the combination of social marginalization and diasporic
media can push immigrants toward enclavism. In the case of Lebanon,
whose situation is applicable to other pluralistic societies (including
Iraq) in the non-West, instead of allocating media resources along sectarian lines, why not decentralize the system and allow truly independent stations to emerge? In Lebanon, these media outlets could express
various ways of being a Maronite, a Shiite, or a Sunnite, exposing the
internal diversity of all confessions. By highlighting intraconfessional
diversity, this approach undercuts the system's raison d'être, which has
hardened into dogma, and makes possible the development of alternative social, political, and media structures. A national audiovisual space
could be rehabilitated by revamping Télé-Liban, making it a public, not
a state/privately owned, institution, committing public funds, and possibly levying a special fee on private broadcasters to raise necessary
monies. In the words of García-Canclini (referring to Latin America but
applicable elsewhere), political and economic conditions must favor the
expansion of multicultural media that express multiple points of view,
in a framework that promotes the "collective public interest rather than
commercial profitability" (1995/2001, p. 133). A media system where
a strong national public service shares the airwaves with a variety of
local, regional, and national stations not exclusively based on sectarian
calculations has the best chance of enhancing political life and public discourse across confessional and other potentially explosive boundaries
of affiliation.

The legal and jurisdictional pluralism advocated by Seyla Benhabib
(2002), as discussed in Chapter Three, provides a conceptual framework that I find applicable to media policy in complex, multicultural
countries. The merit of her model is that it recognizes and encourages
fluidity in cultural identity and mixture between groups, while guar-
anteeing equal rights to all. In Benhabib's view, as long as the system
she describes adheres to the three normative requisites of (1) egalitarian

reciprocity, (2) voluntary self-ascription, and (3) freedom of exit or association (elaborated on in Chapter Three), it is compatible with universally acknowledged human rights and democratic standards.

The fulfillment of these conditions leads to a "complex cultural dialogue" (Benhabib, 2002, p. 22) that repudiates the idea that cultures are discrete and separate entities, historically unchanging wholes into which birth alone secures membership. In contrast, the accomplishment of egalitarian reciprocity, voluntary self-ascription, and freedom of exit and association anchors the recognition of diversity between and within ethnic, religious, and linguistic communities and allows for transcultural mixtures that are bound to take shape with sustained cultural exchange. These positive developments, when they occur at the national level and thus allow for increased translocal exchanges, make the local and national realms less vulnerable to capture by the seductive discourse and reductive structures of globalization. This, in turn, enhances the prospects that hybridity, a condition that is constituted in part by communication, fulfills its social and political potential, mitigating social tensions, expressing the polyvalence of human creativity, and providing a context of empowerment in which individuals and communities are agents in their own destiny. Only then can the unsavory implications of hybridity as the cultural logic of globalization be mitigated. And only then can hybridity—albeit without guarantees—be a progressive, hopeful discourse.

Notes

Preface

Epigraph source: Thomas, 1996, p. 9.

1. Many readers will recognize that this book's title is inspired by Fredric Jameson's *Postmodernism or, The Cultural Logic of Late Capitalism* (1991), in which he charts postmodernism's fragmentation of cultural forms and the transformation of space and the material environment in the age of late capitalism.

2. I borrow this notion from Stuart Hall's widely cited essay "The Problem of Ideology: Marxism without Guarantees," originally published in 1983 and reprinted in 1986 in the *Journal of Communication Inquiry* and in 1996 in *Stuart Hall: Critical Dialogues in Cultural Studies* (Morley and Chen, 1996). In Hall's Gramscian rereading of Marx, the circuit of capital explains the issue of reproduction, "the ways in which the conditions for keeping the circuit moving are sustained" (1996, p. 35). Because this sustenance cannot be preordained, Hall advocates a "Marxism without guarantees" (p. 45). I adapt Hall's idea into "hybridity without guarantees" to argue that the outcome of cultural hybridity cannot be predetermined a priori as dominant, hegemonic, or resistive.

Chapter One

Epigraph source: Tomlinson, 1999, p. 141.

1. In *Hybridity in Theory, Culture, and Race* (1995), Robert Young writes that "hybrid" is a nineteenth-century word that "in Latin . . . meant the offspring of a tame sow and wild boar" (p. 6). The *Webster* defined hybrid in 1828 as "a mongrel or mule; an animal or plant, produced from the mixture of two species" (cited in Young, ibid.). While "hybrid" was used as early as 1813 by one writer who discussed human fertility, the use of "hybrid" to refer to human intermixing was first recorded in the *Oxford English Dictionary* in 1861 (Young, 1995).

2. "Hybridity" is in my opinion a better English translation of the French *métissage* than the usage in English of the Spanish word *mestizaje*. On this point I am in agreement with French Guyanese literary critic Roger Toumson, who in *Mythologie du métissage* (1998) writes: "C'est à la faveur de ce débat qu'a surgi au sein de l'intelligensia européenne, en France et en Angleterre, plus particulièrement, la problématique de l' *'hybridisation'*—c'est le terme dont a usé Salman Rushdie—c'est-à-dire du *'métissage'*" [It is in the wake of this debate (about the end of history) that has emerged, among European intellectuals, most particularly in France and in England, the problematic of hybridity—it is the term used by Salman Rushdie—that is to say *métissage*] (p. 62). Indeed, as a

widely known celebrant of cultural fusion in the West, the Indian-born novelist Rushdie uses the term "hybridity," not "hybridization." Besides, in *La pensée métisse*, French historian Serge Gruzinski (1999) defines "métissage" as "le brassage des êtres et des imaginaires" [mixing of beings and imaginaries] (p. 36); (*brassage* is also the French equivalent of "brewing"). Gruzinski differentiates between "hybridation" and "métissage," defining the former as a "closed imaginary" of cultural diversity, and the latter as an "open horizon." In Gruzinski's view, the first marks the cohabitation of diverse cultural forms, and the second captures a transformative process of fusion (see pp. 190–193). Others concur with the view that "the category of *métissage* . . . cannot be merely translated with the Spanish *mestizaje*" (Rabasa, 2000, p. 315). It is unfortunate, then, that Deke Dusimberre translated Gruzinski's *La pensée métisse* as *The Mestizo Mind* (2002), effectively equating "métissage" and "mestizaje." As used in this book and in the literature about mestizaje, métissage, creolization, or syncretism, "métissage," then, is the French equivalent of "hybridity." Chapter Three will unpack the multiple meanings and applications of these terms.

3. A partial list: anthropology (Thomas, 1996), critical race studies (Werbner and Modood, 1997), cultural studies (Gilroy, 1993), art criticism (Clarke, 1997; Coombes, 1992), popular music and ethnomusicology (Boggs, 1991; Hutnyk, 1997; Nexica, 1997; Salamone, 1998), sociology (Nederveen Pieterse, 1994, 2001), film studies (Marchetti, 1998), literary criticism (Jussawalla, 1995; Moreiras, 1999; Young, 1995), migration studies (Papastergiadis, 2000), postcolonial theory (Ahmad, 1995; Bhabha, 1994; Said, 1994), and performance studies (Joseph and Fink, 1999). Hybridity is also used in studies of tourism (Hollinshead, 1998), folklore (Kapchan and Turner-Strong, 1999), sports (Archetti, 1999), and architecture (Morton, 2000). Finally, discussions of hybridity can be found in books about global corporate competition (Zachary, 2000), popular travel writing (Iyer, 2000), economics (Cowen, 2002a), and mainstream media accounts of global popular culture ("Culture Wars," 1998; Hermes, 1994; Farhi and Rosenfeld, 1998; Waxman, 1998).

4. Users of the concept of hybridity in media studies are still scarce, and most of those working specifically in international communication have merely mentioned or addressed hybridity in a rather limited fashion, an issue I discuss later in this chapter. Nonetheless, since the mid-1990s, hybridity is an emerging issue in media and communication and has appeared regularly at professional conventions of the International Association for Media and Communication Research (IAMCR), the International Communication Association (ICA), the National Communication Association (NCA), and the Society for Cinema Studies (SCS), renamed the Society for Cinema and Media Studies (SCMS). This is in addition to meetings that focus on hybridity, e.g., the "Theorizing the Hybrid" conference held at the University of Texas at Austin in March 1996 and the "Traveling Concepts: Texts, Subjectivity, Hybridity" conference organized in January 2000 at the Amsterdam School of Cultural Analysis (ASCA). Néstor García-Canclini, whose *Hybrid Cultures* (1989/1995) is a founding text of hybridity research, was a keynote speaker at the 1997 IAMCR conference in Oaxaca, Mexico, while the 2001 ICA conference in Washington, D.C., included several papers on hybridity, and the 2003 ICA conference in San Diego featured one theme-session panel devoted to discussing cultural hybridity that attracted

nearly seventy attendants. However, these efforts do not offer a systematic conceptualization of hybridity in international communication and media studies scholarship.

5. In Egypt, *Alif: Journal of Comparative Poetics* published a special issue, "The Hybrid Literary Text: Arab Creative Authors Writing in Foreign Languages" (*Alif* 20, 2000). In France, the journal *Diogène*, published by the Presses Universitaires de France with the assistance of UNESCO, had a 1999 special issue titled "Métissage culturel entre religions écrites et traditions orales" (Cultural Hybridity between Written Religions and Oral Traditions) ("Métissage culturel," 1999). Finally, in the United States, the *Journal of American Folklore* devoted an entire issue to the subject "Theorizing the Hybrid" (Kapchan and Strong, 1999), which carried the proceedings of the conference by the same title, mentioned in the previous note.

6. While a systematic elucidation of postcolonial theory and criticism is beyond the scope of this book, the reader can consult an abundant literature on both the affirmation and contestation of postcolonial theory, including discussions of the value of the term "postcolonialism" itself: See Ahmad, 1992, 1995; Appiah, 1991; Bahri, 1995; Dirlik, 1994; Hall, 1996; McClintock, 1992; Mishra and Hodge, 1991; Miyoshi, 1993; Shohat, 1992. Spivak (1999) succinctly expresses the central question when she writes that discussions of postcolonial theory "often dissimulate the implicit collaboration of the postcolonial in the service of *neo*colonialism" (p. 361). In communication studies, see the exchange between Shome (1998) and Kavoori (1998) in *Critical Studies in Mass Communication*, 15(2), and the special issue of *Communication Theory* "Postcolonial Approaches to Communication" (Drzewiecka and Halualani, 2002; Grossberg, 2002; Kraidy, 2002a; Parameswaran, 2002; Shome and Hegde, 2002; Spivak, 2002). In terms of postcolonial theorists who specifically address hybridity, Homi Bhabha has been both influential and controversial. In his exhaustive survey of postcolonial theory, Tanzanian-British literary critic Bart Moore-Gilbert (1997) devotes a full chapter to Bhabha—Edward Said and Gayatri Chakravarty Spivak, the other members of what British literary critic Robert Young (1995) called the "Holy Trinity" of postcolonial theory, get the same honor—arguing that one of Bhabha's most original contributions is to have emphasized "the mutualities and negotiations across the colonial divide" (p. 116), in contrast to Edward Said's focus on the colonizer (the "early" Said; see Chapter Three) and Frantz Fanon's emphasis on the colonized. However, Bhabha's Lacanian grounding and his focus on the semiotic and textual domains have made him the favorite target of materialist critics such as Aijaz Ahmad (1992, 1995). After acknowledging weaknesses in Bhabha's writing, Moore-Gilbert offers a solid counter-critique of Ahmad.

7. Martín-Barbero's conception of mestizaje is used to describe various objects and phenomena. In *Communication, Culture, and Hegemony: From the Media to Mediations* (Martín-Barbero, 1993a), the author's magnum opus, there are other definitions than the one I just quoted. For example: "the cultural realities of these countries, the new combinations and syntheses—the *mestizajes*—that reveal not just the racial mixture that we come from but the interweaving of modernity and the residues of various cultural periods, the mixture of social structures and sentiments" (p. 2), later elaborated: "*Mestizaje* is not simply a racial fact, but the explanation of our existence, the web of times and places,

memories and imagination which, until now, have been adequately expressed only at a literary level" (p. 188). In other instances there seems to be a slight confusion as to the meaning of "mestizaje," possibly accentuated in the translation from Spanish to English. In one instance Martín-Barbero (1993b) refers to "urban *mestizajes*, . . . the skills, knowledge, and grammars that, constituted in memory, mediate the cultural readings of the different groups, and to the imaginaries from which men and women, young and old, Indians and blacks, peasants and city dwellers project their identities" (p. 25). Elsewhere, Martín-Barbero (2002) writes that identities are constructed in relational and narrative processes, which include "the multimediatic idiom within which today's translations are played out . . . and also that even more complex and ambiguous idiom of appropriations, and miscegenations [*mestizajes*]" (p. 627). For Martín-Barbero, then, "mestizaje" is at once name and adjective, singular and plural, process and product.

8. In my view, the designation "global media studies" (Kraidy, 2002c) reflects a variety of interdisciplinary theories that have widened the scope of research on global media and activated a consideration of the linkages between production, texts, and consumption (for example, Miller, Govil, McMurria, and Maxwell, 2001; Murphy and Kraidy, 2003a), a task that the traditional international communication canon has to a large degree neglected. Different traditions have tended to focus on one out of three stages of the communication process. Cultural imperialism, grounded in critical political economy, focused on production and distribution. In contrast, media criticism, derived from literary and rhetorical criticism, examined the layers of meaning embedded in media texts. Finally, reception studies, rooted in cultural anthropology and sociology, semiotics and reader-response theories, emphasized the creative abilities of active media audiences. In my view, the rubric "global media studies" also encompasses diasporic media research, another area neglected in the study of international communication. Integrating these different aspects can improve our understanding of the links between media culture and broader societal processes in a comparative context. However, "global media studies" should not uncritically give prominence to textual and discursive aspects of global media. At any rate, a full discussion of the benefits and pitfalls of the "global media studies" tag awaits another day.

CHAPTER TWO

Epigraph source: Mattelart, 1998.

1. For his part, Nederveen Pieterse (1996) distinguished between three "paradigms" or "positions" on globalization and culture. The first, "cultural differentialism or lasting difference," refers primarily to Huntington's work. The second, "cultural convergence or growing sameness," echoes the cultural imperialism position. This book falls broadly within the third position that Nederveen Pieterese identifies, "cultural hybridisation or ongoing mixing" (p. 1389). For readers interested in this perspective, *Globalization and Culture: Global Mélange* (Nederveen Pieterese, 2004) repackages the author's articles on cross-cultural encounters and hybridity.

2. In characteristically trenchant style Edward Said (2001) commented in the *Nation* that " 'The Clash of Civilizations' thesis is a gimmick like 'The War of the Worlds,' better for reinforcing defensive self-pride than for critical understanding of the bewildering interdependence of our time." For a sustained critique of Huntington's view on culture and civilization from the standpoint of political theory, the reader can also refer to the Turkish American political theorist Seyla Benhabib (2002), who argues that Huntington's use of culture and civilization is tautological, hence "the concept of cultural civilizational identity is an explanans, as well as explanandum" (p. 188). Also, in *Arab Culture in the Era of Globalization* [in Arabic], the Saudi sociologist and cultural critic Turki al-Hamad (2001) offers a cogent critique of Huntington's thesis, arguing that "it rests on totalistic long-term deductions, based on partial and selective information" (p. 47). Finally, the *Journal of Peace Research* in 2000 published an article whose authors, in their own words, "subjected [Huntington's] argument to a wide variety of systematic empirical tests" and concluded that "civilizations do not define the fault lines along which international conflict occurs" (Russett, Oneal, and Cox, 2000, p. 602).

3. For a thorough discussion of NWICO, including its historical, legal, political, and media coverage dimensions, see Gerbner, Mowlana, and Nordenstreng, 1994. See also Boyd-Barrett 1995 for a sustained analysis of the news aspects of the debate.

4. Straubhaar (1991) concluded his influential article as follows: "we see a qualitative change in world media relations. Although the United States still dominates world media sales and flows, national and regional cultural industries are consolidating a relatively more interdependent position in the world television market . . . . The process remains complex, however. While some producers gain greater independence in some genres with some audiences, some producers and genres fail, and some audiences continue to prefer internationalized production from outside both nation and region. We simply suggest a larger gamut of possibilities, from dependence to relative interdependence, in media relations" (p. 56).

5. A second stage of research on cultural domination, although not formally identified with the cultural imperialism thesis, came to view in the 1990s in association with calls to revive the New World Information and Communication Order debate. What differentiates this discourse from earlier cultural imperialism formulations is its emphasis on the commercialization of the sphere of culture. While cultural imperialism research (see Mattelart, 1983, and Schiller, 1971/1992) has addressed these issues, there has recently developed a deliberate focus on transnational corporations as actors, as opposed to nation-states, and on transnational capital flows, as opposed to image flows. Obviously, the distinction is more a matter of focus than of substance, since it is hard to separate the power of transnational corporations from that of nation-states, and difficult to distinguish clearly between capital flows and media flows.

6. The special issue of *Communication Theory* showcases critical approaches to global communication with a focus on discursive issues and the material-ideational interplay (Kraidy, 2002a; Parameswaran, 2002). Authors in the *Journal of International Communication* have addressed human rights, social justice, and civil society, also looking at customary debates on cultural

influence from alternative vantage points such as feminism, critical theory, queer theory, postcolonialism, and religion. This has showcased interparadigmatic borrowing, where feminist perspectives illuminate issues of citizenship (Sreberny-Mohammadi, 1996), and communication theory explicates aspects of international relations and foreign policy research (Rudock, 1996) and the idea of a global public sphere (Tomlinson, 1994).

7. Virginia Nightingale (1996) argues, not without merit, that despite recent developments, the "sender-message-receiver" model "remains the fundamental assumption of communication studies" (p. 26). In a corrective to the distinction claimed by Hall, Nightingale finds that "encoding/decoding" shares aspects with "sender-receiver-feedback." They are both linear and hierarchical, in the sense that sending and encoding always occur before receiving and decoding. However, the two models differ in that the former is essentially concerned with administrative efficiency whereas the latter seeks to understand the structure of social relations. For a detailed comparative analysis, see Nightingale, 1996, chapter 2, especially pp. 26–31.

8. Literary and philosophical treatments of globalization that focus on the role of communication as hinge between the economic and cultural are instructive in that regard. Literary critic Fredric Jameson has argued that "globalization is a communicational concept, which alternately masks and transmits cultural or economic meanings." He nonetheless warns: "But the communicational focus of the concept of globalization is essentially incomplete." He concludes with a challenge: "I defy anyone to try to think of it in exclusively media or communicational terms" (Jameson, 1998, p. 55). More recent theoretical writings give communication an even more important role in global affairs. In *Empire* (2000), U.S. literary theorist Michael Hardt and Italian political philosopher Antonio Negri write that "communication not only expresses but also organizes the movements of globalization. It organizes the movements by multiplying and structuring interconnections through networks." The authors place communication at the heart of what they call "biopolitical" power, because communication "expresses the movement and controls the sense and direction of the imaginary that runs through these communicative connections; in other words, the imaginary is guided and channeled within the communicative machine" (pp. 32–33). In this context communication functions as a sort of electrical conductor between the material hardware of globalization and the symbolic processes that fill and animate these networks. But beyond mediation, communication has a constitutive role. This is how I understand Hardt and Negri's assertion that "[t]he political synthesis of social space is fixed in the space of communication" (p. 33).

CHAPTER THREE

Epigraph sources: Stewart, 1999, p. 58; Gilroy, 1993, p. 20; and Ahmad, 1995, p. 12.

1. Hannerz (1989) gives examples that undermine a necessary coevality of cultural and political-economic power: the cultural sway of the Soviet Union was

considerably less than its political-military clout, and Japan has only marginal global cultural potency considering it is the world's second most powerful economy. However, in light of the global popularity of *Pokemon*, the subcultural cult status of Japanese anime, and the success of Japanese pop music stars such as Namie Amuro throughout Asia, some observers have pointed to Japan's rising cultural power (see McGray, 2002). Douglas McGray notably argues that "in cultural terms at least, Japan has become one of a handful of perfect globalization nations" (2002, p. 53) and concludes that Japan possesses "the cultural reach of a superpower" (p. 54). Conversely, Britain wields a cultural power disproportionate to its political and military status. As coined by international relations scholar Joseph Nye Jr., "soft power" is not a direct derivative of hard, that is, military, political-economic, and technological power. The rising global tide of anti-Americanism—most acute in the Islamic world but significantly strong in Europe's liberal democracies—demonstrates that the United States' unparalleled might has not necessarily extended to the "hearts and minds" of less potent people. Rather, worldwide opposition to the 2003 U.S. war in Iraq suggests that the single hyperpower may lose in soft power what it gains in material ascendance.

2. Gómez-Peña's title (1996), *The New World Border,* is probably inspired by the sociocultural dynamics of the U.S.-Mexico border, which generated a corpus of scholarship, parts of it invoking mestizaje and hybridity to describe composite border Mexican-U.S. cultural forms. In addition to Gomez-Peña (1996), writings by poet and critic Gloria Anzaldúa (*Borderlands/la Frontera: The New Mestiza*, 1987), anthropologists Renato Rosaldo (*Culture and Truth: The Remaking of Social Analysis*, 1993), and Ruth Behar (*Translated Woman: Crossing the Border with Esperanza's Story*, 1993), in addition to literary scholars Scott Michaelsen and David E. Johnson (*Border Theory: The Limits of Cultural Politics*, 1997), Calderón and Saldívar (*Criticism in the Borderlands: Studies in Chicano Literature, Culture, and Ideology*, 1991), and Claire Fox (*The Fence and the River: Culture and Politics at the U.S.-Mexico Border*, 1999), have explored the cultural politics of the border region. This context has witnessed a similar tension between a celebration of hybridity and concerns about the material inequalities it reflects (see Michaelsen and Johnson, 1997, for a criticism of the more celebratory formulations of the border). For analyses of the border in media research, see Barrera, 1996; Lozano, 1996.

3. Buffon's ideas are elaborated mostly in the third volume, "L'histoire de l'homme," published in 1749, of his thirty-six-volume *L'histoire naturelle*; in his *Essai sur l'inégalité des races humaines* [Essay on the inequality of human races] (1853–1855), the French diplomat and racial ideologue Comte de Gobineau postulates similar claims about the superiority of the white race. The reader interested in the history and details of these racialist theories can refer to Toumson, 1998, and R. Young, 1995.

4. Scholars continue to draw on religious studies to understand cultural mixture (see Stewart and Shaw, 1994). Anthropologist Raquel Romberg (1998), for instance, uses syncretism to frame her study of the political and sociocultural dynamics of contemporary religious practices in Puerto Rico. She distinguishes between "etic" (by which she means denotative) and "emic" (connotative)

meanings of the term "syncretism." In contrast to the etic perspective, where syncretism helps explain mixture, the emic meaning of syncretism adapts to changing intergroup relations.

5. The 2000 U.S. Census offers a propitious opportunity for exploring the tension inherent in the institutionalization of hybrid identities. In 2000, for the first time, respondents who completed census forms had the option to describe themselves in multiracial terms. The new "Check All That Apply" option included 126 ethnic categories (Fears, 2001), which constituted fifty-seven new identity categories (Moore, 2001). This change in census policy came after longtime lobbying efforts from multiracial groups, whose advocacy received a boost in 1990 when that year's census data showed that two million people had checked "Other," making "Other" the third-fastest-growing category. Ten years later, a study found that in some states up to a tenth of the residents were multiracial (Moore, 2001). The issue received intense coverage in the prestige press, with dozens of articles and editorials in the *Washington Post, New York Times, Los Angeles Times, Miami Herald,* and *Chicago Tribune* providing factoids and commenting on the cultural and political implications of new racial categories. Census results in the year 2000 indicated that 2.4 percent of the U.S. population, or approximately seven million people, had selected one of the multiracial options (Funderburg, 2001).

Nonetheless, the new "multiracial" census category is controversial, because census data shape a variety of highly consequential issues, including how federal funds are apportioned, civil rights laws enforced, congressional districts redrawn, and state budgets allocated (Fears, 2001). According to a 1999 report by the General Accounting Office of the United States, census data are used in twenty-two out of the twenty-five large federal grant programs (Cohn and Morello, 2001). Groups like the National Association for the Advancement of Colored People (NAACP) and the Japanese Citizens League went on record against the new category, citing concerns that destabilizing racial categories will lead to lax enforcement of civil rights laws (Moore, 2001) and a decline in the clout of minorities in general. The growing number of Hispanics, who have now replaced African Americans as the largest minority group, also fueled African American opposition to the new category, with some experts warning that up to 70 percent of African Americans are mixed with some other racial group (Fears, 2001). The *Los Angeles Times* summarized it best, citing numerous researchers who said that "multiracial data collection has launched the country into uncharted regions where politics, identity, law and culture will collide with confusing effects" (Moore, 2001).

6. More recently, Gilroy has continued grappling with the fluidity of ethnicity in his book, whose U.S. edition is provocatively titled *Against Race: Imagining Political Culture beyond the Color Line* (2000).

7. Page numbers for quotations from García-Canclini 1989/1995 are from the English translation.

8. I have already explained (in Chapter One) my preference for translating *"métissage,"* used in major French and Francophone works, as "hybridity" (see Gruzinski, 1999; Toumson, 1998).

Chapter Four

Epigraph sources: Doty, 1996, p. 5; Cowen, 2002a, p. 59; and Zachary, 2000, p. xxi.

1. In examining representations of hybridity in elite print media, I believe that representational practices should be integrated in international communication analysis, whose focus hitherto on media institutions and structures has preempted a significant treatment of things discursive. In this respect, there is an interdisciplinary literature that international communication scholars can draw from. For example, critical international relations scholar Roxanne Doty (1996) emphasizes the implications of the West/North's representational power in its dealing with developing countries. She writes that "[o]ne of the most consequential elements present in all of the encounters between the North and the South, has been the practice(s) of *representation* by the North of the South" (p. 2). Escobar (1995) and Said (1994) also stress the importance of representation in international relations.

2. The speaker is Everett Ladd, then executive director of the Roper Center at the University of Connecticut. In addition to Ladd, speakers at the March 1992 AEI conference—"The New Global Popular Culture: Is It American? Is It Good for America? Is It Good for the World?"—included academics, artists, and journalists such as George Gerbner, Todd Gitlin, Pico Iyer, Charles Krauthammer, and Joseph Nye Jr., and the keynote speaker was Sydney Pollack. The notion of hybridity was not central to the conference but was nonetheless broached, when, for example, a speaker said: "Rock and roll, which is one of our greatest cultural exports, is a hybrid of the European sense of melody and harmony and African rhythm" ("The Controversy," 1992, p. 76).

3. In his rant against monoculture, Zachary makes passing swipes at Max Weber and Samuel Huntington (2000, pp. 74, 77) for their views on culture but stops short of a thorough critique. For such an assessment of Huntingtonian views in culture and civilization, the reader may refer to this book's Chapter Two.

4. The Darwinian implications of this view are manifest when Zachary writes: "Mixing and mongrelization make evolutionary sense.... The more genetically diverse a species, the more likely it is to possess an adaptation that helps it survive in a specific environment. This is one way of understanding the phrase 'survival of the fittest'" (2000, p. 77). Also, a business appropriation of the notion of deterritorialization is obvious when Zachary writes that "hybrids are richly particular people adept at fitting into many places precisely because their portable roots give them so much to offer" (pp. xx). There is also a growing corporate trend in the United States to set up "ethnic marketing departments." *Shopping for Identity: The Marketing of Ethnicity* (Halter, 2000) explores how ethnicity has become a marketing tool for U.S. corporations. Notably, chapter 7, "Recipe for Multiethnicity: The Mestiza Makeover," uses the discourse of hybridity to explain trends in ethnic marketing. For more on ethnic marketing, also see Paredes, 2001, and Zachary, 2000, especially pp. 202–205.

5. While this formula is obviously foundational to Zachary's vision of hybridity, he later asserts that "statistically, hybridity doesn't exist" (2000, p. 5).

6. Zachary's argument that "[t]o the receiving nation, the question of national loyalty is irrelevant" (2000, p. 72) is increasingly questionable in light of the

"war on terrorism" and its domestic implications—such as the Patriot Act—in the United States.

7. In their elaboration of the notion of strategic rhetoric, Nakayama and Krizek (1995) draw on French historian, theologian, and cultural researcher Michel de Certeau's distinction between strategy and tactic. In *L'Invention du quotidien* (1980/1990), de Certeau defined strategy as "the calculation (or manipulation) of power relations that becomes possible from the moment that a subject of will and power...is isolatable." A strategy thus carves up a space, "postulates a place that can be circumscribed as its *own* and can be the base from which to manage relations with an *exteriority* of targets or threats" (p. 59, emphasis in original, my translation). In de Certeau's view, enacting a strategy is in short to establish boundaries between "an appropriated space and its other" (p. 59). This implies, first, that spatial logic trumps temporal considerations; second, that this logic constitutes a panoptic practice of surveillance; and third, that it entails the preexistence of a power that arranges and polices the strategically established site (de Certeau, 1990). Strategy is therefore the domain and privilege of the powerful. In contrast, tactic, as "the calculated action determined by the absence of a proper place" (p. 60), constitutes the realm of the weak. It operates on the enemy's own territory, within the other's field of vision, and is not part of an integrated process. It exploits the system's vulnerabilities: there, "[i]t poaches. It creates surprises.... It is trickery" (p. 61). Strategy is conspicuous and its power depends to a large extent on this visibility; in contrast, tactic is stealthy and mobile. "Tactic is determined by the absence of power just as strategy is organized by the postulation of a power" (p. 62). From their space of proprietary power, strategies thus link spaces with discourses, projecting them onto each other in a bid to preserve positions of privilege.

Chapter Five

Epigraph source: Bhabha, 1994, p. 89.

1. I write "slightly modified" because in the rare instances where there is English speech, such as with the Narrator and Voice Trumpets, it has been converted to an American accent.

2. Viselman's comment reflects a strategic ambiguity on the inherent polysemy of television texts, especially *Teletubbies*, on one hand arguing against trying to define the characters, thus acknowledging multiple meanings, on the other hand rejecting politicized readings of the program, thus attempting to fix the fluidity of the program's meanings.

3. Gruzinski is referring to two sites in Mexico. The first, in the colonial city of Puebla, is the Casa del Deán (literally, house of the dean), which was occupied by a clergyman of high stature between 1564 and 1589 and is considered, at least by Gruzinski, "one of the marvels of the Mexican Renaissance" (1999, p. 112). Its interior is adorned with large and unique paintings, the creation of native Indian Mexican painters, including one tableau of monkeys in playful relation to a centauress, which was one of Gruzinski's main inspiration in his analysis of hybridity, hence the quote I use. The second is an Augustinian church in Ixmiquilpan, a town located around 130 miles northwest of Mexico City. The

church contains two very large frescoes that graphically depict bloody war scenes—a highly unusual occurrence in a Catholic church—where European and preconquest Mexican iconic elements mix freely, interpreted by Gruzinski as another manifestation of Mexico's unique hybridity (pp. 116–119). All translations from the French original (Gruzinski, 1999) are mine.

4. According to one source, sales figures for both Televisa and TV Azteca show continued growth. For Televisa, annual sales in \$U.S. millions were \$1,892.4 in 1999, \$2,163.6 in 2000, \$2,147.4 in 2001, and \$2,075.4 in 2002. For TV Azteca, the numbers are \$564.1 in 2000, \$632.6 in 2001, \$643.6 in 2002, and \$648.0 in 2003 (Hoover's Online, 2004a,b).

CHAPTER SIX

Epigraph source: Rushdie, 1994, back cover.

1. Lebanon lies in western Asia on the shores of the Mediterranean Sea. It is bordered by Syria to the north and east, Israel to the south, and the Mediterranean to the west. The country's 10,452 square kilometers (4,015 square miles) make it one of the world's smallest nation-states. Lebanon was a province of the Ottoman Empire for four centuries, enjoying a relatively high degree of autonomy, until the Ottoman defeat in World War 1 brought on the French mandate. The Lebanese constitution was promulgated in 1926, under a French mandate sanctioned by the League of Nations, but Lebanon did not gain independence until 1943.

I prefer the term "confession" to "sect" when writing about the more than eighteen religious groups who live in Lebanon. The country's population can only be estimated, since the last official census was conducted in 1932, at which time it was found that the population was almost evenly divided, with Christians slightly outnumbering Muslims. The main groups are Druze (generally counted as Muslims), Greek Orthodox Christians, Maronite Christians, Shiite Muslims, and Sunni Muslims. Recent estimates put the population at between three and four million—a July 1996 estimate put the population at 3,776,317 (*Lebanon Factbook*, 1997)—and the Muslim-to-Christian ratio at 6 to 4. For more on the issue of confessionalism or sectarianism, see Makdisi (2000).

2. See ("Réfléxions," 1994). In June 2003, the Maronite church officially and publicly renounced any national project for the Maronites, a shift of historical importance but nonetheless one that reflects a fait accompli.

3. I regard the opposition between the critical political economy tradition and cultural studies, as discussed in Chapters One and Two, to be artificial. Approaches that focus on material, discursive, and textual aspects of communication complement each other, as this chapter explicitly attempts to demonstrate, and more broadly as this entire book seeks to substantiate.

4. Whereas in Western public discourse veiling is portrayed as a reactionary practice, there is debate among scholars as to whether veiling is oppressive or progressive. For instance, feminist oral historian Sherna-Berger Gluck (1991), who researches Palestinian women's issues, argues that the veil can have a liberating effect because it provides women with anonymity and mobility. The reader may also consult Amin, 2002, for more on the veil issue in Iran.

5. This resonates, pun intended, with Stuart Hall's rhetorical question: "Are there any musics left that have not heard some other music?" (1991a, p. 38).

6. The globally known Music Television (MTV) should not to be confused with Lebanon's Murr Television, also known as MTV, shut down by authorities on September 4, 2002 (see Kraidy, 2002d).

7. Unfortunately, permission was not granted to quote the lyrics of the two songs. While "Switzerland of the Middle East" and "Paris of the East" were propagated in the international press, metaphors of decay were captured in titles of books about Lebanon: Hudson (1968), *The Precarious Republic,* and Mackey (1989), *Lebanon: Death of a Nation.* See Khalaf, 2002, for more on this issue.

8. I am grateful to Joe Khalil, then executive producer at Murr Television in Lebanon, and now at Al-Arabiya in Dubai, for this insight.

9. Hezbollah-owned Al-Manar's satellite broadcasts are highly popular with Arab audiences, especially in the Levant. While adhering to an Islamist discourse inspired by the Iranian revolution, the station's overt focus is the resistance to Israel, with a backdrop of virulent criticism of U.S. policies in the Middle East. In the early to mid-1990s, Al-Manar dispatched cameramen with commandos who were executing operations against the Israeli army that occupied Southern Lebanon. Vivid, "reality" footage was replayed on nightly newscasts to great effect. Also, Al-Manar has challenged the stereotype of the veiled, subservient Muslim woman by employing articulate women in Islamic dress as program hosts. Unfortunately, however, anti-Israeli rhetoric oftentimes lapses into anti-Semitic propaganda, such as in 2003, when the station aired a Syrian production of the anti-Semitic *Protocols of the Elders of Zion,* called *al-Shatat* [Diaspora].

10. The Lebanese audience is one of the smallest in the world, and breaking it down into confessionally defined segments reduces it even further, bringing advertising rates to nonviably low levels. This was once a central impetus to the 1994 Audio-Visual Media Law. With numerous media outlets vying for a national audience of a couple of million, media proliferation nearly brought Lebanon's once thriving advertising industry to the brink of collapse. For a systematic analysis of the political, economic, and technical forces that led to the establishment of Lebanon's first broadcasting law, see Kraidy (1998a).

11. I borrow the notion of "hegemonic echo" from my colleague and friend Patrick Murphy, who has mentioned it more than once in conversations we have had about common sense in everyday life. Also see Murphy, 2003.

CHAPTER SEVEN

Epigraph source: Said, 1994, p. 58.

1. Michel de Certeau's elaboration of strategy and tactic (1980/1990) (explained in Chapter Four) can help us assess hybridity as a discourse with near-paradigmatic ambitions. The cultural imperialism thesis, having enjoyed a widespread following in the 1960s and 1970s, did in effect enjoy strategic status, in de Certeau's understanding. It occupied the center of the debate on the sociocultural influence of global media, defined its terms, and delineated its boundaries. It also gained institutional support in UNESCO during the years of

the New World Communication and Information Order (NWICO) debate discussed earlier in this book. Arguments against the cultural imperialism thesis appeared on the radar screen from the thesis's inception but were initially without steam. These dissenting voices, following de Certeau's theory, were tactical. Unlike the cultural imperialism thesis's worldwide resonance in both academic and policy communities, its opponents were restricted mostly to the Western academy and did not initially hold considerable sway in conferences and publications. However, the end of the Cold War, a changing ideological climate, the decline and fragmentation of the Left, and new intellectual trends, in addition to the endurance of social scientific mass communication research, have effectively inverted the equation. From the tactical confines of the margins, critics of the cultural imperialism thesis have moved to the strategic center. Since the late 1980s, it has in effect been the turn of critical scholars who adhere to the cultural imperialism thesis to be on the defensive, their school of thought having declined in status, as their erstwhile marginal critics have come to lead the debate from the center.

2. In *Distant Proximities: Dynamics beyond Globalization* (2003), international relations scholar James Rosenau offers a detailed justification (pp. 81–87) for using the local-global dichotomy for analytical purposes. For an in-depth exploration of the epistemological dimensions of this issue, see Mirsepassi, Basu, and Weaver, 2003. On the local-global pair in media and communication studies, see Chan and Ma (1996), Dowmunt (1993), Eade (1997), Ferguson (1995), Gurevitch and Kavoori (1994), Hall (1991a), Thussu (1998), Kraidy (1999a, 2003b), Roome (1999); and Sreberny-Mohammadi (1984). Alternative media have enjoyed a renewed interest over the past few years. See Downing, 2000; Rodríguez, 2001; and Atton, 2002.

3. Australian anthropologist Nicholas Thomas (1996) observed the same phenomenon in the art world, where "the interest in hybridity enables critics and curators to celebrate their own capacity for acknowledging cultural difference, while refraining from engaging with the stories and works that emerge from ground remote from their own" (p. 9). Thomas concludes that "mutual contact between peoples prior to colonization is not seen to generate reflexivity and cultural dynamism; only interaction with the West inaugurates a cultural process that ends up with the most advanced non-European artists engaging with Western styles and traditions" (p. 10).

4. In *Ethnography through Thick and Thin* (1998), anthropologist George Marcus formulates his notion of "multi-sited ethnography," asserting that for ethnography, "there is no global in the local-global contrast now so frequently evoked. The global is an emergent dimension of arguing about the connection among sites in a multi-sited ethnography" (p. 83). Marcus's (p. 71) own differentiation of realist ethnography (the method of traditional ethnography) from a modernist ethnography more concerned with large-scale international processes further helps us in accentuating the distinction between local and translocal ethnography.

5. While in media cultural studies, articulation is associated with Stuart Hall (1985, 1986), he is one of many users of that notion. Others include Louis Althusser and Etienne Balibar (1970), Maurice Bloch (1983), Terry Eagleton

(1976), and Ernesto Laclau and Chantal Mouffe (1985). As Downing has argued (1996, pp. 212–215; 1997, pp. 189–192), articulation is difficult to use in an applied manner to explore a variety of interconnected social forces. Nonetheless, I believe that this notion retains analytical value if we endeavor to specify it. To that end, I use the qualifier "lopsided" to reflect my belief that one of the two poles of any articulation will lead and determine the directionality of the articulation. Hall (1986) himself uses the analogy of the articulated lorry or tractor-trailer to illustrate the notion of articulation, but as Downing pointed out, Hall's analogy suggests that "it is only the hitching of one unit to another which he has in mind, rather than the fact that the truck pulls the trailer hitched up to it" (1996, p. 212). It is indeed one pole of the articulation that decides the direction and speed of the articulated couple. Nonetheless, at the risk of stretching the analogy too far, a very steep upward hill can break the articulation, and the trailer can move in the opposite direction from the tractor, albeit without much control of speed or direction, determined by gravity and geography, and with the likelihood that the movement will end in a crash of some sort. In theoretical terms, this means that contextual factors preempt me from preferring determination to articulation, even though I recognize that in some cases an articulation can be lopsided to the extent of becoming determination. In any case, the notion of "lopsided articulation" must be thoroughly contextualized and not become a formula applied in the same way across historical periods and spatial locations.

Bibliography

Abou, S. (1981). *L'identité culturelle: Relations interethniques et problemes d'acculturation*. Paris: Editions Anthropos.

Abu-Lughod, L. (1999). The interpretation of culture(s) after television. In S. Ortner (Ed.), *The fate of "culture": Geertz and beyond* (pp. 110–135). Berkeley: University of California Press.

Abu-Lughod, L. (2003). Asserting the local as national in the face of the global: The ambivalence of authenticity in Egyptian soap operas. In A. Mirsepassi, A. Basu, and F. Weaver (Eds.), *Localizing knowledge in a globalizing world* (pp. 101–130). Syracuse, N.Y.: Syracuse University Press.

Achcar, G., Gresh, A., Radvanyi, J., Rekacewicz, P., and Vidal, D. (2003, January.) *L'Atlas du monde diplomatique*. Special issue, *Maniere de Voir*.

Affergan, F. (2001). "La mascarade des couleurs: Contribution à une anthropologie du métissage." In J. L. Bonniol (Ed.), *Paradoxes du métissage* (pp. 27–40). Paris: Comité des Travaux Historiques et Scientifiques.

Ahmad, A. (1992). *In theory: Classes, nations, literatures*. London: Verso

Ahmad, A. (1995). The politics of literary postcoloniality. *Race and Class, 36*(3), 1–20.

Ahmed, S. (1999). 'She'll wake up one of these days and find she's turned into a nigger': Passing through hybridity. *Theory, Culture, and Society, 18*(2), 87–106.

A la convention, Paris préserve in extremis "l'exception culturelle." (2003, July 10). *Le Monde*.

Al-Azm, S. J. (1981). Orientalism and Orientalism in reverse. *Khamsin, 8*, 5–26.

Al-I Ahmad, J. (1984). *Occidentosis: A plague from the West*. (H. Algar, Ed.; R. Campbell, Trans.). Berkeley, CA: Mizan Press.

Al-Hamad, Turki. (2001). *Arab culture in the era of globalization*. Beirut: Al-Saqi. (In Arabic).

Alif 20: The hybrid literary text: Arab creative authors writing in foreign languages. (2000). Cairo, Egypt: American University of Cairo Press.

Allen, J. S., and Cheer, S. M. (1996). The non-thrifty genotype. *Current Anthropology, 37*(5), 831–842.

Allor, M. (1988). Relocating the site of the audience. *Critical Studies in Mass Communication, 5*, 217–233.

Althusser, L., and Balibar, E. (1970). *Reading capital*. London: Verso.

America's Best Newspapers. (1999, November/December). *Columbia Journalism Review*, available http://www.cjr.org/year/99/6/**best**.asp.

Amin, C. M. (2002). *The making of the modern Iranian woman: Gender, state policy, and popular culture, 1865–1946*. Gainesville: University Press of Florida.

Anderson, B. (1993). *Imagined communities: Reflections on the origins and spread of nationalism.* London: Verso.

Anderson, B. (2000). Benefits of diversity in a global economy, guest: Greg Pascal Zachary. *CNN International,* transcript accessed through Lexis-Nexis. Retrieved September 12, 2000.

Ang, I. (1985). *Watching Dallas: Soap opera and the melodramatic imagination.* London: Routledge.

Ang, I. (1991). *Desperately seeking the audience.* London: Routledge.

Ang, I. (1996). *Living room wars: Rethinking media audiences for a postmodern world.* London: Routledge.

Antola, A., and Rogers, E. M. (1984). Television flows in Latin America. *Communication Research, 11,* 183–202.

Anzaldua, G. (1987). *Borderlands/La frontera: The new mestiza.* San Francisco: Aunt Lute.

Aparicio, F. R., and Jáquez, C. (Eds.). (2001). *Musical migrations: Transnationalism and cultural hybridity in Latin(o) America.* Philadelphia: Temple University Press.

Appadurai, A. (1991). Global ethnoscapes: Notes and queries for a transnational anthropology. In M. Fox (Ed.), *Recapturing anthropology: Working in the present* (pp. 191–210). Santa Fe, NM: School of American Research Press.

Appadurai, A. (1994). Disjuncture and difference in the global cultural economy. In M. Featherstone (Ed.), *Global culture* (pp. 295–310). London: Sage.

Appadurai, A. (1996). *Modernity at large: Cultural dimensions of globalization.* Minneapolis: University of Minnesota Press.

Appiah, K. A. (1991). Is the post- in postmodernism the post- in postcolonial? *Critical Inquiry, 17*(2), 336–357.

Archetti, E. P. (1999). *Masculinities: Football, polo, and the tango in Argentina.* Oxford, UK, and New York: Berg.

Arron, J. J. (1951). Criollo: Definición y matices de un concepto. *Hispania 34,* 172–176.

Ashcroft, B., Griffiths, G., and Tiffin, H. (1998). *Key concepts in post-colonial studies.* London and New York: Routledge.

Atton, C. (2002). *Alternative media.* London: Sage.

Aune, J. A. (2001). *Selling the free market: The rhetoric of economic correctness.* New York: Guilford.

Bahri, D. (1995). One more time with feeling: What is postcolonialism? *Ariel, 26*(1), 51–82.

Baines, J. (Trans.). (1999a). On understanding syncretism. *Orientalia, 68*(3), 181–198. (Original work by Bonnet, H. (1939). Zum Verständnis des Synkretismus. *Zeitschrift für Ägyptische Sprache und Altertumstunde, 75,* 40–52.)

Baines, J. (1999b). Egyptian syncretism: Hans Bonnet's contribution. *Orientalia, 68*(3), 199–214.

Baker, M. (1997, November 21). Dyke: A long-running TV drama. *Broadcast.*

Bakhtin, M. (1981). *The dialogical imagination: Four essays.* (M. Holquist, Ed.; C. Emerson and M. Holquist, Trans.). Austin: University of Texas Press.

Bamyeh, M. A. (2000). *The ends of globalization.* Minneapolis: University of Minnesota Press.

Bandura, A., and Huston, A. C. (1961). Identification as a process of incidental learning. *Journal of Abnormal and Social Psychology, 63*(2), 311–318.

Barber, B. (1996). *Jihad vs. McWorld: How globalism and tribalism are reshaping the world.* New York: Ballantine.

Barber, B. (2003, February 2). Creative destruction: How globalization is changing the world's cultures. [Review of the book by Tyler Cowen]. *Los Angeles Times,* p. R3.

Barnett, G. A., and McPhail, T. L. (1980). An examination of the relationship of United States television and Canadian identity. *International Journal of Intercultural Relations, 4,* 219–232.

Barnett, S., and Curry, A. (1994). *The battle for the BBC.* London: Aurum Press.

Barrera, C. (1998, October 7). TV Azteca to raise advertising rates by 40 pct. Mexico City: Reuters.

Barrera, E. (1996). The U.S.-Mexico as a post-NAFTA Mexico. In E. G. McAnany and K. Wilkinson (Eds.), *Mass media and free trade: NAFTA and the cultural industries* (pp. 187–220). Austin: University of Texas Press.

Baudrillard, J. (1968). *Le système des objets* [The system of objects]. Paris: Éditions Gallimard.

Baudrillard, J. (1972). *Pour une critique de l'economie politique du signe* [For a critique of the political economy of the sign]. Paris: Éditions Gallimard.

Baudrillard, J. (1983). *Simulations.* New York: Semiotext(e).

Baudrillard, J. (1987a). *The ecstasy of communication.* New York: Semiotext(e).

Baudrillard, J. (1987b). *Forget Foucault.* New York: Semiotext(e).

Bauman, Z. (1994). Modernity and ambivalence. In M. Featherstone (Ed.), *Global culture: Nationalism, globalization, and modernity* (pp. 143–170). London and Newbury Park, CA: Sage.

Behar, R. (1993). *Translated woman: Crossing the border with Esperanza's story.* Boston: Beacon.

Beltrán, L. R. (1975). Research ideologies in conflict. *Journal of Communication, 25*(2), 187–193.

Beltrán, L. R. (1978a). TV etchings in the minds of Latin Americans: Conservatism, materialism, and conformism. *Gazette, 24*(1), 61–85.

Beltrán, L. R. (1978b). Communication and cultural domination: U.S.–Latin America case. *Media Asia, 5,* 183–192.

Benhabib, S. (1999). The liberal imagination and the four dogmas of multiculturalism. *Yale Journal of Criticism, 12*(2), 401–413.

Benhabib, S. (2002). *The claims of culture: Equality and diversity in the global era.* Princeton, NJ: Princeton University Press.

Bentley, J. H. (1993). *Old World encounters: Cross-cultural contacts and exchanges in pre-modern times.* New York: Oxford University Press.

Berelson, B. (1952). *Content analysis in communication research.* Glencoe, IL: Free Press.

Bernabé, J., Chamoiseau, P., and Confiant, R. (1989). *Éloge de la Créolité.* Paris: Gallimard.

Berry, E. E., and Epstein, M. N. (1999). *Transcultural experiments: Russian and American models of creative communication.* New York: St. Martin's Press.

Berthet, D. (Ed.). (2002). *Vers une esthétique du métissage.* Paris: L'Harmattan.

Bhabha, H. (1994). *The location of culture.* London and New York: Routledge.

Bielby, D. D., and Harrington, C. L. (2002). Markets and meanings: The global syndication of television programming. In D. Crane et al. (Eds.), *Global culture: Media, arts, policy, and globalization* (pp. 215–232). London: Routledge.

Bilby, K. (1999). "Roots explosion": Indigenization and cosmopolitanism in contemporary Surinamese popular music. *Ethnomusicology, 43*(2), 256–296.

Biltereyst, D., and Meers, P. (2000). The international telenovela debate and the contra-flow argument: A reappraisal. *Media, Culture, and Society, 22*(4), 392–414.

Blair, T. (1998). *The third way: New politics for a new century.* Fabian Pamphlet 588. London: Fabian Society.

Blanchard, M. A. (1986). *Exporting the First Amendment: The press-government crusade of 1945–1952.* New York: Longman.

Blevins, J. P. (1995). Syncretism and paradigmatic opposition. *Linguistics and Philosophy, 18,* 113–152.

Bloch, M. (1983). *Marxism and anthropology.* Oxford: Oxford University Press.

Blumler, J. G., and Katz, E. (Eds.). (1974). *The uses of mass communications: Current perspectives on gratifications research.* Beverly Hills, CA: Sage.

Boggs, V. W. (1991, Winter). Musical transculturation: From Afro-Cuban to Afro-Cubanization. *Popular Music and Society, 15*(4), 71–83.

Bolke Turner, C., and Turner, B. (1994). The role of mestizaje of surnames in Paraguay in the creation of a distinct New World ethnicity. *Ethnohistory, 41*(1), 139–165.

Bongie, C. (1998). *Islands and exiles: The Creole identities of post/colonial literature.* Stanford: Stanford University Press.

Bonniol, J. L. (Ed.). (2001). *Paradoxes du métissage.* Paris: Comité des Travaux Historiques et Scientifiques.

Bosrock, R. M. (1999, April 26). As cultural borders fade, cultural differences re-emerge. *Minneapolis Star Tribune.*

Boulos, J. C. (1995). *La Télé: Quelle histoire!* [Television: What a story]. Beirut: Fiches du Monde Arabe.

Bourdieu, P. (1979). *Distinction: Critique sociale du jugement.* Paris: Minuit. (Translated as *Distinction: A social critique of the judgment of taste.* (Richard Nice, Trans.) London: Routledge and Kegan Paul, 1987.

Boyd, D. (1991). Lebanese broadcasting: Unofficial electronic media during a prolonged civil war. *Journal of Broadcasting and Electronic Media, 35*(3), 269–287.

Boyd-Barrett, O. (1977). Media imperialism: Towards an international framework for the analysis of media systems. In J. Curran, M. Gurevitch, and J. Woollacott (Eds.), *Mass communication and society* (pp. 116–135). London: Arnold.

Boyd-Barrett, O. (1981/2). Western news agencies and the "media imperialism" debate: What kind of data-base? *Journal of International Affairs, 35*(2), 247–260.

Boyd-Barrett, O. (1995). NWICO strategies and media imperialism: The case of regional news exchange. In K. Nordenstreng and H. Schiller (Eds.),

Beyond national sovereignty: International communication in the 1990s (pp. 177–192). Norwood, NJ: Ablex.

Boyd-Barrett, O. (1997). International communication and globalization: Contradictions and directions. In A. Mohammadi (Ed.), *International communication and globalization* (pp. 11–26). London: Sage.

Boyd-Barrett, O. (1998). Media imperialism reformulated. In D. K. Thussu (Ed.), *Electronic empires: Global media and local resistance* (pp. 157–176). London: Arnold.

Brah, A., and Coombes, A. E. (2000). Introduction: The conundrum of "mixing." In A. Brah and A. E. Coombes (Eds.), *Hybridity and its discontents: Politics, science, culture* (pp. 1–16). London: Routledge.

Brah, A. and Coombes, A. E. (Eds.) (2000). *Hybridity and its discontents: Politics, science, culture*. London: Routledge.

Braman, S. (1990). Trade and information policy. *Media, Culture, and Society, 12,* 361–385.

Braman, S. (1996). Interpenetrated globalization, in S. Braman and A. Sreberny-Mohammadi (Eds.), *Globalization, communication, and transnational civil society* (pp. 21–36). Cresskill, NJ: Hampton Press.

Braman, S. (2002). A pandemonic age: The future of international communication theory and research. In W. B. Gudykunst and B. Mody (Eds.), *Handbook of international and intercultural communication* (2d ed.) (pp. 399–413). Thousand Oaks, CA, and London: Sage.

Braman, S., and Sreberny-Mohammadi, A. (Eds.). (1996). *Globalization, communication, and transnational civil society*. Cresskill, NJ: Hampton Press.

Braxton, G. (2002, January 21). Networks' showcases aim to improve diversity effort. *Los Angeles Times*.

Braxton, G. (2002, January 30). Director diversity seen as lacking. *Los Angeles Times*.

Bremmer, C. (1999, September 24). French unite against U.S. trade domination. *London Times*.

Brenkman, J. (1987). *Culture and domination*. Ithaca, NY, and London: Cornell University Press.

Brewer, A. (1990). *Marxist theories of imperialism: A critical survey*. New York: Routledge.

Briggs, C. L., and Bauman, R. (1992). Genre, intertextuality, and social power. *Journal of Linguistic Anthropology, 2*(2), 131–172.

Brown, A. (2000, Winter). Transforming business structures to hyborgs. *Employment Relations Today,* 5–14.

Brown, C. (Ed.). (1995). *Co-production international*. London: 21st Century Business Publications.

Brunel, J., and Lefort, R. (2000, May). Ocimar Versolato: Rêves, métissage et sensualité. *Courier de l' Unesco*, pp. 47–50.

Brunsdon, C., and Morley, D. (1978). *Everyday television: "Nationwide."* London: BFI.

Buckingham, D. (1987). *Public secrets: EastEnders and its audience*. London: BFI.

Budd, M., Entman, R. M., and Steinmas, C. (1990). The affirmative character of U.S. cultural studies. *Critical Studies in Mass Communication, 7,* 169–184.

Buell, F. (1998). Nationalist postnationalism: Globalist discourse in contemporary American culture. *American Quarterly, 50*(3), 548–591.

Butler, J. (1998, January–February). Merely cultural. *New Left Review, 227*, 33–44.

Calderon, H., and Saldivar, J. D. (Eds.). (1991). *Criticism in the borderlands: Studies in Chicano literature, culture, and ideology.* Durham, NC: Duke University Press.

Caldwell, J. T. (1995). Hybridity on the superhighway: Techno-futurism and historical agency. *Quarterly Review of Film and Video, 16*(1), 103–111.

Calif. resolution backs Teletubbie. (1999, February 23). Berkeley, CA: Associated Press.

Cantor, P. (2004, December 2). Review of Creative destruction: How globalization is changing the world's cultures, by Tyler Cowen. *Humane Studies Review,* available http://www.theihs.org/libertyguide/article.php/503.html.

Caplan, L. (1995). Creole world, purist rhetoric. *JRAI, 1,* 743–762.

Carey, J. W., and Kreiling, A. L. (1974). Popular culture and uses and gratifications. In J. G. Blumler and E. Katz (Eds.), *The uses of mass communication* (pp. 249–268). Beverly Hills, CA: Sage.

Carey, J. W. (1989). *Communication as culture.* Boston: Unwin Hyman.

Carey, J. W. (1995). Abolishing the old spirit world. *Critical Studies in Mass Communication, 12*(1), 82–88.

Cassirer. H. R. (1977). Radio as the people's medium. *Journal of Communication, 27*(2), 151–154.

Chabry, L., and Chabry, A. (1987). *Politique et minorités au Moyen-Orient: Les raisons d'une explosion.* Paris: Maisonneuve et Larose.

Chadha, K., and Kavoori, A. (2000). Media imperialism revisited: Some findings from the Asian case. *Media, Culture, and Society, 22*(4), 415–416.

Chambers, I. (1994). *Migrancy, culture, identity.* London and New York: Routledge.

Chan, J. M., and Ma, E. K. W. (1996). Asian television: Global trends and local processes. *Gazette, 58,* 45–60.

Chaney, D. (1972). *Processes of mass communication.* London: Macmillan.

Chang, B. G. (1996). *Deconstructing communication: Representation, subject, and economies of exchange.* Minneapolis: University of Minnesota Press.

Chang, N. (2002). *Silencing political dissent: How post–September 11 anti-terrorism measures threaten our civil liberties.* New York: Seven Stories Press.

Charles, J., Shore, L., and Todd, R. (1979). The *New York Times* coverage of Equatorial and lower Africa. *Journal of Communication, 29*(2), 148–155.

Chateau, D. (2002). Métissage ou pluralisme. In D. Berthet (Ed.), *Vers une esthétique du métissage* (pp. 39–52). Paris: L'Harmattan.

Chaudenson, R. (1992). *Des îles, des hommes, des langues: Essai sur la créolisation linguistique et culturelle.* Paris: L'Harmattan.

Chicago Cultural Studies Group. (1992). Critical multiculturalism. *Critical Inquiry, 18*(3), 530–555.

Chow, R. (1993). *Writing diaspora: Tactics of intervention in contemporary cultural studies.* Bloomington and Indianapolis: Indiana University Press.

Chuh, K. (1996). Transnationalism and its past. *Public Culture, 9*(1), 209–232.

Clarke, D. (1997). Varieties of cultural hybridity: Hong Kong art in the late colonial era. *Public Culture, 9*(2), 395–416.

Cohen, J. R. (1991). The "relevance" of cultural identity in audiences' interpretations of mass media. *Critical Studies in Mass Communication, 8*(4), 442–454.

Cohn, D., and Morello, C. (2001, March 9). N.Va.'s growth outpaces state's; census shows huge jump in minorities. *Washington Post*, p. A01.

Comor, E. (1997). The re-tooling of American hegemony: U.S. foreign communication policy from free flow to free trade. In A. Sreberny-Mohammadi et al. (Eds.), *Media in a global context: A reader* (pp. 194–206). London: Arnold.

Comor, E. (2002). Media corporations in the age of globalization. In W. B. Gudykunst and B. Mody (Eds.), *Handbook of international and intercultural communication* (2d ed.) (pp. 309–324). Thousand Oaks, CA, and London: Sage.

Condit, C. M. (1994). Hegemony in a mass-mediated society: Concordance about reproductive technologies. *Critical Studies in Mass Communication, 11*(3), 205–230.

The controversy over popular culture. (1992, March 10). *American Enterprise, 3*(3), 72.

Coombes, A. E. (1992). Inventing the "postcolonial": Hybridity and constituency in contemporary curating. *New Formations, 10*, 39–53.

Cooper, Laura E., and Cooper, B. Lee. (1993). The pendulum of cultural imperialism: Popular music interchanges between the United States and Britain, 1943–1967. *Journal of Popular Culture, 27*(3), 61–78.

Corradi, J. E. (1971). Cultural dependency and the sociology of knowledge: The Latin American case. *International Journal of Contemporary Sociology, 8*, 35–55.

Cowen, T. (2002a). *Creative destruction: How globalization is changing the world's cultures.* Princeton, NJ, and Oxford: Princeton University Press.

Cowen, T. (2002b, November 2). Creative destruction: The idea that globalization will produce a bland McWorld is a myth. *National Post*, p. A21.

Crane, D., Kawashima, N., and Kawasaki, K. (Eds.). (2002). *Global culture: Media, arts, policy, and globalization.* London: Routledge.

Culture wars (1998, September 12). *Economist*, pp. 97–99.

Cunningham, S., and Sinclair, J. (2000). *Floating lives: The media and Asian diasporas.* Australia: University of Queensland Press and Australian Key Center for Cultural and Media Policy.

Curran, J. (1990). The new revisionism in mass communication research. *European Journal of Communication, 5*, 135–164.

Curran, J., and Park, M. J. (2000). *De-Westernizing media studies.* London: Routledge.

Curtin, M. (1993, Spring). Beyond the vast wasteland: The policy discourse of global television and the politics of American empire. *Journal of Broadcasting and Electronic Media.* 37(2), 127–145.

Curtin, M. (1999). Feminine desire in the age of satellite television. *Journal of Communication, 49*(2), 55–70.

Darryl Slack, J. (1996). The theory and method of articulation in cultural studies. In D. Morley and K. H. Chen (Eds.), *Stuart Hall: Critical dialogues in cultural studies* (pp. 112–127). London and New York: Routledge.

De Certeau, M. (1980/1990). *L' Invention du quotidien: 1. Arts de faire, nouvelle édition*. Paris: Gallimard. (Translated as part of *The Practice of Everyday Life* [1984]. Berkeley: University of California Press.)

De Certeau, M., Giard, L., and Mayol, P. (1980/1990). *L' Invention du quotidien: 1. Habiter, cuisiner, nouvelle édition*. Paris: Gallimard. (Translated as part of *The Practice of Everyday Life* [1984]. Berkeley: University of California Press.)

Deleuze, G. (1994). *Difference and repetition*. (P. Patton, Trans.). New York: Columbia University Press.

Deleuze, G., and Guattari, F. (1980). *Mille plateaux* [A thousand plateaus]. Paris: Les Éditions du Minuit.

Deleuze, G., and Guattari, F. (1986). *Nomadology: The war machine*. (B. Massumi, Trans.). New York: Semiotext(e).

Demers, D. (1999). *Global media: Menace or messiah?* Cresskill, NJ: Hampton Press.

DePalma, A. (1999, July 14). Tough rules stand guard over Canadian culture. *New York Times*.

Derrida, J. (1972). *Marges de la philosophie*. Paris: Éditions de Minuit. (Translated as *Margins of Philosophy* [1982]. [A. Bass, Trans.]. Chicago: University of Chicago Press.)

Derrida, J. (1972). *Positions*. Paris: Éditions de Minuit. (Translated as *Positions* [1981] [A. Bass, Trans.]. Chicago: University of Chicago Press.)

Derrida, J. (1976). *Of grammatology* (G. C. Spivak, Trans.). Baltimore: Johns Hopkins University Press.

Derrida, J. (1980). The law of genre. *Glyph, 7*, 202–232.

Desmond, J. C., and Domínguez, V. G. (1996). Resituating American studies in a critical internationalism. *American Quarterly, 48*(3), 475–490.

Deutschman, A. (2000, August 30). Bring on the misfits. *Salon.com*. Retrieved April 4, 2003, from http://archive.salon.com/business/feature/2000/08/30/global_me/print.html.

Development communication. (1997). Special issue, *Journal of International Communication, 4*(2).

Dirlik, A. (1994). The postcolonial aura: Third world criticism in the age of global capitalism. *Critical Inquiry, 20*(2), 328–356.

Dissanayake, W. (1977). New wine in old bottles: Can folk media convey modern messages? *Journal of Communication, 27*(2), 122–136.

Dobbs, M. (2003, June 26). Iranian exiles sow change via satellite. *Washington Post*, p. A1.

Dominguez, V. (1986). *White by definition: Social classification in Creole Louisiana*. New Brunswick, NJ: Rutgers University Press.

Doremus, A. (2001). Indigenism, mestizaje, and national identity in Mexico during the 1940s and the 1950s. *Mexican Studies/Estudios Mexicanos, 17*(2), 375–402.

Dorfman, A., and Mattelart, A. (1971). *Para leer al pato Donald*. Santiago de Chile: Ediciònes Universitarias de Valparaíso. (Translated as *How to read Donald Duck: Imperialist ideology in the Disney comic*. [1975]. [D. Kunzle, Trans.]. New York: International General.)

Dorst, J. D. (1999). Which came first, the chicken device or the textual egg? Documentary film and the limits of the hybrid metaphor. *Journal of American Folklore, 112*(445), 268–281.

Doty, R. L. (1996). *Imperial encounters: The politics of representation in North-South relations*. Minneapolis: University of Minnesota Press.

Dowmunt, T. (Ed.). (1993). *Channels of resistance: Global television and local empowerment*. London: British Film Institute and Channel 4.

Downing, J. D. H. (1996). *Internationalizing media theory*. London: Sage,

Downing, J. D. H. (1997). Cultural studies, communication, and change: Eastern Europe to the Urals. In M. Ferguson and P. Golding (Eds.), *Cultural studies in question* (pp. 187–204). Thousand Oaks, CA, and London: Sage.

Downing, J. D. H. (2000). *Radical media: Rebellious communication and social movements*. London: Sage.

Drell, J. H. (1999). Cultural syncretism and ethnic identity: The Norman "conquest" of southern Italy and Sicily. *Journal of Medieval History, 25*(1), 203–213.

Drotner, K. (1994). Ethnographic enigmas: "The everyday" in recent media studies. *Cultural Studies, 8*, 208–225.

Drotner, K. (2000). Less is more: Media ethnography and its limits. In I. Hagen and J. Wasko (Eds.), *Consuming audiences? Production and reception in media research* (pp. 165–188). Cresskill, NJ: IAMCR and Hampton Press.

Drummond, L. (1980). The cultural continuum: A theory of intersystems. *Man 5*, 352–374.

Drzewiecka, J. A., and Halualani, R. T. (2002). The structural-cultural dialectic of diasporic politics. *Communication Theory, 12*(3), 340–366.

Duboux, R. (1994). *Métissage ou barbarie*. Paris: L'Harmattan.

During, S. (1997). Popular culture on a global scale: A challenge for cultural studies? *Critical Inquiry, 23*, 808–833.

Eade, J. (Ed.). (1997). *Living the global city: Globalization as local process*. London: Routledge.

Eagleton, T. (1976). *Criticism and ideology: A study in Marxist literary theory*. London: Verso.

Elasmar, M., and Hunter, J. (1997). The impact of foreign TV on a domestic audience: A meta-analysis. In *Communication Yearbook, 20*, pp. 47–69. Thousand Oaks, CA: Sage.

Elliott, P. (1974). Uses and gratifications research: A critique and a sociological alternative. In J. G. Blumler and E. Katz (Eds.), *The uses of mass communication* (pp. 249–268). Beverly Hills, CA: Sage.

Ellwood, D. W. (2000). Comparative anti-Americanism in Western Europe. In H. Fehrenbach and U. G. Poigier (Eds.), *Transactions, transgressions, transformations: American culture in Western Europe and Japan* (pp. 26–44). New York: Berghahn.

Embracing our diversity (2001, May 19). *Irish Times*, p. 62.

Enzensberger, H. M. (1984). *The consciousness industry*. New York: Seabury Press.

Enzensberger, H. M. (1992). *Mediocrity and delusion: Collected diversions* (M. Chalmers, Trans.). New York: Verso.

Erni, J. (1989). Where is the "audience"?: Discerning the (impossible) subject. *Journal of Communication Inquiry, 13*(2), 30–42.

Escobar, A. (1995). *Encountering development: The making and unmaking of the Third World*. Princeton, NJ: Princeton University Press.

Escobar, A. (2003). Place, nature, and culture in discourses of globalization. In A. Mirsepassi, A. Basu, and F. Weaver (Eds.), *Localizing knowledge in a globalizing world* (pp. 37–59). Syracuse, NY: Syracuse University Press.

Falwell denies "outing" Teletubbies, defends warning. (1999, February 25). Lynchburg, VA: Reuters.

Farhi, P., and Rosenfeld, M. (1998, October 25). American pop penetrates worldwide. *Washington Post*, p. A1.

Fears, D. (2001, April 16). Mixed-race heritage, mixed emotions. *Washington Post*, p. A1.

Featherstone, M. (Ed.). (1994). *Global culture: Nationalism, globalization, and modernity*. London and Newbury Park, CA: Sage.

Fehrenbach, H. (2000). Persistent myths of Americanization: German reconstruction and the renationalization of postwar cinema, 1945–1965. In H. Fehrenbach and U. G. Poigier (Eds.), *Transactions, transgressions, transformations: American culture in Western Europe and Japan* (pp. 81–108). New York: Berghahn.

Fehrenbach, H., and Poigier, U. G. (Eds.). (2000a). *Transactions, transgressions, transformations: American culture in Western Europe and Japan*. New York: Berghahn.

Fehrenbach, H., and Poigier, U. G. (2000b). Introduction: Americanization reconsidered. In H. Fehrenbach and U. G. Poiger (Eds.), *Transactions, transgressions, transformations: American culture in Western Europe and Japan* (pp. xiii–xxxix). New York: Berghahn.

Fejes, F. (1981). Media imperialism: An assessment. *Media, Culture, and Society*, 3(3), 281–289.

Ferguson, M. (1995). Media, markets, and identities: Reflections on the global -local dialectic. *Canadian Journal of Communications*, 20(4), available http://www.cjc-online.ca/viewarticle.php?id=313.

Ferguson, M., and Golding, P. (Eds.). (1997). *Cultural studies in question*. London and Thousand Oaks, CA: Sage.

Firro, K. M. (2003). *Inventing Lebanon: Nationalism and the state under the mandate*. London: I. B. Tauris.

Fischer, J. (1995). Some thoughts on contamination [Editorial]. *Third Text, 32*, 3–7.

Fiske, J. (1987). *Television culture*. London and New York: Routledge.

Fiske, J. (1988). Meaningful moments. *Critical Studies in Mass Communication, 5*, 246–250.

Fiske, J. (1991). *Understanding popular culture*. London and New York: Routledge.

Fiske, J. (1994). *Media matters: Everyday culture and political change*. Minneapolis: University of Minnesota Press.

Foucault, M. (1972). *The archaeology of knowledge and the discourse on language*. (A. M. Sheridan Smith, Trans.). New York: Pantheon.

Fox, C. F. (1999). *The fence and the river: Culture and politics at the U.S.-Mexico border*. Minneapolis: University of Minnesota Press.

Fox, E. (1975). Multinational television. *Journal of Communication, 25*(2), 122–127.

Fraser, N. (1997). *Justice interruptus: Critical reflections on the "postsocialist" condition*. New York and London: Routledge.

Freedman, D. (2001). Who wants to be a millionaire? The politics of television exports [Paper presented at the International Studies Association Convention, Chicago, February 20–24].

Frémeaux, J. (2002). *Les empires coloniaux dans le processus de la mondialisation*. Paris: Maisonneuve et Larose.

Freyre, G. (1936/1986). *The mansions and the shanties*. (Harriet de Onis, Trans.). Berkeley: University of California Press. (Originally published as *Sobrados e mucambos* [Brazilia: Companhia Editora Nacional]).

Friedman, J. (1994). *Cultural identity and global process*. London and Thousand Oaks, CA: Sage.

Friedman, J. (1997). Global crises, the struggle for cultural identity, and intellectual porkbarrelling: Cosmopolitans versus locals, ethnics, and nationals in an era of de-hegemonisation. In P. Werbner and T. Moddod (Eds.), *Debating cultural hybridity: Multi-cultural identities and the politics of anti-racism* (pp. 70–89). London and Atlantic Heights, NJ: Zed Books.

Fukuyama, F. (1992). *The end of history and the last man*. New York: Avon.

Funderburg, L. (2001, March 26). I am what I say I am. *Time*, p. 82.

Galtung, J. (1971). A structural theory of imperialism. *Journal of Peace Research*, 2, 81–117.

Gamio, M. (1916/1992). *Forjando patria* (4th ed.). México, DF: Editorial Porrúa. (Originally published México, DF: Porrúa Hermanos.)

García-Canclini, N. (1989). *Culturas híbridas: Estratgegias para entrar y salir de la modernidad*. Mexico City: Grijalbo. (Translated as *Hybrid cultures: Strategies for Entering and Leaving Modernity*. [1995]. [S. López and E. Schiappari, Trans.]. Minneapolis: University of Minnesota Press.]

García-Canclini, N. (1990). Cultural reconversion (H. Staver, Trans.). In G. Yúdice, J. Franco, and J. Flores (Eds.), *On edge: The crisis of Latin American culture*. Minneapolis: University of Minnesota Press.

García-Canclini, N. (1995/2001). *Consumidores y ciudadanos: Conflictos Multiculturales de la globalización*. México, DF: Grijalbo [G. Yudice et al. (2001). *Consumers and citizens: Globalization and multicultural conflicts*. Minneapolis: University of Minnesota Press.].

García-Canclini, N. (1997). Hybrid cultures and communicative strategies. *Media Development*, 44(1): 22–29.

García-Canclini, N. (1999). *La globalización imaginada*. Mexico City, Buenos Aires, and Barcelona: Paidos.

Garnham, N. (1995a). Political economy and cultural studies: Reconciliation or divorce? *Critical Studies in Mass Communication*, 12(1), 62–71.

Garnham, N. (1995b). Reply to Grossberg and Carey. *Critical Studies in Mass Communication*, 12(1), 95–100.

Garten, J. E. (1998, November 30). Cultural imperialism is no joke (Economic viewpoint). *Business Week*.

Gay Tinky Winky bad for children. (1999, February 10). *BBC Online*.

Geertz, C. (1973). *The interpretation of cultures*. New York: Basic Books.

Geertz, C. (1983). *Local knowledge*. New York: Basic Books.

Geertz, C. (1995). *After the fact: Two countries, four decades, one anthropologist*. Cambridge: Harvard University Press.

Geertz, C. (2003, February 17). Off the menu [Review of Creative destruction: How globalization is changing the world's cultures, by Tyler Cowen]. *New Republic, 228*(6), 27.

Gemayel, N. (1984a). *Les échanges culturels entre les Maronites et l'Europe, deuxième partie: Les contributions des élèves du Collège Maronite de Rome à l'essor du mouvement culturel au Liban).* Beirut: Author.

Gemayel, N. (1984b). *Les échanges culturels entre les Maronites et l'Europe: Du Collège Maronite de Rome (1584) au Collège de Ayn Warqa (1789).* Beirut: Author.

Gerbner, G. (1994). UNESCO in the U.S. press. In G. Gerbner, H. Mowlana, and K. Nordenstreng (Eds.), *The global media debate: Its rise, fall, and renewal* (pp. 111–122). Norwood, NJ: Ablex.

Gerbner, G., Mowlana, H., and Nordenstreng, K. (1994). *The global media debate: Its rise, fall, and renewal.* Norwood, NJ: Ablex.

Giddens, A. (1990). *The consequences of modernity.* Stanford, CA: Stanford University Press.

Gillespie, M. (1995). *Television, ethnicity, and cultural change.* London and New York: Routledge.

Gillespie, N. (2003, August–September). Really creative destruction: Economist Tyler Cowen argues for the cultural benefits of globalization. *Reason,* http://reason.com/0308/cr.ng.really.shtml

Gillespie, P. (2002, November 2). Lessons from history— The Wild Geese and the Irish in Europe. *Irish Times,* p. 9.

Gilroy, P. (1993). *The black Atlantic: Modernity and double consciousness.* Cambridge: Harvard University Press.

Gilroy, P. (2000). *Against race: Imagining political culture beyond the color line.* Cambridge: Harvard University Press.

Glissant, É. (1981). *Le discours Antillais.* Paris: Seuil.

Glissant, E. (1993). *Le tout-monde.* Paris: Gallimard.

Globalization. (2000). Special issue, *Third World Quarterly, 21*(6).

Globalizations are plural. (2000). Special issue, *International Sociology, 2*(15).

Gluck, S-B. (1991). Advocacy oral history: Palestinian women in resistance. In S. B. Gluck and D. Patai (Eds.), *Women's words: The feminist practice of oral history* (pp. 205–220). New York and London: Routledge

Gluck, S. B., and Patai, D. (Eds.). (1991). *Women's words: The feminist practice of oral history.* New York and London: Routledge.

Goff, P. M. (2000). Invisible borders: Economic liberalization and national identity. *International Studies Quarterly, 44,* 533–562.

Golding, P. (1994). The communication paradox: Inequality at the national and international levels. *Media Development, 4,* 7–9.

Golding, P., and Harris, P. (1997). *Beyond cultural imperialism: Globalization, communication, and the new international order.* London and Thousand Oaks, CA; Sage.

Goldman, A. (1993). Implications of Japanese total quality control for Western organizations: Dimensions of an intercultural hybrid. *Journal of Business Communication, 30*(1), 29–43.

Gómez-Peña, G. (1996). *The new world border: Prophecies, poems, and loqueras for the end of the century.* San Francisco: City Lights.

Gossiaux, J. F. (2001). Les logiques "antimétisses" de l'éthnicité: Le paradigme multinational. In J. L. Bonniol (Ed.), *Paradoxes du métissage* (233–240). Paris: Comité des Travaux Historiques et Scientifiques.

Graham, D. (1999). *Building a global audience: British television in overseas markets.* London: Department of Media, Culture, and Sports.

Granzberg, G. (1982). Television as storyteller: The Algonkian Indians of central Canada. *Journal of Communication, 32*(1), 43–52.

Gray, H. (1995). *Watching race: Television and the struggle for "blackness."* Minneapolis: University of Minnesota Press.

Grossberg, L. (1988). Wandering audiences, nomadic critics. *Cultural Studies, 2*(3), 377–390.

Grossberg, L. (1993). Cultural studies and/in new worlds. *Critical Studies in Mass Communication, 10*(10), 1–22.

Grossberg, L. (1995). Cultural studies vs. political economy: Is anyone else bored with this debate? *Critical Studies in Mass Communication, 12*(1), 72–81.

Grossberg, L. (1999). Speculations and articulations of globalization. *Polygraph, 11*, 11–48.

Grossberg, L. (2002). Postscript. *Communication Theory, 12*(3), 367–370.

Gruzinski, S. (1995). Images and cultural *mestizaje* in colonial Mexico. *Poetics Today, 16*(1), 53–77.

Gruzinski, S. (1999). *La pensée métisse.* Paris: Fayard. (Translated as *The Mestizo Mind.* [2002]. [D. Dusimberre, Trans.]. London and New York: Routledge.)

Guback, T., and Varis, T. (1986). *Transnational communication and cultural industries* [No. 92]. Paris: UNESCO Reports and Papers on Mass Communication.

Guinier, L. (1998). *Lift every voice: Turning a civil rights setback into a new vision of social justice.* New York: Simon and Schuster.

Gurevitch, M., and Kavoori, A. (1994). Global texts, narrativity, and the construction of local/global meanings. *Journal of Narrative and Life History, 4*, 9–24.

Gutierrez, F. F., and Schement, J. R. (1984). Spanish International Network: The flow of television from Mexico to the United States. *Communication Research, 11*(2), 241–258.

Hagen, I., and Wasko, J. (Eds.). (2000a). *Consuming audiences? Production and reception in media research.* Cresskill, NJ: IAMCR and Hampton Press.

Hagen, I., and Wasko, J. (2000b). Introduction: Consuming audiences? Production and reception in media research. In I. Hagen and J. Wasko (Eds.), *Consuming audiences? Production and reception in media research* (pp. 3–29). Cresskill, NJ: IAMCR and Hampton Press.

Hale, C. (1999). Travel warning: Elite appropriations of hybridity, mestizaje, antiracism, equality, and other progressive-sounding discourses in highland Guatemala. *Journal of American Folklore 112*(445), 297–315.

Hall, S. (1985). Signification, representation, ideology: Althusser and the post-structuralist debates. *Critical Studies in Mass Communication, 2*(3), 91–114.

Hall, S. (1986). On postmodernism and articulation: An Interview with Stuart Hall. (Lawrence Grossberg, Ed.). *Journal of Communication Inquiry, 10*(2), 45–60.

Hall, S. (1991a). The local and the global: Globalization and ethnicity. In A. D. King (Ed.), *Culture, globalization, and the world-system: Contemporary conditions for the representation of identity* (pp. 19–40). London: Macmillan.

Hall, S. (1991b). Old and new identities, old and new ethnicities. In A. D. King (Ed.), *Culture, globalization, and the world-system: Contemporary conditions for the representation of identity* (pp. 41–68). London: Macmillan.

Hall, S. (1992). Cultural studies and its theoretical legacies. In L. Grossberg, C. Nelson, and P. Treichler (Eds.), *Cultural studies* (pp. 277–294). New York and London: Routledge.

Hall, S. (1993). Minimal selves. In A. Gray and J. McGuigan (Eds.), *Studying culture: An introductory reader* (pp. 134–138). London and New York: Edward Arnold.

Hall, S. (1996a). The problem of ideology: Marxism without guarantees. In D. Morley and K. H. Chen (Eds.), *Stuart Hall: Critical dialogues in cultural studies* (pp. 25–46). London and New York: Routledge.

Hall S. (1996b). When was the post-colonial? Thinking at the limit. In L. Curti and I. Chambers (Eds.), *The postcolonial question* (pp. 242–260). London: Routledge.

Hall, S. (1990/1997). Encoding/Decoding. In A. Gray and J. McGuigan (Eds.), *Studying culture: An introductory reader* (pp. 90–103). London: Arnold.

Halloran, J. (1997). International communication research: Opportunities and obstacles. In A. Mohammadi (Ed.), *International communication and globalization* (pp. 27–47). London: Sage.

Halter, M. (2000). *Shopping for identity: The marketing of ethnicity.* New York: Schocken.

Hamelink, C. J. (1983). *Cultural autonomy in global communications.* New York: Longman.

Hannerz, U. (1987). The world in creolization. *Africa, 54*(4), 546–559.

Hannerz, U. (1989). Notes on the global ecumene. *Public Culture, 1*(2), 66–75.

Hannerz, U. (1992). *Cultural complexity: Studies in the social organization of meaning.* New York: Columbia University Press.

Hannerz, U. (1994). Notes on the global ecumene. In M. Featherstone (Ed.), *Global modernities* (pp. 237–252). London: Sage.

Hardt, H. (1988). Comparative media research: The world according to America. *Critical Studies in Mass Communication, 5*(2), 129–146.

Hardt, M., and Negri, A. (2000). *Empire.* Cambridge: Harvard University Press.

Harik, E. (1994). Pluralism in the Arab world. *Journal of Democracy, 4*(3), 43–56.

Haugerud, A. (2003). The disappearing local: Rethinking global-local connections. In A. Mirsepassi, A. Basu, and F. Weaver (Eds.), *Localizing knowledge in a globalizing world* (pp. 60–81). Syracuse, NY: Syracuse University Press.

Havens, T. (2000). "The biggest show in the world": Race and the global popularity of *The Cosby Show. Media, Culture, and Society, 22*(4), 371–392.

Havens, T. (2002). "It's still a white world out there": The interplay of culture and economics in international television trade. *Critical Studies in Media Communication, 19*(4), 377–397.

Hebdige, D. (1988). *Hiding in the light: On images and things.* New York: Routledge.

Hebdige, D. (1991). *Subculture: The meaning of style.* London and New York: Routledge.

Heelas, P., Lash, S., and Morris, P. (Eds.). (1996). *Detraditionalization*. Oxford, UK: Blackwell.

Hegde, R. S. (1998). A view from elsewhere: Locating difference and the politics of representation from a transnational feminist perspective. *Communication Theory, 8*(3), 271–297.

Henderson, D. R. (2002, December 12). An invasion without guns: Cultural imperialism is a red herring in today's global economy. *Wall Street Journal*. Retrieved June 19, 2003, from http://www.fcpp.org/publications_detail_print.php?PubID=483.

Henri, H. (2002). Anthropophagies et hybridations. In D. Berthet (Ed.), *Vers une esthétique du métissage* (pp. 91–106). Paris: L'Harmattan.

Henry, J. M., and Bankston, Carl L., III (1998). Propositions for a structuralist analysis of creolism. *Current Anthropology, 39*(4), 558–566.

Herman, E., and McChesney, R. (1997). *The global media: Missionaries of corporate capitalism*. London: Cassell.

Hermes, W. (1994, November–December). Imperialism: Just part of the mix? (American pop culture). *Utne Reader*, pp. 19–20.

Herold, C. M. (1988). The "Brazilianization" of Brazilian television: A critical review. *Studies in Latin American Popular Culture, 7*, 41–58.

Hicks, D. E. (1991). *Border writing: The multidimensional text*. Minneapolis: University of Minnesota Press.

Highlights of the Mexican Federal Copyrights Law (1998). *The U.S.-Mexico Legal Reporter*. Gray Cary Ware and Freidenrich LLP. Retrieved June 10, 2003, from http://library.lp.findlaw.com/articles/file/firms/graycary/gcwf000155.

Hobson, D. (1982). *Crossroads: The drama of a soap opera*. London: Methuen.

Hogan, J. (1999). The construction of gendered national identities in the television advertisements of Japan and Autralia. *Media, Culture, and Society, 21*, 743–758.

Hollinshead, K. (1998). Tourism, hybridity, and ambiguity: The relevance of Bhabha's 'third space' cultures. *Journal of Leisure Research, 30*(1), 121–156.

Hood, J. N., and Koberg, C. S. (1994). Patterns of differential assimilation and acculturation for women in business organizations. *Human Relations, 47*(2), 159–179.

Hoover's Online (2004a). Grupo Televisa, S.A. Retrieved March 3, 2004, from http://www.hoovers.com/grupo-televisa.-s.a./–ID_51043–/free-co-factsheet.xhtml.

Hoover's Online (2004b). TV Azteca S.A. de C.V. Retrieved March 3, 2004, from http://www.hoovers.com/tv-azteca.-s.a./–ID_53615–/free-co-fin-factsheet.xhtml.

Hubka, D. (2002). Globalization of cultural production: The transformation of children's animated television, 1980 to 1995. In D. Crane et al. (Eds.), *Global culture: Media, arts, policy, and globalization* (pp. 233–255). London: Routledge.

Hudson, M. (1968). *The precarious republic*. New York: Random House.

Huey, J. (1990, December 31). America's hottest export: Pop culture. *Fortune*, pp. 50–60.

Human rights. (1999). Special issue, *Journal of International Communication, 6*(1).

192   BIBLIOGRAPHY

Hunter, S. (2000, March 26). East meets West in Chan's "Shanghai Noon." *Washington Post*, p. C5.

Huntington, S. (1993, Summer). The clash of civilizations? *Foreign Affairs, 72*(3), 22–28.

Huntington, S. (1996). *The clash of civilizations and the remaking of world order.* New York: Touchstone.

Huntington, S. (2000). Try again: A reply to Russett, Oneal, and Cox. *Journal of Peace Research, 37*(5), 609–610.

Hutnyk, J. (1997). Adorno at Womad: South Asia crossovers and the limits of hybridity-talk. In P. Werbner and T. Moddod (Eds.), *Debating cultural hybridity: Multi-cultural identities and the politics of anti-racism* (pp. 106–138). London and Atlantic Highlands, NJ: Zed Books.

Hutnyk, J. (1999/2000). Hybridity saves? Authenticity and/or the critique of appropriation. *Amerasia Journal, 25*(3), 39–58.

Hymes, D. (1971). *Pidginization and creolization of languages.* Cambridge: Cambridge University Press.

Inglehart, R., and Baker, W. E. (2000). Modernization, cultural change, and the persistence of traditional values. *American Sociological Review, 65*, 19–51.

International Teletubbies celebration at FAO Schwartz is fantasy come true for kids. (1999, March 24). [Press release]. New York: Microsoft.

Iyer, P. (2000). *The global soul: Jet lags, shopping malls, and the search for home.* New York: Knopf.

Jacka, E. (Ed.). (1992). *Continental shift: Globalisation and culture.* Double Bay, Australia: Local Consumption.

Jacobson, T. L. (1999). Cultural imperialism, hybridity, and the reflective appropriation of tradition. In K. G. Wilkins (Ed.), *Redeveloping communication for social change.* Lanham, MD: Rowman and Littlefield.

James, B. (1995). Learning to consume: An ethnographic study of cultural change in Hungary. *Critical Studies in Mass Communication, 12*(3), 287–304.

Jameson, F. (1981). *The political unconscious: Narrative as a socially symbolic act.* Ithaca, NY: Cornell University Press.

Jameson, F. (1991). *Postmodernism, or The cultural logic of late capitalism.* Durham, NC: Duke University Press.

Jameson, F. (1998). Globalization as a philosophical issue. In F. Jameson and M. Miyoshi (Eds.), *The cultures of globalization* (pp. 54–80). Durham, NC: Duke University Press.

Jameson, F., and Miyoshi, M. (Eds.) (1998). *The cultures of globalization.* Durham, NC: Duke University Press.

Jay, P. (2001). Beyond discipline? Globalization and the future of English. *PMLA, 11*(1), 32–47.

Joseph, M. (1994). Introduction: Diaspora, new hybrid identities, and the performance of citizenship. *Women and Performance Quarterly, 14/15*, 3–13.

Joseph, M. (1999). Introduction: New hybrid identities and performance. In M. Joseph and J. N. Fink, (Eds.), *Performing hybridity* (pp. 1–24). Minneapolis: University of Minnesota Press.

Joseph, M., and Fink, J. N. (Eds.). (1999). *Performing hybridity.* Minneapolis: University of Minnesota Press.

Jourdan, C. (1991). Pidgins and Creoles: The blurring of categories. *Annual Review of Anthropology, 20*, 187–209.

Jussawalla, F. (1995). Of the Satanic Verses' Mohajirs and Migrants: Hybridity vs. syncretism and indigenous aesthetics in postcoloniality. *Third Text, 32*, 94.

Kamalipour, Y. R. (Ed.). (1995). *The U.S. media and the Middle East: Image and perception*. Westport, CT: Praeger.

Kang, J. G., and Morgan, M. (1988). Culture clash: Impact of U.S. television in Korea. *Journalism Quarterly, 65*, 431–438.

Kapchan, D. (1993). Hybridization and the marketplace: Emerging paradigm in folkloristics. *Western Folklore 52*, 303–326.

Kapchan, D., and Turner-Strong, P. (Eds.). (1999). Theorizing the hybrid. Special issue, *Journal of American Folklore, 112*(445).

Kaplan, A. (1993). "Left alone in America": The absence of empire in the study of American culture. In A. Kaplan and D. E. Pease (Eds.), *Cultures of United States imperialism* (pp. 3–21). Durham, NC, and London: Duke University Press.

Kaplan, A., and Pease, D. E. (Eds.) (1993). *Cultures of United States imperialism*. Durham, NC, and London: Duke University Press.

Kapner, S. (2003, January 3). U.S. TV shows losing potency around world. *New York Times*, http://www.nytimes.com/2003/01/02/businessspecial/02TUBE.html.

Katz, E. (1959). Mass communication research and popular culture. *Studies in Public Comunication, 2*, 1–6.

Katz, E. (1977). Can authentic cultures survive new media? *Journal of Communication, 27*(2), 113–121.

Katz, E., Blumler, J. G., and Gurevitch, M. (1974). Utilization of mass communication by the individual. In J. G. Blumler and E. Katz (Eds.), *The uses of mass communication* (pp. 19–32). Beverly Hills, CA: Sage.

Katz, E., and Lazarsfeld, P. (1955). *Personal influence*. New York: Free Press.

Kavoori, A. P. (1998). Getting past the latest "post": Assessing the term "post-colonial." *Critical Studies in Mass Communication, 15*(2), 195–202.

Kellogg, S. (2000). Depicting *mestizaje*: Gendered images of ethnorace in colonial Mexican texts. *Journal of Women's History, 12*(3), 67–92.

Khalaf, S. (1987). *Lebanon's predicament*. New York: Columbia University Press.

Khalaf, S. (2002). *Civil and uncivil violence in Lebanon: A history of the internationalization of communal conflict*. New York: Columbia University Press.

Khalil, J. (2002). The search for ideas: Aspects of program exchange on Arab satellite channels [Paper presented at the annual meeting of the Arab U.S. Association of Communication Educators (AUSACE), Beirut, Lebanon, October 31–November 1].

King, A. (1990/1997). *Culture, globalization, and the world-system*. Minneapolis: University of Minnesota Press.

Kipling, R. (1901). *Kim*. London: Macmillan.

Klapper, J. (1960). *The effect of mass communication*. Glencoe, IL: Free Press.

Kleinwachter, W. (1994). Three waves of the debate. In G. Gerbner, H. Mowlana, and K. Nordenstreng (Eds.), *The global media debate: Its rise, fall, and renewal* (pp. 13–20). Norwood, NJ: Ablex.

Knox, R. (1850). *The races of men: A fragment*. London: Renshaw.

Kohl, P. R. (1997). Reading between the lines: Music and noise in hegemony and resistance. *Popular Music and Society, 21*(3), 3–17.

Kolar-Panov, D. (1996). Video and the diasporic imagination of selfhood: A case study of the Croatians in Australia. *Cultural Studies, 10*(2), 288–314.

Kolar-Panov, D. (1997). *Video, war, and the diasporic imagination.* London and New York: Routledge.

Kraidy, M. M. (1998a). Broadcasting regulation and civil society in post-war Lebanon. *Journal of Broadcasting and Electronic Media, 42*(3), 387–400.

Kraidy, M. M. (1998b). Intertextual maneuvers around the subaltern: *Aladdin* as a postmodern text. In Cristina Degli-Esposti (Ed.), *Postmodernism and the cinema* (pp. 45–59). Oxford, UK, and New York: Berghahn.

Kraidy, M. M. (1999a). The local, the global, and the hybrid: A native ethnography of glocalization. *Critical Studies in Media Communication, 16*(4), 456–477.

Kraidy, M. M. (1999b). State control of television news in 1990s Lebanon. *Journalism and Mass Communication Quarterly, 76*(3), 485–498.

Kraidy, M. M. (2000). Television and civic discourse in postwar Lebanon. In L. A. Gher and H. Y. Amin (Eds.), *Civic discourse and digital age communications in the Middle East* (pp. 3–18). Stamford, CT: Ablex.

Kraidy, M. M. (2001). National television between localization and globalization. In Y. Kamalipour and K. Rampal (Eds.), *Media, sex, and drugs in the global village* (pp. 261–272). Lanham, MD: Rowman and Littlefield.

Kraidy, M. M. (2002a). Hybridity in cultural globalization. *Communication Theory, 12*(3), 316–339.

Kraidy, M. M. (2002b). Arab satellite television between globalization and regionalization. *Global Media Journal, 1*, 1, http://lass.calumet.purdue.edu/cca/gmj/new_page_1.htm.

Kraidy, M. M. (2002c). Ferment in global media studies. *Journal of Broadcasting and Electronic Media, 46*(4), 630–640.

Kraidy, M. M. (2002d). State-media relations in Lebanon: National, regional, and global dimensions of the shutdown of MTV [Paper presented at the convention of the Middle East Studies Association, Washington, D.C., November 23–26].

Kraidy, M. M. (2003a). Globalization *avant la lettre?* Cultural hybridity and media power in Lebanon. In P. D. Murphy and M. M. Kraidy (Eds.), *Global media studies: Ethnographic perspectives* (pp. 276–296). London and New York: Routledge.

Kraidy, M. M. (2003b). Glocalization: An international communication framework? *Journal of International Communication, 9*(2), 29–49.

Kraidy, M. M. (2004). From culture to hybridity in international communication. In M. Semati (Ed.), *New frontiers in international communication theory* (pp. 247–262). Laurel, MD: Rowman and Littlefield.

Kraidy, M. M., and Murphy, P. D. (2003). Media ethnography: Global, local, or translocal. In P. D. Murphy and M. M. Kraidy, *Global media studies: Ethnographic perspectives* (pp. 299–307). London and New York: Routledge.

Kraniaukas, J. (2000). Hybridity in transnational frame: Latin-Americanist and post-colonial perspectives on cultural studies. In A. Brah and A. E. Coombes

(Eds.), *Hybridity and its discontents: Politics, science, culture* (pp. 235–256). London: Routledge.

Kumar, S., and Curtin, M. (2002). "Made in India": Between music television and patriarchy. *Television and New Media, 3*(4), 345–366.

Kuper, A. (2000). *Culture: The anthropologist's account.* Cambridge: Harvard University Press.

Laclau, E. (1977). *Politics and ideology in Marxist theory.* London: New Left Books.

Laclau, E., and Mouffe, C. (1985). *Hegemony and socialist strategy: Towards a radical democratic politics.* London and New York: Verso.

LaFranchi, H. (2000, July 24). Freedom of expression? Jerry Springer–style programs invade Mexico. *Christian Science Monitor.*

Laing, D. (1986). The music industry and the "cultural" imperialism thesis. *Media, Culture, and Society, 8,* 331–341.

Lancaster, J. (1998, October 27). Barbie, "Titanic" show good side of the U.S. *Washington Post,* p. A1.

Laroche, E. (1949). *Histoire de la racine nem- en grec ancien* [A history of the root nem-in ancient Greek]. Paris: Klincksieck.

Larson, F. (1979). International affairs coverage on U.S. network television. *Journal of Communication, 29*(2), 136–147.

Lauer, M. (1993). Modernity, a foreign body: Néstor García Canclini's *Culturas híbridas. Traversia, 3,* 125–133.

Lazarsfeld, P., Berelson, B., and Gaudet, H. (1944). *The people's choice.* New York: Duell, Sloan and Pearce.

Lebanon factbook. (1997). Langley, VA: Central Intelligence Agency.

Lee, B. (1995). Critical internationalism. *Public Culture, 7*(3), 559–592.

Lee, C. C. (1980). *Media imperialism reconsidered: The homogenizing of television culture.* Beverly Hills, CA: Sage.

Lee, P. S. N. (1991). The absorption and indigenization of foreign media cultures: A study of a cultural meeting point of the East and West: Hong Kong. *Asian Journal of Communication, 1*(2), 52–72.

Leeds-Hurwtiz, W. (1990). Notes on the history of intercultural communication: The Foreign Service Institute and the mandate for intercultural training. *Quarterly Journal of Speech, 76,* 262–281.

Lemish, D., and Tidhar, C. E. (2001). How global does it get? The Teletubbies in Israel. *Journal of Broadcasting and Electronic Media, 45*(4), 558–574.

Leung, L., and Wei, R. (2000). More than just talk on the move: Uses and gratifications of the cellular phone. *Journalism and Mass Communication Quarterly, 77*(2), 308–320.

Levitt, T. (1983). The globalization of markets. *Harvard Business Review, 63*(3), 92–102.

Lewis, G. H. (1991, Winter). Ghosts, ragged but beautiful: Influences of Mexican music on American country-western and rock 'n' roll. *Popular Music and Society, 15*(4), 86–103.

Liebes, T. (1988). Cultural differences in the retelling of television fiction. *Critical Studies in Mass Communication, 5*(4), 277–292.

Liebes, T., and Katz, E. (1990). *The export of meaning: Cross-cultural readings of "Dallas."* London and New York: Oxford University Press.

Livingston, R. E. (2001). Glocal knowledges: Agency and place in literary studies. *PMLA, 116*(1), 145–157.

Lomelí, A. (2003). The internationalization of Mexican television [Paper presented at the Global Fusion 2003 conference, Austin, TX, November 1–3].

Longley, E., and Kiberd, D. (2001). *Multi-culturalism: The view from the two Irelands.* Cork: Cork University Press.

Lotman, Y. (1991). *The universe of the mind* (A. Shukman, Trans.). London: Taursus Press.

Lozano, J. C. (1996). Media reception on the Mexican border with the United States. In E. G. McAnany and K. Wilkinson (Eds.), *Mass media and free trade: NAFTA and the cultural industries* (pp. 157–186). Austin: University of Texas Press.

Lukacs, G. (1994). *Historical consciousness: The remembered past.* New Brunswick, NJ: Transaction.

Lull, J. (1988). *World families watch television.* Newbury Park, CA: Sage.

Mackenzie, H. (1999, March 16). U.S. seen as cultural imperialist. Available http://www.globalpolicy.org/globaliz/cultural/cultimp.htm.

Mackey, S. (1989). *Lebanon: Death of a nation.* Chicago: Congdon and Weed.

Makdissi, U. (2000). *The culture of sectarianism.* Berkeley: University of California Press.

Marchetti, G. (1998). Transnational cinema, hybrid identities, and the films of Evans Chan. *Postmodern Culture,* available http://jefferson.village.virginia.edu/pmc/text-only/issue.198/8.2marchetti.

Marcus, G. E. (1998). *Ethnography through thick and thin.* Princeton, NJ: Princeton University Press.

Martin, T. H., Byrne, R. B., and Wedemeyer, D. J. (1977). Balance: An aspect of the right to communicate. *Journal of Communication, 27*(2), 155–159.

Martín-Barbero, J. (1993a). *Communication, culture, and hegemony: From the media to mediations.* London and Newbury Park, CA: Sage.

Martín-Barbero, J. (1993b). Latin America: Cultures in the communication media. *Journal of Communication, 43*(2), 18–30.

Martín-Barbero, J. (2000). The cultural mediations of television consumption. In I. Hagen and J. Wasko (Eds.), *Consuming audiences? Production and reception in media research* (pp. 145–162). Cresskill, NJ: IAMCR and Hampton Press.

Martín-Barbero, J. (2002). Identities: Traditions and new communities. *Media, Culture, and Society, 24*(5), 621–642.

Martínez-Echazábal, L. (1998). *Mestizaje* and the discourse of national/cultural identity in Latin America. *Latin American Perspectives, 25*(3), 21–42.

Masmoudi, M. (1979). The new world information order. *Journal of Communication, 29*(2), 172–179.

Mattelart, A. (1979). *Multinational corporations and the control of culture.* Atlantic Highlands, NJ: Humanities Press.

Mattelart, A. (1983). *Transnationals and the third world: The struggle for culture.* South Hadley, MA: Bergin and Harvey.

Mattelart, A. (1994). *Mapping world communication: War, progress, culture.* Minneapolis: University of Minnesota Press.

Mattelart, A. (1998). Généalogie des nouveaux scénarios de la communication. In J. Berdot, F. Calvez, and I. Ramonet (Eds.), *L'après-télévision: Multimedia, virtual, Internet. Acts du Colloquia "25 images/seconded."* Valence, France: CRAC.

Mattelart, A. (2002). An archeology of the global era: Constructing a belief. *Media, Culture, and Society, 24*(5), 591–612.

Maser, M. J. (1996, Spring). Culture in international relations. *Washington Quarterly.*

Mayo, J. K, Oliveira, J. B. A., Rogers, E. M., Guitarist, S. D. P., and Monett, F. (1984). The transfer of Sesame Street to Latin America. *Communication Research, 11*(2), 259–280.

McAllister, M. P. (1992). Recombinant television genres and Doogie Howser, M. D. *Journal of Popular Film and Television, 20*(3), 61–69.

McAnany, E., and Wilkinson, K. (1992). From cultural imperialism to takeover victims? Questions of Hollywood's buyouts from the critical tradition. *Communication Research, 19*(6), 724–748.

McAnany, E., and Wilkinson, K. (Eds.). (1996). *Mass media and free trade: NAFTA and the cultural industries.* Austin: University of Texas Press.

McClintock, A. (1992). The angel of progress: Pitfalls of the term "post-colonialism." *Social Text, 31/32,* 1–15.

McComb, D. (Ed.). (1989). Cultural studies and ethnography. Special issue, *Journal of Communication Inquiry, 13*(2).

McFadyen, S., Hoskins, C., and Finn, A. (1998). The effects of cultural differences on the international co-production of television programs and feature films. *Canadian Journal of Communication, 23*(4).

McGee, J. (2001, November 4). An intelligence giant in the making. *Washington Post,* p. A4.

McGee, M. C. (1980). The "ideograph": A link between rhetoric and ideology. *Quarterly Journal of Speech, 66,* 1–16.

McGray, D. (2002, May–June). Japan's gross national cool. *Foreign Policy,* pp. 44–54.

McGuigan, J. (1992). *Cultural populism.* London and New York: Routledge.

McQuail, D. (1984). *Mass communication theory: An introduction.* London: Sage.

McQuail, D., and Gurevitch, M. (1974). Explaining audience behavior: Three approaches considered. In J. Blumler and E. Katz (Eds.), *The uses of mass communications: Current perspectives on gratifications research* (pp. 287–301). Beverly Hills, CA: Sage.

McQueen, D. (1984). With the benefit of hindsight: Reflections on uses and gratifications research. *Critical Studies in Mass Communication, 1*(1), 77–93.

McQueen, D., and Gurevitch, M. (1974). Explaining audience behavior. In J. G. Blumler and E. Katz (Eds.), *The uses of mass communication* (pp. 287–306). Beverly Hills, CA: Sage.

Mélia, J. (1986). *Chez les Chrétiens d'Orient* [At the Christians of the Orient]. Beirut: Dar al Majani.

Merton, R. (1946). *Mass persuasion.* New York: Free Press.

Metcalf, P. (2001). Global "disjuncture" and the "sites" of anthropology. *Cultural Anthropology, 16*(2), 165–182.

Métissage culturel entre religions écrites et traditions orales. (2000). Special issue, *Diogène, 187.*

México en el mundo: Nos sirve ser uno de los campeones mundiales en la negotiación de acuerdos de libre comercio? [Mexico in the world: Is it in our interest to be one of the world champions in negotiating free trade agreements]. (2000, June 7). *Expansión, 31*(792), 1.

Mexico's Televisa shares rally on restructure. (1999, February 1). Mexico City: Reuters.

Mexico's TV Azteca shares rise 10 percent. (1999, December 15). Mexico City: Reuters.

Michaelsen, S. (1998). Hybrid bound. *Postmodern Culture, 8*(3), available http//: www.iath.Virginia.edu/pmc/text-only/issue.598/8.3.r_michaelsen.txt.

Michaelsen, S., and Johnson, D. E. (Eds.). (1997). *Border theory: The limits of cultural politics.* Minneapolis: University of Minnesota Press.

Mighty is the mongrel? Winning in the global economy (2000, November 20). Cato Institute Book Forum, Cato Institute. Retrieved April 4, 2003, from http://www.freetrade.org/pubs/speeches/cf-112000.html.

Mignolo, W. D. (2000). *Local histories/Global designs: Coloniality, subaltern knowledges, and border thinking.* Princeton, NJ: Princeton University Press.

Miller, D. (Ed.). (1995). *Worlds apart: Modernity through the prism of the local.* London: Routledge.

Miller, T., Govil, N., McMurria, J., and Maxwell, R. (2001). *Global Hollywood.* London: British Film Institute.

Minganti, F. (2000). Jukebox boys: Postwar Italian music and the culture of covering. In H. Fehrenbach and U. G. Poiger (Eds.), *Transactions, transgressions, transformations: American culture in Western Europe* (pp. 148–165). New York: Berghahn.

Minority roles in movies, TV dip in 1998. (1999, May 4). Los Angeles: Reuters.

Mirsepassi, A., Basu, A., and Weaver, F. (Eds.). (2003). *Localizing knowledge in a globalizing world.* Syracuse, NY: Syracuse University Press.

Mishra, V., and Hodge, B. (1991). What is post(-) colonialism? *Textual Practice, 5*(3), 399–414.

Miyoshi, M. (1993). A borderless world? From colonialism to transnationalism and the decline of the nation-state. *Critical Inquiry, 19,* 726–750.

Mohammadi, A. (Ed.). (1997). *International communication and globalization.* London: Sage.

Mohammadi, A. (1995). Cultural imperialism and cultural identity. In J. Downing, A. Sreberny-Mohammadi, and A. Mohammadi, *Questioning the media* (pp. 362–378). Newbury Park, CA: Sage.

Molína-Enríquez, A. (1909/1978). *Los grandes problemas nacionales.* Mexico: Ediciones Era.

Moore, S. (2001, March 5). New census' options challenge traditional thinking. *Los Angeles Times,* http://www.latimes.com.

Moore-Gilbert, B. (1997). *Postcolonial theory: Contexts, practices, politics.* London and New York: Verso.

Moran, A. (1998). *Copycat TV: Globalisation, program formats, and cultural identity.* Luton, UK: University of Luton Press.

Moreau, A. S. (2000). Syncretism. In *Evangelical Dictionary of World Missions.* Grand Rapids, MI: Baker Book House.

Moreiras, A. (1999). Hybridity and double consciousness. *Cultural Studies,* 13(3), 373–407.

Morelo, C. (2001, April 1). Census snapshot frames the future. *Washington Post,* p. A1.

Morgan, R. (1999, June 7). Teletubbies promo items prove too popular. New York: Reuters.

Morley, D. (1980). *The "nationwide" audience: Structure and decoding.* London: BFI.

Morley, D. (1983). Cultural transformations: The politics of resistance. In H. Davis and P. Walton (Eds.), *Language, image, media* (pp. 104–119). London: Blackwell.

Morley, D. (1992). *Television, audiences, and cultural studies.* London: Routledge.

Morley, D. (1995). Active audience theory: Pendulums and pitfalls. *Journal of Communication* 43(4), 255–261.

Morley, D. (1996). EurAm, modernity, reason, and alterity, or postmodernism, the highest stage of cultural imperialism? In D. Morley and K. H. Chen (Eds.), *Stuart Hall: Critical Dialogues in Cultural Studies.* London and New York: Routledge.

Morley, D. (1997). Theoretical orthodoxies: Textualism, constructivism, and the "new ethnography" in cultural studies. In M. Ferguson and P. Golding (Eds.), *Cultural studies in question* (pp. 121–137). Thousand Oaks, CA, and London: Sage.

Morley, D., and Brunsdon, C. (1978). *Everyday television "nationwide."* London: BFI.

Morley, D., and Chen, K. H. (Eds.). (1996). *Stuart Hall: Critical dialogues in cultural studies.* London and New York: Routledge.

Morris, N. (2002). The myth of unadulterated culture meets the threat of imported media. *Media, Culture, and Society, 24,* 278–289.

Morris, N., and Waisbord, S. (2001). *Media and globalization: Why the state matters.* Lanham, MD: Rowman and Littlefield.

Morris, R. (1997). Educating savages. *Quarterly Journal of Speech, 83,* 152–171.

Morton, P. A. (2000). *Hybrid modernities: Architecture and representation at the 1931 Colonial Exposition, Paris.* Cambridge: MIT Press.

Mosco, V., and Kaye, L. (2000). Questioning the concept of the audience. In I. Hagen and J. Wasko (Eds.), *Consuming audiences? Production and reception in media research* (pp. 31–46). Cresskill, NJ: IAMCR and Hampton Press.

Mosco, V., and Schiller, D. (2001). *Continental order? Integrating North America for cybercapitalism.* Lanham, MD: Rowman and Littlefield.

Mouffe, C. (1994). For a politics of nomadic identity. In Robertson et al. (Eds.), *Travelers' tales: Narratives of home and displacement* (pp. 105–113). London and New York: Routledge.

Mummery, J. (1966, October 27). The protection of ideas, I. *New Law Journal,* pp. 1455–1456.

Murdock, G. (1995). Across the great divide: Cultural analysis and the condition of democracy. *Critical Studies in Mass Communication, 12(1),* 89–94.

Murphy, P. D. (2003). Chasing echoes: Culture reconversion, self-representation, and mediascapes in Mexico. In P. D. Murphy and M. M. Kraidy (Eds.), *Global media studies: Ethnographic perspectives* (pp. 257–275). London and New York: Routledge.

Murphy, P. D., and Kraidy, M. M. (2003a). *Global media studies: Ethnographic perspectives.* London and New York: Routledge.

Murphy, P. D., and Kraidy, M. M. (2003b). International Communication, Ethnography, and the Challenge of Globalization. *Communication Theory, 13*(3), 304–323.

Naficy, H. (1993). *The making of exile cultures: Iranian television in Los Angeles.* Minneapolis: University of Minnesota Press.

Nakayama, T. R., and Krizek, R. L. (1995). Whiteness: A strategic rhetoric. *Quarterly Journal of Speech, 81,* 291–309.

Natsis, J. J. (1999). Legislation and language: The politics of speaking French in Louisiana. *French Review, 73*(2), 325–331.

Nederveen Pieterse, J. (1994). Globalisation as hybridisation. *International Sociology, 9*(2), 161–184.

Nederveen Pieterse, J. N. (1996, June 8). Globalisation and culture: Three paradigms. *Economic and Political Weekly, 31*(23), 1389–1393.

Nederveen Pieterse, J. N. (2001). Hybridity, so what? The anti-hybridity backlash and the riddles of recognition. *Theory, Culture, and Society, 18*(2), 219–245.

Nederveen Pieterse, J. N. (2004). *Globalization and culture: Global mélange.* Lanham, MD: Rowman and Littlefield.

Nexica, I. J. (1997). Music marketing: Tropes of hybrids, crossovers, and cultural dialogue through music. *Popular Music and Society, 21*(3), 61–82.

Nightingale, V. (1996). *Studying audiences: The shock of the real.* London: Routledge.

Nisan, M. (1992). *Minorities in the Middle-East: A history of struggle and self-expression.* Jefferson, NC: MacFarland.

Noble, G., Pynting, S., and Tabar, P. (1999). Youth, ethnicity, and the mapping of identities: Strategic essentialism and strategic hybridity among male Arabic-speaking youth in southwestern Sydney. *Communal/Plural, 7*(1), 29–44.

Nordenstreng, K. (2001). Epilogue. In N. Morris and S. Waisbord (Eds.), *Media and globalization: Why the state matters* (pp. 155–160). Boulder, CO: Rowman and Littlefield.

Nordenstreng, K., and Schiller, H. (Eds.). (1979). *National sovereignty and international communication.* Norwood, NJ: Ablex.

Nordenstreng, K., and Varis, T. (1973). Television traffic: A one-way street? *Reports, Papers on Mass Communication #70.* Paris: UNESCO.

Nurse, K. (1999). Globalization and Trinidad carnival: Diaspora, hybridity, and identity in global culture. *Cultural Studies, 13*(4), 661–690.

Nye, J. S., Jr. (1990, October 3). No, the U.S. isn't in decline. *New York Times,* p. A33.

Obeyesekere, G. (1992). *The apotheosis of Captain Cook: European mythmaking in the Pacific.* Princeton, NJ: Princeton University Press.

O'Brien, R. C. (1977). Professionalism in broadcasting in developing countries. *Journal of Communication, 27*(2), 138–152.

Ogan, C. (1988). Media imperialism and the videocassette recorder: The case of Turkey. *Journal of Communication, 38*(2), 93–106.

Ogan, C. (2001). *Communication and identity in the diaspora.* Laurel, MD: Lexington.

Oliveira, O. S. (1988). Brazilian media usage as a test of dependency theory. *Canadian Journal of Commmunication, 13,* 16–27.

Oliveira, O. S. (1989). Media and dependency: A view from Latin America. *Media Development,* no. 1, 10–13.

Oliveira, O. S. (1990). "Brazilian soaps outshine Hollywood: Is cultural imperialism fading out? In K. Nordenstreng and H. Schiller (Eds.), *Beyond national sovereignty: International communication in the 1990s* (pp. 116–131). Norwood: Ablex.

Olson, S. (1999). *Hollywood planet: Global media and the competitive advantage of narrative transparency.* Mahwah, NJ: Lawrence Erlbaum Associates.

The one where Pooh goes to Sweden (2003, April 3). *Economist,* p. 73.

Oneal, J. R., and Russett, B. M. (2000). A response to Huntington. *Journal of Peace Research, 37*(5), 611–612.

Ortiz, F. (1940/1995). *Cuban counterpoint: Tobacco and sugar.* Durham, NC: Duke University Press. (Originally published as *Contrapunteo cubano del tabaco y el azúcar,* Havana: J. Montero.)

Ortiz, F. (1952). La Transculturación Blanca de los Tambores de los Negros [White transculturation of drums of the blacks]. *Archivos Venezolanos de Folklore, 1*(2), 235–265.

Østerud, S. (2000). How can audience research overcome the divide between macro- and micro-analysis, between social structure and action? In I. Hagen and J. Wasko (Eds.), *Consuming audiences? Production and reception in media research* (pp. 123–144). Cresskill, NJ: IAMCR and Hampton Press.

Palmer, A. W. (1995). The Arab image in newspaper political cartooons. In Y. R. Kamalipour (Ed.), *The U.S. media and the Middle East: Image and perception* (pp. 139–150). Westport, CT: Praeger.

Palumbo-Liu, D., and Gumbrecht, H. U. (1997). *Streams of cultural capital.* Stanford, CA: Stanford University Press.

Pang, A. S. K. (2000, November). Mongrel capitalism. *Atlantic Monthly,* pp. 118–120.

Papacharisi, Z., and Rubin, A. M. (2000). Predictors of Internet use. *Journal of Broadcasting and Electronic Media, 44*(2), 175–198.

Papastergiadis, N. (1995). Restless hybrids. *Third Text, 32,* 9–18.

Papastergiadis, N. (1997). Tracing hybridity in theory. In P. Werbner and T. Moddod (Eds.), *Debating cultural hybridity: Multi-cultural identities and the politics of anti-racism,* pp. 257–281. London and Atlantic Highlands, NJ: Zed Books.

Papastergiadis, N. (2000). *The turbulence of migration: Globalization, deterritorialization, and hybridity.* Cambridge: Polity Press.

Parameswaran, R. (1997). Colonial interventions and the postcolonial situation in India. *Gazette, 59*(1), 21–42.

Parameswaran, R. (1999). Western romance fiction as English-language media in postcolonial India. *Journal of Communication, 49*(3), 84–105.

Parameswaran, R. (2002). Local culture in global media: Excavating colonial and material discourses in *National Geographic. Communication Theory, 12*(3), 287–315.

Paredes, M. C. (2001). The reorganization of Spanish-language media marketing in the United States. In V. Mosco and D. Schiller (Eds.), *Continental order? Integrating North America for cybercapitalism* (pp. 120–135). Lanham, MD: Rowman and Littlefield.

Participatory communication. (2001). Special issue, *Journal of International Communication, 8*(2).

Paulis, C. (2001). De l'hybride au schizophrène. In J. L. Bonniol (Ed.), *Paradoxes du métissage* (pp. 93–104). Paris: Comité des Travaux Historiques et Scientifiques.

Payne, D. E., and Peake, C. A. (1977). Cultural diffusion: The role of U.S. TV in Iceland. *Journalism Quarterly, 54,* 523–531.

Paxman, A., and Saragoza, A. M. (2001). Globalization and Latin media powers: The case of Mexico's Televisa. In V. Mosco and D. Schiller (Eds.), *Continental order? Integrating North America for cybercapitalism* (pp. 64–85). Lanham, MD: Rowman and Littlefield.

Pease, D. E. (1993). New perspectives on U.S. culture and imperialism. In A. Kaplan and D. E. Pease (Eds.), *Cultures of United States imperialism* (pp. 22.–40). Durham, NC, and London: Duke University Press.

Pells, R. (1997, May 2). The local and global loyalties of Europeans and Americans. *Chronicle of Higher Education,* p. B4

Petterson, J. (2000). No more song and dance: French radio broadcast quotas, *chansons,* and cultural exceptions. In H. Fehrenbach and U. G. Poigier (Eds.), *Transactions, transgressions, transformations: American culture in Western Europe and Japan* (pp. 109–126). New York: Berghahn.

Phares, W. (1995). *Lebanese Christian nationalism: The rise and fall of an ethnic resistance.* Boulder, CO: Lynne Reiner.

Phoenix, A., and Owen, C. (2000). From miscegenation to hybridity: Mixed relationships and mixed parentage in profile. In A. Brah and A. E. Coombes (Eds.), *Hybridity and its discontents: Politics, science, culture* (pp. 72–95). London: Routledge.

Pingree, S., and Hawkins, R. (1981). U.S. programs on Australian television: The cultivation effect. *Journal of Broadcasting, 31,* 97–105.

Poiger, U. G. (2000). *Jazz, rock, and rebels: Cold war politics and American culture in a divided Germany.* Berkeley: University of California Press.

Pokémania v globophobia (1999, November 20–26). Editorial. *Economist.*

Polgreen, L. (2003, July 27). For mixed-race South Africans, equity is elusive. *New York Times.*

Pool, I. De S. (1977). The changing flow of television. *Journal of Communication, 27*(2), 137–147.

Pool, I. De S. (1983). What ferment? A challenge for empirical research. *Journal of Communication, 33*(3), 258–261.

Portella, E. (2000, April). Cultural cloning or hybrid cultures? *UNESCO Courier,* p. 9.

Postcolonial hybrids. (2001, March 8–14). *Al-Ahram Weekly On-Line,* no. 524.

Pratt, M. L. (1992). *Imperial eyes: Travel writing and transculturation.* New York: Routledge.

Rabasa, J. (2000). A new look at *mestizaje. Colonial Latin American Review, 9(2),* 315–318.

Radway, J. (1984). *Reading the romance: Feminism and the representation of women in popular culture.* Chapel Hill: University of North Carolina Press.

Radway, J. (1989). Ethnography among elites: Comparing discourses of power. *Journal of Communication Inquiry, 13(2),* 3–11.

Raschka, M. (1988, June 19). Hold your fire, it's Cosby time: TV show's popularity cuts across all factions in Beirut. *Chicago Tribune,* p. C16.

Ravault, R. J. (1987). International information: Bullet or boomerang? In D. L. Paletz (Ed.), *Communication research: Approaches, studies, assessments* (pp. 245–265). Norwood, NJ: Ablex.

Reed, D. (1999, February 10). Falwell's newspaper attempts to label 'Teletubbies' character as gay. Roanoke, VA: Associated Press.

Réfléxions sur la crise de la communauté maronite [Reflections on the crisis of the Maronite community]. (1993, third trimester/1994, first trimester). *Les Cahiers de L'Orient,* pp. 221–251.

Riding, A. (1999, December 14). The French fume over popularity of U.S. films. *New York Times.*

Rieff, D. (1999, Summer). A new age of liberal imperialism. *World Policy Journal, 16(2),* 1–10.

Roach, C. (1997). Cultural imperialism and resistance in media theory and literary theory. *Media, Culture, and Society, 19,* 47–66.

Robertson, R. (1992). *Globalization.* London and New York: Sage.

Robertson, R. (1994). Globalisation or glocalisation? *Journal of International Communication, 1(1),* 3–6.

Rodríguez, C. (2001). *Fissures in the mediascape: An international study of citizens' media.* Cresskill, NJ: Hampton Press.

Rodríguez, C., and Murphy, P. D. (1997). The study of communication and culture in Latin America: From laggards and the oppressed to resistance and hybrid cultures. *Journal of International Communication, 4(2),* 24–45.

Rogers, E., and Schement, J. R. (1984). Introduction to "Media flows in Latin America." Special issue, *Communication Research, 11(2),* 159–162.

Romberg, R. (1998). Whose spirits are they? The political economy of syncretism and authenticity. *Journal of Folklore Research, 35(1),* 69–82.

Rosa, A. J. (1996, November). El que no tiene dingo, tiene mandingo: The inadequacy of the "mestizo" as a theoretical construct in the field of Latin American studies—The problem and solution. *Journal of Black Studies, 27(2),* 278–291.

Rosaldo, R. (1993). *Culture and truth: The remaking of social analysis* (2d ed.). Boston: Beacon.

Rosaldo, R. (1995). Foreword to *Hybrid cultures: Strategies for entering and leaving modernity.* (S. López and E. Schiappari, Trans.) (pp. xi–xvii). Minneapolis: University of Minnesota Press,

Rosenau, J. N. (2003). *Distant proximities: Dynamics beyond globalization.* Princeton, NJ, and Oxford: Princeton University Press.

Rosenfeld, M. (1998, October 26). Malaysians create hybrid culture with American imports. *Washington Post*, p. A23.

Rosengren, K. E., Wenner, L. A., and Palmgreen, P. (Eds.). (1985). *Media gratifications research*. Beverly Hills, CA: Sage.

Rothkop, D. (1997, June 22, Summer). In praise of cultural imperialism. *Foreign Policy, 107*, 38–53.

Rouse, R. (1995). Thinking through transnationalism: Notes on the cultural politics of class relations in the contemporary United States. *Public Culture, 7*(2), 353–402.

Roush, W. (2000, September/October). Mongrel 'r' us. *Technology Review*, pp. 125–126.

Rudock, A. (1996). Seems like old times: U.S. foreign policy, media audiences, and the limits of resistance. *Journal of International Communication, 3*(2), 94–113.

Rushdie, S. (1994). *East, west: Stories*. New York: Vintage.

Rushdie, S. (1999, March 5). Rethinking the war on American culture. *New York Times*.

Russett, B. M., Oneal, J. R., and Cox, M. (2000). Clash of civilizations, or realism and liberalism déjà vu? Some evidence. *Journal of Peace Research, 37*(5), 583–608.

Sahlins, M. (1981). *Historical metaphors and mythical realities: Structure in the early history of the Sandwich Islands*. Ann Arbor: University of Michigan Press.

Sahlins, M. (1985). *Islands of history*. Chicago: University of Chicago Press.

Sahlins, M. (1995). *How "natives" think: About Captain Cook, for example*. Chicago: University of Chicago Press.

Said, E. (1978). *Orientalism*. New York: Pantheon.

Said, E. (1984). *The world, the text, and the critic*. Cambridge: Harvard University Press.

Said, E. (1994). *Culture and imperialism*. New York: Knopf.

Said, E. (2001, October 22). The clash of ignorance. *Nation*, pp. 11–13.

Sakamato, R. (1996). Japan, hybridity, and the creation of colonialist discourse. *Theory, Culture, and Society, 13*(3), 113–128.

Salamone, F. A. (1998, Fall). Nigerian and Ghanaian popular music: Two varieties of creolization. *Journal of Popular Culture, 32*(2), 11–25.

Salibi, K. S. (1971). The Lebanese identity. *Journal of Contemporary History, 6*(1), 76–86.

Salibi, K. S. (1988). *A house of many mansions: The history of Lebanon reconsidered*. Berkeley: University of California Press.

Salwen, M. (1991). Cultural imperialism: A media effects approach. *Critical Studies in Mass Communication, 8*(1), 29–38.

Samama, C. R. (2001). *Développement mondial et culturalités*. Paris: Maisonneuve et Larose.

Sánchez-Ruiz, E. E. (2001). Globalization, cultural industries, and free trade: The Mexican audiovisual sector in the NAFTA age. In V. Mosco and D. Schiller (Eds.), *Continental order? Integrating North America for cybercapitalism* (pp. 86–119). Lanham, MD: Rowman and Littlefield.

Sands, D. (2002, December 29). Review of the book *Creative destruction*. *Washington Times*.

Schement, J. R., Gonzalez, I. N., Lum, P.A., and Valencia, R. (1984). The international flow of television programs. *Communication Research, 11*(2), 159–162.

Schement, J. R., and Rogers, E. M. (1984). Media flows in Latin America. *Communication Research, 11*(2), 305–320.

Schiller, D. (1985). The emerging global grid: Planning for what? *Media, Culture, and Society, 7*, 105–125.

Schiller, H. (1974). Freedom from the "free flow." *Journal of Communication, 24*(1), 110–117.

Schiller, H. (1976). *Communication and cultural domination.* New York: Sharpe.

Schiller, H. (1991). Not yet the post-imperialist era. *Critical Studies in Mass Communication, 8*(1), 13–28.

Schiller, H. (1971/1992). *Mass communication and American empire* (2d ed., updated). Boulder: Westview.

Schiller, H. (1989). *Culture, Inc.: The corporate takeover of public expression.* New York: Oxford University Press.

Schiller, H. (2000). The social context of research and theory. In I. Hagen and J. Wasko (Eds.), *Consuming audiences? Production and reception in media research* (pp. 111–122). Cresskill, NJ: IAMCR and Hampton Press.

Schineller, P. (1992). Inculturation and syncretism: What is the real issue? *International Bulletin of Missionary Research, 16*, 50–53.

Schreiter, R. J. (1993, April). Defining syncretism: An interim report. *International Bulletin of Missionary Research*, 50–53.

Seamann, W. R. (1992). Active audience theory: Pointless populism. *Media, Culture, and Society, 14*(2), 301–311.

Sepstrup, P. (1990). *Transnationalisation of television in Western Europe.* London: John Libby.

Serge Adda, président de TV5 Monde: "Il y de la place pour plusieurs formats de chaînes françaises mondiales" (2003, July 4). *Le Monde.*

Serres, M. (1969). *Hermès I: La communication.* Paris: Éditions de Minuit.

Serres, M. (1972). *Hermès II: L'interférence.* Paris: Éditions de Minuit.

Serres, M. (1974). *Hermès III: La traduction.* Paris: Éditions de Minuit.

Serres, M. (1977). *Hermès IV: La distribution.* Paris: Éditions de Minuit.

Serres, M. (1980). *Hermès V: Le passage du Nord-Ouest.* Paris: Éditions de Minuit.

Shannon, C., and Weaver, W. (Eds.). (1949). *The mathematical theory of communication.* Urbana: University of Illinois Press.

Shohat, E. (1992). Notes on the "post-colonial." *Social Text, 31/32*, 99–113.

Shohat, E., and Stam, R. (1994). *Unthinking Eurocentrism: Multiculturalism and the media.* London and New York: Routledge.

Shome, R. (1996). Postcolonial interventions in the rhetorical canon: An "Other" view. *Communication Theory, 6*(1), 40–59.

Shome, R. (1998). Caught in the term "post-colonial": Why the "post-colonial" still matters. *Critical Studies in Mass Communication, 15*(2), 203–212.

Shome, R., and Hegde, R. S. (2002). Postcolonial approaches to communication: Charting the terrain, engaging the intersections. *Communication Theory, 12*(3), 249–270.

Sid-Ahmed, M. (1998, August 6–12). Globalising culture: A non-starter? *Al-Ahram Weekly*, issue 384.

Silverstone, R. (1992). *Television and everyday life.* London: Routledge.

Sinclair, J. (1982, February). From "modernization" to cultural dependence: Mass communication studies and the third world. *Media Information Australia, 23,* 12–18.

Sinclair, J. (1992). The decentering of cultural imperialism: Televisa-ion and globo-ization in the Latin world. In E. Jacka (Ed.), *Continental shift: Globalisation and culture* (pp. 89–116). Double Bay, Australia: Local Consumption.

Sinclair, J. (1997). The business of international broadcasting: Cultural bridges and barriers. *Asian Journal of Communication, 7*(1), 137–155.

Sinclair, J., Jacka, E., and Cunningham, S. (Eds.). (1996). *Peripheral vision: New patterns in global television.* New York and London: Oxford University Press.

Skidmore, D. (1998). Huntington's clash revisited. *Journal of World-Systems Research, 4*(2), 181–188.

Skovmand, M., and Schroder, K. C. (Eds.). (1992). *Media cultures: Reappraising transnational media.* London: Routledge.

Smith, A. D. (1994). Towards a global culture? In M. Featherstone (Ed.), *Global culture: Nationalism, globalization, and modernity* (pp. 171–192). London and Newbury Park, CA: Sage.

Smythe, D. W. (1981). *Dependency road: Communication, capitalism, consciousness, and Canada.* Norwood, NJ: Ablex.

Sollors, W. (1986). *Beyond ethnicity.* Oxford and New York: Oxford University Press.

Spanos, W. V. (2000). *America's shadow: An anatomy of empire.* Minneapolis: University of Minnesota Press.

Sparks, C. (1989). Experience, ideology, and articulation: Stuart Hall and the development of culture. *Journal of Communication Inquiry, 13*(2), 79–87.

Spitta, S. (2001). Of brown buffaloes, cockroaches, and others: *Mestizaje* north and south of the Río Bravo. *Revista de Estudios Hispánicos, 35,* 333–346.

Spivak, G. C. (1999). *A critique of postcolonial reason: Toward a history of the vanishing present.* Cambridge: Harvard University Press.

Spivak, G. C. (2002). Postcolonial scholarship—Productions and directions: An interview with Gayatri Chakravorty Spivak (with R. S. Hegde and R. Shome). *Communication Theory, 12*(3), 271–286.

Sreberny-Mohammadi, A. (1984). The global and the local in international communications. In J. Curran and M. Gurevitch (Eds.), *Mass media and society* (pp. 136–152). London and New York: Arnold.

Sreberny-Mohammadi, A. (1996). International feminism(s). *Journal of International Communication, 3*(1), 1–4.

Sreberny-Mohammadi, A. (1997). The many cultural faces of imperialism. In P. Golding and P. Harris, *Beyond cultural imperialism: Globalization, communication, and the new international order* (pp. 49–68). London and Thousand Oaks, CA: Sage.

Sreberny-Mohammadi, A., Winseck, D., McKenna, J., and Boyd-Barrett, O. (Eds.). (1996). *Media in a global context: A reader.* London: Arnold.

Stevenson, R. L. (1983). A critical look at critical analysis. *Journal of Communication, 33*(3), 262–269.

Stevenson, R. L. (1988). *Communication, development, and the third world.* New York: Longman.

Stewart, C. (1999, Fall). Syncretism and its synonyms: Reflections on cultural mixture. *Diacritics, 29*(3), 40–62.

Stewart, C., and Shaw, R. (Eds.). (1994). *Syncretism/Anti-syncretism: The politics of religious synthesis.* London and New York: Routledge.

Stoddard, E., and Cornwell, G. H. (1999). Cosmopolitan or mongrel? Créolité, hybridity, and "douglarisation" in Trinidad. *European Journal of Cultural Studies, 2*(3), 331–353.

Straubhaar, J. (1982). The development of the telenovela as the pre-eminent form of popular culture in Brazil. *Studies in Latin American Popular Culture, 1,* 138–150.

Straubhaar, J. (1984). Brazilian television: The decline of American influence. *Communication Research, 11*(2), 221–240.

Straubhaar, J. (1991). Beyond media imperialism: Asymmetrical interdependence and cultural proximity. *Critical Studies in Mass Communication 8*(1), 39–59.

Straubhaar, J., and Viscasillas, G. M. (1991). Class, genre, and the regionalization of television programming in the Dominican Republic. *Journal of Communication, 41*(1), 53–69.

Streeter, T. (1989). Polysemy, plurality, and media studies. *Journal of Communication Inquiry, 13*(2), 88–106.

Stross, B. (1999). The hybrid metaphor: From biology to culture. *Journal of American Folklore, 112*(445), 254–257.

Struck, D. (2000, January 20). Think American, Japanese are advised; government panel says traditional values impede progress. *Washington Post,* p. A01.

Subliminal Messages? (1999, February 16). *Washington Post,* p. A16.

Swanson, D. L. (1977). The uses and misuses of uses and gratifications. *Human Communication Research, 3,* 214–221.

Tabar, P. (1994). The image of power in Maronite political discourse. *Beirut Review, 7,* 91–114.

Tan, A. S., Tan, G. K., and Tan, A. S. (1987). American TV in the Philippines: A test of cultural impact. *Journalism Quarterly, 64,* 229–238.

Taylor, P. J. (1999). *Modernities: A geohistorical interpretation.* Minneapolis: University of Minnesota Press.

Taylor, P. W. (1995). Co-productions—Content and change: International television in the Americas. *Canadian Journal of Communication, 20*(3).

Teletubbies declare war. (1999, March 23). *BBC Online.*

Teletubby mania on QVC. (1998, December 28). [Press release]. West Chester, PA: Itsy Bitsy Entertainment and QVC.

Televisa Mexico to cut $80 mln in costs in 99/2000. (1999, April 28). Mexico City: Reuters.

Tempelman, S. (1999). Constructions of cultural identity: Multiculturalism and exclusion. *Political Studies, 47,* 17–31.

Terry, S. (2000, August 28). Mix 'n' match society: Going "transcultural." *Christian Science Monitor.*

Thomas, N. (1996). Cold fusion (cultural hybridity). *American Anthropologist, 98,* 9–16.

Thomas, N. (1998). Hybrid histories: Gordon Bennett's critique of purity. *Communal/Plural, 6*(1), 107–116.

Thompson, G. (2002, March 12). Vatican seeks to curb Mexico's Indian deacons. *New York Times,* http://www.nytimes.com/2002/03/12/international/americas/12MEXl.html.

Thussu, D. K. (Ed.). (1998). *Electronic empires: Global media and local resistance.* London: Arnold.

Tinky Winky, Dipsy, Laa-Laa, and Po say 'Eh-oh' to Microsoft. (1999, January 6). [Press release]. New York: Itsy Bitsy Entertainment.

Todd, E. (2002). *Apres l'empire: Essai sur la decomposition du systeme americain.* Paris: Gallimard.

Tomlinson, J. (1991). *Cultural imperialism.* Baltimore, MD: Johns Hopkins University Press.

Tomlinson, J. (1994). Mass communication and the idea of a global public sphere. *Journal of International Communication, 1*(2), 57–70.

Tomlinson, J. (1997). Cultural globalization and cultural imperialism. In A. Mohammadi (Ed.), *International communication and globalization* (pp. 170–190). London: Sage.

Tomlinson, J. (1999). *Globalization and culture.* Chicago: University of Chicago Press.

Toumson, R. (1998). *Mythologie du métissage.* Paris: Presses Universitaires de France.

Toumson, R. (2001). Les archétypes du métissage. In J. L. Bonniol (Ed.), *Paradoxes du métissage* (pp. 65–70). Paris: Comité des Travaux Historiques et Scientifiques.

Tracey, M. (1985). The poisoned chalice? International television and the idea of dominance. *Daedalus, 114*(4), 17–56.

Tracey, M. (1988, March). Popular culture and the economics of global television. *Intermedia,* pp. 19–25.

Trueheart, C. (1998, October 27). With popularity come pitfalls. *Washington Post,* p. A19.

Tsai, M. K. (1970). Some effects of American television programs on children in Formosa. *Journal of Broadcasting, 14,* 229–238.

Tufte, T. (1995). How do telenovelas serve to articulate hybrid cultures in contemporary Brazil? *Nordicom Review, 2,* 29–35.

Tunstall, J. (1977). *The media are American.* Beverly Hills, CA, and London: Sage/Constable.

TV Azteca and Canal 40 announce joint venture; TV Azteca purchases 10% of Channel 40. (1998, July 29). Mexico City: TV Azteca and S.A. de C.V.

TV Azteca denies wrongdoing in Chile. (1999, January 27). Mexico City: Reuters.

TV Azteca signs exclusive free TV licensing agreement for Disney programming. (1998, November 5). Mexico City: TV Azteca and S.A. de C.V.

UNESCO (United Nations Educational Scientific and Cultural Organization). (1982). *Proceedings of the Mexico conference on cultural policies.* Paris: UNESCO.

Un recensement "ethnique" contesté en Nouvelle-Calédonie. (2003, August 4). *Le Monde.*

Valdman, A. (1978). *Pidgin and Creole linguistics*. Bloomington: Indiana University Press.

Valognes, J. P. (1994). *Vie et mort des Chrétiens d'Orient: Des origines a nos jours* [Life and death of the Christians of the Orient: From the outset to the present]. Paris: Fayard.

Van der Lee, P. (1997, Summer). Latin American influences in Swedish popular music. *Popular Music and Society, 21*(2), 17–45.

Van der Veer, P. (1997). "The enigma of arrival": Hybridity and authenticity in the global space. In P. Werbner and T. Moddod (Eds.), *Debating cultural hybridity: Multi-cultural identities and the politics of anti-racism* (pp. 90–105). London and Atlantic Heights, NJ: Zed Books.

Van Dijk, T. A. (1993). Principles of critical discourse analysis. *Discourse and Society, 4*(2), 249–283.

Van Elteren, M. (1996). Conceptualizing the impact of U.S. popular culture globally. *Journal of Popular Culture, 30*(1), 47–90.

Varan, D. (1998). The cultural erosion metaphor and the transcultural impact of media systems. *Journal of Communication, 48*(2), 58–85.

Varis, T. (1974). Global traffic in television. *Journal of Communication, 24*(1), 102–109.

Varis, T. (1984). The international flow of television programs. *Journal of Communication, 34*(1), 143–152.

Vasconcélos, J. (1925/1997). *The cosmic race/La raza cosmica*. (Didier T. Jaen, Trans.). Baltimore: Johns Hopkins University Press.

Wagnleitner, R., and May, E. T. (Eds.). (2000). *"Here, there, and everywhere": The foreign politics of American popular culture*. Hanover, NH: University Press of New England.

Wallerstein, I. (1994). Culture as the ideological battleground of the modern world-system. In M. Featherstone (Ed.), *Global culture: Nationalism, globalization, and modernity* (pp. 31–56). London and Newbury Park, CA: Sage.

Wallerstein, I. (2000). *The essential Wallerstein*. New York: New Press.

Wallis, R., and Malm, K. (1990). *On record: Rock, pop, and the written word*. Boston: Kegan Paul.

Wal-mart had legal ok on Teletubbies look-alikes. (1999, March 23). Chicago: Reuters.

Wal-mart to destroy Teletubby look-alikes. (1999, May 19). New York: Reuters.

Wang, G. (1997). Beyond media globalization: A look at cultural integrity from a policy perspective. *Telematics and Informatics, 14*(4), 309–321.

Ware, W., and Dupagne, M. (1994). Effects of U.S television programs on foreign audiences: A meta-analysis. *Journalism and Mass Communication Quarterly, 71*(4), 947–959.

Warmbold, J. (1992). If only she didn't have Negro blood in her veins: The concept of *métissage* in German colonial literature. *Journal of Black Studies, 23*(2), 200–209.

Warsh, D. (2000, July 9). Against purity. *Boston Globe*, p. G1.

Wasko, J. (1994). *Hollywood and the information age*. Cambridge: Polity Press.

Wasser, F. (1995). Is Hollywood America? The transnationalization of the American film industry. *Critical Studies in Mass Communication, 12*(4), 423–437.

Waters, M. (1995). *Globalization*. London: Routledge.

Wayne, M. (2003). Postfordism, monopoly capitalism, and Hollywood's media-industrial complex. *International Journal of Cultural Studies, 6*(1), 82–103.

Wax, E. (2003, July 14). An African "Big Brother" unites and delights. *Washington Post*, p. A1.

Waxman, S. (1998, October 26). Hollywood tailors its movies to sell in foreign markets. *Washington Post*, p. A1.

Weeks, L. (2002, January 31). Frappe society: The trend to blend. *Washington Post*, pp. C1–C2.

Weimann, G. (1984). Images of life in America: The impact of American TV in Israel. *International Journal of Intercultural Relations, 8*, 185–197.

Werbner, P. (1997). Introduction: The dialectics of cultural hybridity. In P. Werbner and T. Modood (Eds.), *Debating cultural hybridity: Multi-cultural identities and the politics of anti-racism* (pp. 1–26). London and Atlantic Highlands, NJ: Zed Books.

Werbner, P., and Modood, T. (Eds.). (1997). *Debating cultural hybridity: Multi-cultural identities and the politics of anti-racism*. London and Atlantic Highlands, NJ: Zed Books.

Wilkie, L. A. (2000). Culture bought: Evidence of creolization in the consumer goods of an enslaved Bahamian family. *Historical Archaeology, 34*(3), 10–26.

Willis, P. (2000). *The ethnographic imagination*. Cambridge: Polity Press.

Willnat, L., Hje, Z., and Xiaoming, H. (1998). Foreign media exposure and perceptions of Americans in Hong Kong, Shenzhen, and Singapore. *Journalism and Mass Communication Quarterly, 74*, 738–756.

Wilson, R., and Dissanayake, W. (Eds.). (1996). *Global/Local: Cultural production and the transnational imaginary*. Durham, NC: Duke University Press.

Wuthnow, R. (1992). Infrastructure and superstructure: Revisions in Marxist sociology of culture. In R. Munsch and N. J. Smelser (Eds.), *Theory of culture* (pp. 145–177). Berkeley: University of California Press.

Young, L. (2000). Hybridity's discontents: Rereading science and "race." In A. Brah and A. E. Coombes (Eds.), *Hybridity and its discontents: Politics, science, culture* (pp. 154–170). London: Routledge.

Young, R. (1995). *Colonial desire: Hybridity in theory, culture, and race*. London: Routledge.

Zachary, G. P. (2000). *The global me: New cosmopolitans and the competitive edge: Picking globalism's winners and losers*. New York: Public Affairs.

Zamir, M. (2000). *Lebanon's quest: The road to statehood, 1926–1939*. London: I. B. Tauris.

Zassoursky, Y., and Losev, S. (1981). Information in the service of progress. *Journal of Communication, 31*(4), 118–121.

Ziff, B., and Rao, P. V. (1997). *Borrowed power: Essays on cultural appropriation*. New Brunswick, NJ: Rutgers University Press.

Zompetti, J. P. (1997). Toward a Gramscian critical rhetoric. *Western Journal of Speech Communication, 61*(1), 66–68.

Index

Abu Lughod, Lila, 125

Abu Melhem, 123, 142

Active audience research: x, 21, 44; and agency, 38; in Britain, 36; and consumer freedom, 38; criticism of, 37; and cultural populism, 37; discursive bases of, 37; and encoding-decoding model, 36; and global media studies, 33; international contributions to, 38; and media production, 37; pitfalls of, 37; U.K. and U.S. variants of, 37; in uses and gratifications, 34

Ad-Dunia Hayk, 123, 142

Adorno, Theodor, 33

Afghanistan, 17

Africa, 68; and African Americans, 82–83, 159

Africans, 48

Agency: in active audience research, 38; and American studies, 33; and consumption, 151; and contingency, 67; and critical transculturalism, 96, 149, 151–153; and cultural globalization, 149, 150–151; and cultural imperialism, 33, 149, 150–151; and cultural pluralism, 149, 150–151; and cultural production, 12; definition of, 151; and global culture, 15; and hybridity, 12, 58, 66, 149–153, 161; of international audiences, 94; in international communication, 3; links to communication, 12; and Maronites, 158; and multiculturalism, 149, 150–151; of nation–states, 19, 41; of reader, 17; relation to structure, 13, 149–151, 158; and resistance, 67; site of, 149–151; and *Tele Chobis* viewers, 12

Agency-structure relation, 13, 29, 149–151, 158

Ahmad, Aijaz, 45, 46, 66, 70, 165n6

Al-Arabiya, 99

Al-Hamad, Turki, 3, 167n2

Al-Hayat, 99

Al-I Ahmad, 3

Alif, 165n5

Al-Jazeera, 99

Allor, Martin, 37

Al-Manar, 122, 145, 174n9

Althusser, Louis, 175n5

American Enterprise, 74, 78

American Enterprise Institute, 90

American Quarterly, 32

American Spectator, 73

American studies, x, 32–33

American television, and race issues, 82–83

American University of Beirut, 138

Americanization: and class differences in Britain, 35; of Europe, 35; and French radio, 35; and German cinema, 35; of global culture, 17; and Hollywood studios, 81; of Italy, 60–61

Amin, Samir, 45

Amoeba, as pattern of cultural indigenization, 6

Anderson, Benedict, 51, 56

Ang, Ien, 35, 36

Anthropology: cultural, 4; and cultural globalization, 16; of Hawaii, 61; historical, 61; and modernity-tradition relation, 64; and syncretism, 50

Antihybridity backlash, xi, 65–67

Anzaldúa, Gloria, 169n2

Appadurai, Arjun, 10, 15, 39, 40, 41, 153, 154, 155, 156

Arab satellite television industry, 123

Arab world, 59; and Arab identity, 120; media policy in, 159; and nationalism, 127; oligarchical capitalism in, 159; satellite television in, 99; size of audience in, 99

Arabs: and tradition, 129–131; values of, 128–129

Arab-Western dialogism, 12, 116, 127–133

Archetti, Eduardo, 51

Argentina, 63

Armstrong, Louis, 60

Articulation: and critical transculturalism, 150–156; criticism of, 176n5; definition of, 156; and encoding-decoding model, 36; and hegemony, 36; and hybridity-power nexus, 156; and interpellation, 36; lopsided, 150–156, 176n5; in media and communication studies, 175–176n5

Asians, 48

Asmar, Simon, 123

Atlas du Monde Diplomatique, 10

Audience: activity of, x, 13, 21; ethnography, 37; passivity of, 26. *See also* Active audience research
Audio-Visual Media Law, 123–124, 144, 174n10
Australia: diasporic media in, 10; indigenous people of, 48;
Axis of Evil, 25, 79

Baines, John, 49
Bakhtin, Mikhail, x, 3, 46, 53, 110, 128, 152, 153
Balibar, Etienne, 175n5
Bamyeh, Mohammed, 41
Bandura, Albert, 34
Bankston, Carl, III, 56, 57
Barber, Benjamin, 17, 86
Basic Instinct, 132
Bastian, Adolf, 46
Basu, Amrita, 154
Baudrillard, Jean, 138
Bauman, Zygmunt, 39
BBC, 103; and *Teletubbies*, 104, 106
Beavis and Butthead, 122, 137
Behar, Ruth, 169n2
Beltrán, Luis Ramiro, 26
Ben Jalloun, Tahar, 134
Benhabib, Seyla, 54, 153, 160, 161, 167n2
Benny Hill Show, 122
Bentley, Jerry, and cross-cultural encounters, 3, 47
Bercy, 136
Berelson, Bernard, 34
Berlin School of Ethnology, 46
Bernabé, Jean, 68
Berri, Nabih, 124
Berry, Ellen, 14
Beverly Hills 90210, 132, 137, 138
Bhabha, Homi, x, 46, 58, 66, 67, 114, 165n6
Bhagwati, Jagdish, 87
Billboard, 73
Black Atlantic, 57–58
Blackness, 82
Blair, Tony, 102
Blanchard, Margaret, 98
Blevins, James, 50
Bloch, Maurice, 175n5
Blumler, Jay, 34
Boggs, Vernon, 53
Bolke-Turner, Christina, 51, 52
Bonet, Lisa, 132
Bonnet, Hans, 49
Boston Globe, 73, 90
Boulos, Jean-Claude, 121, 123
Boyd, Douglas, 121

Boyd-Barrett, Oliver, 4, 22, 25, 27, 29, 30, 167n3
Braman, Sandra, 14, 29, 43, 154, 157
Brazil, 93, 94, 99; 1824 constitution of, 63; and creolization, 56; and cultural imperialism thesis, 28; as emerging giant, 28; as regional media center, 6; slavery in, 63; transculturation in, 53
Britain. *See* United Kingdom
Broadcasting. *See* Electronic media
Brundson, Charlotte, 36
Bubbly Chubbies, 105–106
Buckingham, David, 36
Buffon, Conte de, 46, 48, 169n3
Bush, George W., 25
Butterfly, as pattern of cultural indigenization, 6
Byzantines, 119

Canada: and coproductions, 102; cultural and media policy in, 159; and global media debate, 23; and NAFTA, 9
Canal Plus, 122
Captain Cook, 61
Carey, James, 35
Carmichael, Hoagie, 60
Carnival, 110
Carosone, Renato, 60
Catholicism, 35, 49
Catholics, 20
Cato Institute, 90
Cedrus Libani, 137
Cellular phones: in global culture, 15; uses and gratifications of, 34
Césaire, Aimé, 69
Chabry, Annie, 119
Chabry, Laurent, 119
Chamoiseau, Patrick, 68
Chaudenson, Robert, 55, 56
Chiapas, 50
Chicago Cultural Studies Group, 150
Children's television, 111–112
Chile, 113
China: as Confucianist civilization, 20; and cultural imperialism thesis, 28; as great power, 28
Chow, Rey, 67
Christian Science Monitor, 73
Christianity, 49
Citizenship, and global culture, 15
Civilisation, French notion of, 45; and négritude, 69
Civilization: Confucianist, 20; as culture, 19; Islamic, 19, 20; and négritude, 69; Western, 19

France: and coproductions, 102; cultural
identity, 17; and culture, 17; and global
media debate, 23; immigrants in, 10; and
imperialism, 59, 68; postcolonies of, 68; and
public diplomacy, 17
Francophonie, 131, 132
Frankfurt School: criticism of, 33; and cultural
imperialism, 22; and fascist exploitation, 33;
and media effects, 33; and Nazism, 33
Fraser, Nancy, 158
Free flow doctrine: and global media debate,
16; and New World Information and
Communication Order, 23; and prior
consent principle, 98; as rhetorical strategy,
29; and transnational television, 98; as U.S.
policy, 98; and Western governments, 29
Freedman, Des, 102, 103
Freedom of association, or of exit, 55
French CNN, 17
French enlightenment, 48, 69
French film industry, 84–85
French postcolonies, 68
French rationalism, 45
Freyre, Gilberto, 14, 53
Friedman, Jonathan, 66
Fundamentalism, 18
Future television, 144; as Sunnite television
station, 124

Galtung, Johann, 22, 25, 155
Gamio, Manuel, 52
García-Canclini, Néstor, 1, 3, 46, 52, 62–65,
159, 160, 164n4
Geertz, Clifford, xiii, 45, 86, 153
Gemayel, Nasser, 119
Genres, impure, 62–63
Geography, and cultural globalization, 16
Gerbner, George, 167n3
German romanticism, 45
Germany: and coproductions, 102; Frankfurt
School in, 33; immigrants in, 10; as
monoculture, 88, 89
Giddens, Anthony, 39, 43
Gillespie, Marie, 5, 10, 11
Gilroy, Paul, 45, 57–58, 170n6
Glissant, Edouard, 68
Global civil society, 29
Global culture, 171n2; ambivalence in, 39;
Americanization of, 17; Anglophone debate
on, 39; Big Mac as icon of, 15; and The Clash
of Civilizations, 17, 19–21; Coca-Cola as icon
of, 15; cohesion vs. dispersal in, 39;
communicative space of, 21; and complex
connectivity, 21; concept of, 39; and

consumerism, 18; and corporate
transculturalism, 93–96; deterritorialization
in, 39; disjunction in, 39; dystopian view of,
15, 45; and electronic media, 21; fabric of,
21; and governance, 16; and
homogenization, 21; homogenization vs.
heterogenization in, 39; and hybridity, 39;
and hybridization, 21; individual auteurs
of, 78; and Jihad vs. McWorld, 17–19; and
MTV generation, 15; and multinationals,
78; and national identity, 16; paradigms of,
166n1; and particularism, 21; scenarios of,
16–17; in Theory, Culture and Society, 39; and
transnational capitalism, 18; and tribalism,
18; and universalism, 21; utopian view of,
15, 45
Global media: deregulation of, 98, 100; and
free flow doctrine, 98; global structure of,
114; horizontal integration of, 98; as
industry, 98; liberalization of, 98, 100; and
multinational corporations, 98; official U.S.
policy on, 31, 98; and post-Fordism, 98; and
prior consent principle, 98; and program
internationalization, 100; vertical
integration of, 98
Global media debate, 16; France in, 23; and
free and balanced flow doctrine, 16; and
free flow doctrine, 16; United Kingdom in,
23; United States in, 23. See also New World
Information and Communication Order
Global media studies, 13; and active
audience, 33; and communication process,
166n8; definition of, 166n8; as
interdisciplinary configuration, 41; and
international communication, 41, 166n8
Global popular culture. See Global culture
Global television. See Global media
Globalization: as alternative to cultural
imperialism, 38; as Americanization, xi;
benefits and dangers of, 9; commercial
imperatives of, 8; communication
dimensions of, 41, 168n8; conceptual
ambiguity of, 39; as corporate
transculturalism, 151; and counterflow,
76–77; and cultural change, 84; and cultural
industries, 15; and diversity, 79, 84; as
ecumene, 39; first dictionary definition of,
38; and free trade, 76–78; idealist view of,
42; and information, 41; and information
networks, 98; interpenetrated, 154; multiple
dimensions of, 42; as pandisciplinary
preoccupation, 40; and protectionism, 77; as
reductive structure, 161; in relation to
culture, 41–44; "scapes" of, 15; as seductive